# Teaching Your Children to Fish

# Teaching Your Children to Fish by Jack Fallon

Winchester Press

Copyright © 1974 by John W. Fallon
All rights reserved

Library of Congress Catalog Card Number: 73-78834
ISBN: 0-87691-130-0

Book and jacket typography by M. F. Gazze

Published by Winchester Press
460 Park Avenue, New York 10022

Printed in the United States of America

# Contents

~~~~~~~~~~~~~~~~~~~~~~~~~~~~~~~~~~~~~~~~~~~~~~~~~~~~~~~~~~~~

# Preface

~~~~~~~~~~~~~~~~~~~~~~~~~~~~~~~~~~~~~~~~~~~~~~~~~~

This book began with a letter. After reading my "Sea Fare for Seafarers" in the June 1971 issue of *Yachting,* in which I described a weekend of fishing and sailing with my son Jack, Richard Chapin, President of Boston's Emerson College, wrote to me about his ten-year-old son who "hankers to fish and is pretty disappointed that I cannot help him select rod, line, bait, lures, etc. for even the most ordinary circumstances. Daddy is just not quite living up to what he ought to be."

A lot of other parents share Mr. Chapin's problem. The more of them I asked, the more apparent it became that many of them either are discouragingly unsuccessful at fishing with their children or don't do it at all for fear of being unsuccessful. Chapter 1, therefore, is about ways parents sometimes go wrong in their attempts to fish with their children. Having made all the mistakes myself, I can discuss errors with plenty of egg-on-the-face authority.

Fortunately I also have done a lot of right things, so I am able to offer the fruits of my experience in the form of positive suggestions. If they don't work for you, you're probably doing—or thinking or feeling—something wrong. Looking back on a lot of years, I find that every time fishing with my children has not been jam-packed with joy—even when it has rained, even when I've fallen in, even when we haven't caught fish—the fault invariably has been my own. I've been too impatient, too demanding, too insensitive, or just not appreciative enough of the privilege of sharing the simple peripheral pleasures of counting stars and contemplating quiet and midwifing new mornings.

If fishing with three sensational sons and three delightful daughters has taught me anything, it's that there's no such thing as an unsuccessful fishing session with a child. Some are just more successful than others.

Fishing tackle is covered in Chapter 2, and fishing techniques in Chapter 3. Here I aim my advice principally at those parents who have never fished themselves or are baffled by how complex fishing has become since their barefoot days. For the five methods most likely to interest a child—plug casting, spin casting, spinning, surf casting, and fly-fishing—I discuss the basics of equipment and how to use it. There's plenty of information here to launch a youngster successfully into an angling orbit, but elaborate formulas—"a 4-ounce pyramid sinker 18 inches above a #3/0 Siwash hook should be cast at an angle of 40 degrees above the horizontal," and so on—are kept to a minimum. Formula fishing is as artificial as formula kissing. A child never will grow to love fishing if he is overwhelmed with precise instructions and not allowed to develop his skills naturally.

I also offer some suggestions on how to buy equipment. Sometimes—but not always—cheap lures are a better buy than their established but expensive equivalent. Sometimes it's smartest to shop from catalogs, sometimes at tackle stores, sometimes at chain stores. If it's properly done, selecting the equipment is an important part of the fun of fishing.

In Chapter 4 you meet some of my favorite species and learn a little bit about how to fool them. Stripers, trout, and the other classic game species are there, but I've concentrated heavily on the less "prestigious" fish that are actually usually more fun for children and are neglected in most how-to books. If your own personal favorite is not among my selections, you'll probably find one of its close kin. Despite much of the mystique that's been manufactured about fishing, most of the techniques that work for one type of fish can be employed with minor modifications on its cousins. Northern pike, for example, are just as receptive to a shiny spoon skittered along the outside edge of a patch of weeds as are chain pickerel, and a small silver jig jerked and fluttered through a mildly turbulent tideway is as likely to entice an Atlantic mackerel in Boston harbor as it is a Pacific mackerel off Baja California.

Chapter 5 gave me perhaps the most fun to write, because in it I recount many angling experiences that my children and I have shared: backwoods, brook, surf, from a skiff in a bay, from the shore of a pond, through the ice, etc. It explains how best to take advantage of each type of fishing locale.

The Epilogue, a short chapter, describes a fishing trip with grownup children. This may seem out of place in such a book, but it is not, because it is well known that all adult anglers are really nine years old. (This is known as Fallon's Law, in honor of my wife, who discovered it.) A glossary of terms completes the book.

It should be obvious from the frequent mentions of my wife, my daughters, and other lady anglers that this book is written for females just as much as males. However, very early in the book I ran out of genderless references such as "child" and "youngster" and needed a few synonyms. Using "boy" and "girl" interchangeably would have made it seem that I was differentiating between the two, recommending one thing for boys and another for girls, when in actuality I mean everything for both. Also it is very difficult to write a book without using singular pronouns. So I settled on "boy" and "he." I tried "girl." So help me, I did. But it sounded contrived and even a little conciliatory. Our language, I guess, is no more ready for sexual equality than is our society. So let's understand that when I say "boy," I also mean "girl." If this upsets any militant Mss., I'm sorry, but I'm not going to worry about it. I'll be busy fishing.

Paragraphs here and there have been plucked from articles I have published in *Outdoor Life, Salt Water Sportsman, Northeast Outdoors, Massachusetts Out-of-Doors, Soundings,* and *KOA Handbook.* In particular, the story of the Lake Boon ice-fishing expedition in Chapter 5 appeared originally in the February 1973 *Outdoor Life* © 1973, Popular Science Publishing Company, Inc. I am grateful to the editors of these publications for permitting me to use this material.

I also am grateful to Mr. and Mrs. J. Stanley Upton of Chelmsford. Most of this book was written in a quiet cloistered room of their house down the street, where peace and quiet take the place of the jangling phones and blaring phonographs in my own menagerie. To Stan and Grace, my eternal thanks.
—J. F.
Chelmsford, Massachusetts
October 1973

# Teaching Your Children to Fish

# I.
# Fundamentals

~~~~~~~~~~~~~~~~~~~~~~~~~~~~~~~~~~~~~~~~~~~~~~~~~~~~

"There's fishing and there's fishing with children" is the way a friend puts it. "Separately," he says, "they're among life's most pleasurable pursuits: fishing alone or with a compatible adult companion is like a romp with a spunky pup; fishing with a child is like dangling a string in front of a frisky kitten. But mix them, and brother, you've got yourself nothing but a plain old cat-and-dog fight."

Wise words, these. And like most wisdom, which always seems to come in disarmingly simple packages, more often than not it's ignored.

I ignored it the first time I fished with my sons. Pulling up alongside a small neighborhood pond, I distributed a few cursory instructions—"Bait up and let's go, guys . . . last one to land a lunker is a clunker"—and proceeded to cast my plug alongside some lily pads. The poor kids, only five and six at the time, were thoroughly confused. Not only did they not know what a lunker was, they barely were aware of which end of their rods they should be holding. Nevertheless, they charged right down the bank to emulate Daddy, and before I could say "Backlash," Danny fell in, Jack started laughing, Danny got sore, and I spent the rest of the abbreviated afternoon refereeing.

My mistake, a common one, was that instead of taking my sons fishing, I really was *going* fishing and inviting the boys to come along and watch. Oh, sure, I conveniently rationalized my way into believing that it's best to leave the boys alone, to let them do their own discovering, but the plain fact was, I was being selfish. When an afternoon's fishing comes as an all-too-brief reward for a long week's work, it's easy to convince yourself that you can tote your tots along without missing a cast, but you're only kidding yourself.

Closely related to this kind of selfishness is bringing your youngster along with your grown-up buddies before he's either emotionally or physically up to it. I'm not referring, of course, to when a pair of adult pals who are concerned about their lack of expertise seek mutual support by joining up for some tandem father-and-son fishing. First time or two out, in fact, this might be a good way to go. If, however, you're just trying to have your cake and eat it too by bringing your boy, say, backpacking for trout through dense bug-infested woods or casting all night into a cold October surf, then you're not being fair to either your buddies or your boy.

Men like to be loose, unencumbered, uninhibited; to say what they want in the language they choose and to show off their strength and endurance. A boy feels burdensome when he can't keep up, awkward when he can't contribute to the conversation, left out when he doesn't understand why grown-ups are laughing, embarrassed when language gets lusty.

There's an enormous potential for pleasure in fishing with children, pleasure for both parties, but it's a particular kind of pleasure, one that's alien to the wild rivers and churning surfs, the ice-in-the-guides and cast-till-you-collapse kind of fishing that hairy-chested males conventionally crave. To reap its rewards you have to be patient, selfless, restrained—no small feat when you're convinced that alongside that log over there lies the biggest largemouth outside of the Okefenokee.

Don't worry—you'll know when your boy is big enough to join in, not just tag along. He'll get the message across. A joke, a challenge, a "You mean to tell me, Dad, that you can't even cast an ounce-and-a-half plug to the edge of that sandbar?" and you'll suddenly find yourself experiencing the same pride I felt on that long-ago March morning when Jack accompanied me to the Plum Island surf and beat his old man's britches off.

A third way in which parents often err when fishing with their youngsters is by expecting to get too much out of the experience. If you and your boy happen to be estranged, for example, or if crushing business commitments always seem to keep you apart, you can't expect a few hours of fishing to provide instant intimacy. All those cute calendar photos to the contrary—the ones where never is heard a discouraging word, and dads and lads revel in sunny, bugless, fish-filled, tangle-free contentment—an afternoon of worm-dunking with your young son is not likely to patch any big holes in the canvas of your compatibility. It can help. It can lay the groundwork. Words come easy and honest while you and your boy sit watching bobbers on a quiet pond, but fishing can only provide the forum for your reconciliation. Chances are, if you haven't been able to work things out between you on the living-room couch, you won't have much better success from a few hours on the thwarts of a skiff.

You might, if you're mercilessly honest with yourself, even have to admit to being a little bit like that comic-strip character who feels *obligated* to take his son fishing. "Part of growing up," he insists. "Every boy should learn to lay out 50 feet of matched double-tapered flyline before he has his first date." Usually this oration concludes with a reminder to less perceptive parents not to forget that wise old outdoor aphorism, "Spare the rod and spoil the child, heh, heh." Then he goes out and buys the poor kid a $250 split-bamboo instrument to do his learning on.

Fishing for this father is an entry on a checkoff list entitled CHILDHOOD. It's wedged between *Smallpox Vaccination* and *Birds and Bees, Talk About*. Somehow he has convinced himself that catching a trout on a well-presented fly will ensure for his son a lifetime of health, wealth, and wisdom untainted by the tawdriness that lurks beyond the banks of sylvan trout streams.

Baloney! The outdoors, despite its being a great breeding ground for brotherhood and all the beautiful golden-rule qualities that this over-worked word implies, is no convenient cloister against greed, selfishness, or that "to hell with the other guy" attitude that's at the root of most of the world's agonies. The ubiquitous spoor of beer cans and candy wrappers that desecrates our outdoors quickly dispels this illusion.

Furthermore, no dad *owes* his son fishing any more than his son owes him the opportunity of sharing in his simple unspoiled world of wonder. If this is the attitude with which you're inviting your boy, then he's better off turning you down. The pity of it is that he probably won't. Wanting to avoid hurting your feelings, he'll endure a day of your well-intentioned overindulgence and vow never to fish again.

If you're not selfish, unreasonable, unrealistic, or misguided and you still find fishing with your son—or the prospect of it—unsatisfying, then you're probably ignorant. And before you start swinging a gaff in my direction, let me hasten to emphasize that I mean *uninformed*-ignorant, not *stupid*-ignorant: you'd love to take your son fishing, but you simply don't know how to go about it. You can't even tell a bank sinker from a pyramid, a dry fly from a wet. Lures with their vast variety of designs, shapes, colors, sizes, and actions (and prices!) bewilder you, and you see a high order of impenetrable mystery in the conversation of two fly-fishermen discussing such esoterica as matched outfits, shooting heads, roll casts, and 3X tippets. Popping corks make you think of champagne, not busting bass, and if someone asked you to identify a bucktail jig, you'd probably say it's a male deer doing an Irish dance.

Okay, so you don't know much about the mechanics of fishing. This is easily remedied, and will be to the degree you desire in subsequent chapters. The main obstacles to enjoyment when fishing with children, though, are not mechanical. They're things like wet feet and overcomplicated equipment and never catching any fish. It took me many years to find this out, and considering some of my early flops, I sometimes marvel that Jack and Dan ever fished again. Apparently, though, I was doing enough right things along with the wrong ones and I corrected most of the wrong ones before the scars became permanent, because today fishing appears to occupy an appropriately important place in their young-adult lives.

After our first few tries, though, it was obvious that Jack and Dan were heading at flank speed down the road to disillusionment. Even after I had acknowledged my selfishness and done my best to compensate for it, our trips were only sporadically satisfying. Sure, Dan nearly exploded with excitement when he caught his first striper from the surf, but the seemingly endless empty hours of prospecting that led up to it were dull and frustrating for a boy who hadn't yet caught his quota of ordinary fish by ordinary methods. Jack too was overjoyed when he caught his first brightly speckled brook trout from a mountain stream, but even the prospect of more and bigger trout from up-country lakes couldn't convince him that trolling was anything but tedious.

"Can't understand those boys," I told myself. "Lord knows I certainly enjoyed fishing when I was their age. . . ."

. . . Sunfish finning in a New Hampshire pond . . . small mottled ovals of excitement . . . pectorals vibrating . . . flanks aflame in incandescent orange . . . darting with a sweep of their tails toward tiny bits of bread . . . nipping, nibbling, expelling, then ingesting again. . . .

These were my first fish. I was four, maybe five years old at the time, spending a few days with friends at their summer camp set back among the pines. The memory is as bright as the sun that baked my bare back while I lay for hours at the end of that dock watching my first authentically wild creatures from close up, as clear as the almost illusory water in which they swam. I don't remember my first ice cream or my first pair of long pants. I don't even remember the first girl I kissed. But even today I can almost count the scales on those fascinating little fish.

A few years later when I commenced a four-year succession of summer vacations on the Massachusetts seashore, I had pretty well learned the rudiments of freshwater fishing. Hooked by my first session with sunfish, I had been delighted to learn on coming home that the Merrimack River, practically at my doorstep in Lawrence, fairly teemed with sunnies, and thereafter I lost few opportunities to exploit this knowledge. Weekends when the Tower Hill Gladiators didn't have a ball game against the Spicket River Indians or the South Lawrence Bulldogs, afternoons when the good nuns of St. Augustine's weren't keeping me after school for some delinquency, and holidays with only rare exceptions I could be found with the rest of the local Huck Finns—Tom (Molly) Muldoon, Bob (Fat) Gibbons, Dick (Hector) Parthenais—clustered around the sewage outlet at the foot of Strathmore Road floating our bobbers through the gray foamy flow.

In retrospect it's a pretty unappetizing picture, but the kivvers (the Big Guys told us that this was their real name) didn't seem to care, so why, we figured, should we. Before long we even learned to endure the dull gagging stench, because here, we found, was the lair of larger, more enchanting species like yellow perch ("zebrafish" we dubbed them) and, if we could bump our worms along the bottom without losing our hard-to-come-by hooks on an old tire or a rusty oil drum, eels ("snakefish").

In time we found a weedy backwater from which crappies and pickerel could be coaxed, the former on grasshoppers, the latter on live frogs. Once one of the gang caught a hornpout during a stay at a relative's cottage, but of course none of us would believe him. "A fish with a mustache? C'mawwn."

It was like a Klondike gold rush when Parthenais discovered that he could catch big brown scaly fish (carp)—"Honestagawd, thi-i-i-s long!"—on doughballs at the intake tank of the municipal water-treatment plant alongside the Merrimack, and once, when the river went on a rampage, flooding streets, inundating entire blocks, driving families from their homes and merchants from their stores, we had the time of our lives catching suckers from downtown Lawrence's sidewalks.

The seashore, I soon learned, was different. Bobbers didn't float well from a wave-walloped beach, quarter-ounce egg-shaped sinkers couldn't cope with strong tidal currents, and my telescopic steel rod and bait-casting reel with which I had learned to cast beyond the outermost lily pads back home couldn't come close to dropping my sand eels and clam necks into the trough beyond the barrier bar where I sensed that fish must be feeding.

I had to serve my apprenticeship all over again, and ah, what a joyous education it was. Creeks, I found, contained tommycod and colorful little killifish, and harbors held flounder. At night the beach often would be full of whiting and tinker mackerel, driven ashore, I presume, by marauding stripers, although few spoke or even knew about stripers back in the late 1930s, when this superb species was in decline.

The discovery that my old sweetheart, the Merrimack, met the Atlantic only a few miles from where we were staying enabled me to resume my red-hot puppy-love affair and also, I am told, gave my parents cause to wonder if they had reared the first pre-teen dropout of his generation. Every day, with time out only for Sunday services, Fourth of July fireworks, and occasionally the supreme adventure of fishing from a boat, I would rise before daybreak, fry myself a couple of eggs, and head south along the dawn-dappled beach wearing only a pair of salt-encrusted shorts with dried sand eels and rusty hooks in all of their pockets.

The Merrimack's broad mouth, churning between the jettied jaws of Salisbury on the north and Plum Island on the south, was my Oz, the Salisbury jetty my Yellow Brick Road. With the agility and surefootedness of a Dall ram, I ran barefooted along its jagged jumble of weedy barnacled boulders, learning the location of every sandbar and backwater, getting cut off occasionally when the tide came in faster than I did but always diving unconcernedly across the breaches while the sea sighed between swells, and always at low tide replenishing my sinker and hook supplies from other anglers' broken-off hangups.

Droplines were my weapons then, coils of strong brown twine that snarled like matted hair and smelled strongly of the sea. With them I learned to send 4 to 6 ounces of lead soaring at just the right up-current angle to ensure that my clam neck would swing through troughs and pockets I had discovered when the tide was low.

Though I rarely brought along more than a candy bar or two to eat, I never went hungry. I became a sort of puerile panhandler, exploiting adults on porches who just loved to invite tanned little towheads in for lunch. My poor mother, bless her, surely one of the world's ablest cooks and most hospitable hostesses, must have been scorned many times *in absentia* by my benefactors while they watched me wolf down their handouts.

"Poor little thing," I could almost hear them whispering, "he must have a very unhappy home life."

One family, whose son Fred became my close pal, fed me regularly in their riverside cottage until I wore out my welcome one day by covering their flat roof on a hot July morning with what Fred and I had concluded was ambergris, that gray, waxy, and very rare whale regurgitation used in making perfume. Had it really been ambergris, our rooftop treasure might have been worth the millions Fred and I had already spent (a party boat trip every day for the rest of our lives!) when we sat down with Fred's mother and older sister for lunch. Alas, it was not, and the longer we sat, the more obvious it became that what was baking in the sun 10 feet above us bore not even a remote resemblance to perfume. After we had carried out our orders to "get that horrible stuff off that roof this instant, every last lump of it, and bury it, bury it deep, do you hear me?" we were reminded that in the Merrimack, anything resembling ambergris is more likely to have been expelled by upriver humans than downriver whales.

Looking back on how I learned to fish, then, I concluded that freedom must have been what I liked best about my boyhood fishing: setting my own pace; following my own flexible-as-I-cared-to-make-it schedule; defining and delineating my own world of wonder and excitement. Maybe, I thought, this is what my sons are missing. Maybe I just ought to keep my nose out and let them locate their own Yellow Brick Roads. Maybe, I concluded, with a sudden sense of loss, adults and children shouldn't even try to fish together.

But the fallacy of this reasoning wasn't hard to find. . . .

. . . Cap, the man I met on the beach whose inexhaustible patience in untying my tangles showed me that fishing is not all just casting and catching . . . Chet, father of the family with whom we shared our cottage, spending a rare Sunday off with his sons, Sonny and Donald, and me in a rented skiff so we could catch our first flounder . . . Midge, Sonny's and Don's uncle, who treated us to the ultimate adventure of our first party boat trip. . . .

Even my own father tried fishing once, and for a man so totally unsuited for the outdoors, this was a genuinely heroic gesture. It was not at the beach. These were Depression years, and an hour or two of an occasional evening was the most that this marvelous man could squeeze in between his eighteen-hours-every-day drudgeries at his diner. But years later, when his workload had diminished to a mere ten or twelve hours a day with a day off every month or so for good behavior, he spent a night with me under the stars on an island in New Hampshire's Lake Winnipesaukee.

Fishing, unfortunately, was out of the question. Dad was completely preoccupied with fending off the Stuka attacks of insatiable swarms of mammoth mosquitos. Although a tough and talented former prizefighter, he had a hide as soft and bitable as a baby's behind. Not only did insects find it irresistible, but the hard Granite State ground crushed it like putty.

"Cooked by too many hours over that steam table," he used to say when I ribbed him about it years later.

And do you know, I wasn't really disappointed that Dad couldn't share my love for fishing. I was just pleased and proud that this great guy, who had had to hustle for the better part of his parentless childhood in mills and restaurants and haberdasheries and boxing rings to earn his kid sister's five-dollar-a-week rent, had loved me enough to endure what must have been his most unpleasant experience since the trenches of World War I.

Conclusion: Some fathers shouldn't go fishing with their sons, or, for that matter, with anyone else.

Cranking this into my cranial computer, I asked myself, "And what about children? Mightn't there be some children, too, who shouldn't go fishing?"

The answer, of course, was yes. Sonny and Donald, I remembered, fished with me only occasionally, and even then not for very long. (Later I would have even more vivid evidence in my own son Matt, who, through some genetic mixup, has all the interest in fishing that his father once had in the study of differential equations.)

Another input for my computer.

By comparing what I liked about fishing as a boy with what I enjoy about it as an adult, I came up with these additional inputs:

1. Men are stronger than children, able to walk faster, cast further, wade deeper, climb higher, carry heavier loads. But children are more agile. A child is likely to fuel his endurance with spunk rather than strength, and pay the price in exhaustion later on.

2. An adult's experience is likely to make him confident but cautious. A child's lack of it can make him either frightened or reckless.

3. Grownups, because they are committed to fishing, are impatient of distractions. Children, because they have not yet eaten beyond the appetizers of life's banquet, are easily distracted.

4. Children, however, can concentrate longer and harder on something

that intrigues them than can adults, whose thoughts often are assailed by reminders of the leak in the roof, the knock in the car, the pain in the chest, the bills in the mailbox.

5. Adults seek silence, solitude, contemplation in the outdoors. Children seek excitement.

6. The four ingredients of successful fishing for both adults and children are: appealing environment, free mind and conscience, physical and emotional comfort, and a reasonable chance of catching good fish.

With a whirring of my mental wheels, out came these ten suggestions for fishing successfully with children:

1. Let them do their own fishing.
2. Make sure they have action.
3. Keep them comfortable.
4. Don't force them.
5. Start them in gentle waters with simple methods.
6. Equip them properly.
7. *Make* time, *take* time.
8. Learn as well as teach.
9. Include your daughters.
10. Enjoy them while you can.

## LET THEM DO THEIR OWN FISHING

The two fathers fishing with their young sons were as different in their approaches as a butcher and a brain surgeon. One, hip-high in waders, was casting a bushy fly alongside a distant weedbed as he lectured to his son, who stood shivering in the shallows, on the intricacies of pickups and backcasts, shooting heads and tapered leaders. The other sat silently on the rocky elbow of a quiet cove watching his boy dangle a worm from his bamboo pole and wait for his bobber to start dancing.

The first boy was so cold and confused that his day of fun and excitement quickly deteriorated into an ugly academic exercise. When he grows up he'll probably look back on his fishing experiences with the same degree of fondness with which he recalls algebra exams and dental appointments. The other boy—comfortable, unpressured, and catching fish—probably will evolve into an accomplished and enthusiastic angler. Firmly founded in fundamentals and learning them in his own way at his own pace, he will inherit the legacy of his dad's devotion to the outdoors.

Once you've explained the basics to your son—hook, line, bait, rod, reel, where the fish are likely to be and what is likely to entice them—leave

Once you've taught them the fundamentals, let them do their own fishing. If they need help, they'll call. If not, then playing and landing their own fish unassisted will bring a greater sense of accomplishment. (Photo: Milt Rosko)

the lad alone. Let him learn his own lessons, discover his own delights. He'll holler for help when he gets hung up or his line snarls, but unless he asks for your aid, let him bait his own hook, cast his own lure, play his own fish, and yes, even lose a few in the process. Backlashes and falling in the water and the sudden sickening limpness when a carelessly tied knot unravels—these constitute the curriculum in the school of angling experience. As a wise fisherman once commented, "In order to angle, you have to untangle."

Still, there is a lot a parent can teach a child—about fishing, about nature, and in turn about life and the living of it. It's not the learning that a child objects to, it's the lecturing. His eager, interested mind is receptive as a blotter to new ideas, especially on a subject as fascinating as fishing, but admonitions, exhortations, orders—these belong back in the stern, structured environment of the schoolroom. Learning in relaxed, roll-up-your-sleeves places like ponds and streams and bays and beaches is best accomplished by the osmosis of example, observation, and gentle reminders.

A flower, for example. Say you and your son are wading a woodland brook when through a tangle of brush you see a tiny patch of pink: a lady's slipper, that shy, royal recluse of the northern forests. You pause, you kneel in silent homage; you bend, look, touch. Suddenly your son is kneeling beside you.

"What is it, Dad?" he asks eagerly, and there's your invitation to enter his fertile little mind and sow the seeds of knowledge, respect, appreciation.

Or a trout. One of those irritating escape artists that used to drive you ding-dong till you learned how to mend your line and strike a split second sooner, and now this fish is irritating your son the same way. What are you going to do? Are you going to wade in alongside him and administer a patronizing pat on the head with your "Here, son, let me show you how to do it right"?

Much as you hate to admit it, that might be exactly what you would do. You're a father, and fathers are smarter than their sons, and being human (vain, arrogant, insensitive, etc.), they like to let their sons know it. Ironically, the contrary is also true: sons enjoy being reminded of their dads' superiority. Dads are supposed to be big and strong and smart, benevolent protectors with all the answers, and it's reassuring for a boy to know that his dad fills the bill.

But boys also are sensitive. Their psyches are as bruisable as berries. The reassurance you give them by showing them the right way can quickly be counterbalanced by the kick you give them in their tender little confidences.

So what do you do? To a great extent it depends on what kind of son you've got. Is he fragile? Is he resilient? Is he shy? Is he cocky? (And if so, is his cockiness an overcompensation for a lack of confidence?) No, I can't prescribe a universal treatment, and thank heaven I can't. Coming up with solutions to perplexing predicaments is part of the adventure of being a parent. But I *can* suggest that you don't teach your youngster about fishing in a way that will embarrass him or make him feel inferior. And I *can* tell you about the day Jack and Dan learned how to catch striped bass from a rocky beach.

It was a banner day for Dad, one of those inspired occasions when I could do no wrong and my sons could do no right. After two rainy hours in a chill Atlantic surf during which I hit for the circuit—worms, popping plugs, swimming plugs, and streamer flies—the boys were ready to acknowledge that maybe the old man knew something about fishing after all. Through it all Jack was stubbornly sticking with his 9-foot fly rod. Because he was using it like the 7-foot freshwater wand he was used to, his timing was all off. Because he was wading waist deep, he was flogging the water on every backcast. Because he wanted more than anything to catch a striper on one of his own-tied flies, he was getting madder—and messier—by the minute.

When Jack watched me catch my fourth fish, he revealed to me by the sudden slump of his shoulders that his scales had tipped: just the catching of a bass now meant more than catching one on his streamer fly.

"C'mon," I said, offering him the plugging rod I was using, "catch yourself a couple. You can go back to flies later."

A half-dozen heaves and he was on. Ten minutes later he had another. I, meanwhile, had ascended a half-submerged boulder close enough to Jack so that I knew he would observe how, because my backcasts were aimed higher and retained a little longer than his, my line would uncoil smoothly toward my target a few feet off the water, dropping my fly far out and right at the edge of the rip where I aimed it.

When I slid my first striper onto the rock, I suggested that we swap again, and soon afterward Jack was playing his own fly-caught striper . . . from atop the same rock.

Dan, meanwhile, couldn't buy a strike. His casts with his 9-foot spinning rod were long and accurate, his retrieves were careful and spiced with occasional well-timed changes of pace, but for the bass in front of us his 6-inch swimming plug seemed to have all the appeal of a killer whale. After another half-hour without a strike, while I took two more fish while standing only a few feet to his right, Dan was beyond mere frustration. Disappointed, discouraged, demoralized, he needed action and he needed it fast.

"Here," I said, handing him my 6-foot rod, "you'll feel more comfortable with this." Tying on a 3-inch plug that more closely resembled the baitfish on which I had seen the bass feeding, I said, "Lay it right out there, right at the head of that rip. Let it set for a second or two, then pull it hard, for about five feet. Bass will think their dinner is getting away."

Fifteen minutes later Dan had three fish on his stringer and a smile as big as a sunrise on his face.

Silence and solitude might be enough for you, but not for your youngster. In the early stages he craves action, any kind of action.

## MAKE SURE THEY HAVE ACTION

Imagine you're bowling and the pins refuse to topple. Imagine you're golfing and your ball won't drop into the hole.

This has to be how it is for children who can't catch fish. Oh, granted their failures are at least partly attributable to ineptitude: their casts are clumsy, their lures inappropriate, they rattle the oarlocks. But you see, they don't know this. They don't discern, or even look for, or in the beginning even care much about the subtle differences between their unrefined techniques and your own. They want to catch fish, and it's up to you to make sure they do.

I should have been more concerned about action for Dan when he and I fished a dark north-of-Boston beach for striped bass. He must have come perilously close to quitting fishing altogether after four actionless hours of celebrating his twelfth birthday with a session of my—not his, but my—favorite brand of fishing. Fortunately, just before midnight an accommodating 8-pounder pasted his plug as it wobbled along the down-tide edge of a sandy slope. Dan was so delighted with his first striper that he kissed it flush on its mouth as we headed homeward over the dunes. When Peg served it the following evening—not filleted into a couple of anonymous slabs of meat, but stuffed and baked so Dan could still identify his prize—he must have felt that first flush of the hunter's atavistic exhilaration when he provides food for his family.

If, like most anglers, you've brought home more than your share of empty stringers, my exhortation to make sure your child catches fish must sound highly hypothetical. It shouldn't. There are plenty of species that your boy and you almost always can catch by easy-to-master methods. So okay, sunfish on a lily-padded pond might be a little elementary for your refined trout-taking talents. So granted, dunking mud worms for flounder is minor-league stuff compared to trolling big rips for bull bluefish. But these quiet compromises are part of the price you pay for the privilege of being a parent. Furthermore, any form of fishing can be enthrallingly enjoyable if you adapt your tackle, techniques, and attitude. Finally, be grateful for the honor of being welcomed into your child's world. It's a very exclusive domain. For adults, entry is by invitation only.

Action for a youngster can include many things besides catching fish. For Dan that night, casting into the eerie infinity a few feet in front of him was a challenge. Exploring a busy beach that had been transformed by the alchemy of night into a jungle of terrifying delight was a spooky adventure. And as No. 2 sibling in a large family, he experienced the emotional reassurance of a private all-for-him party with no competition from his older brother.

Nevertheless, as his ten, twenty, thirty casts grew to forty, fifty, sixty, each punctuated by an unspoken plea for that yank that never came, the challenge and adventure grew progressively less important, the catching of a fish progressively more. Thank heaven for that birthday bass!

Today, at the top of his teens, Dan occasionally accompanies me to the ocean's edge for stripers, but mostly it's to enjoy the ocean rather than the fishing. Today it's obvious to me (and would have been then if I had stopped casting long enough to notice) that Dan is a physical fisherman. For him the continuous computation of azimuth and elevation and retrieve speed as tide and wind and topography change is a tedious mechanical chore. But if I should invite him to plug a pickerel-filled pond, he'd be in the driveway honking the horn before I could grab my tackle box. Fortunately in the early years, Dan and I shared enough of these occasions too.

## KEEP THEM COMFORTABLE

"Clothes," some enterprising haberdasher once said, "make the man." On a frozen lake, clothes make—or break—the day.

Since cold is the arch foe of comfort, in ice fishing proper dress is of prime importance. No need to overdo it by stocking up like an army quartermaster depot, but don't underdo it either; the same outfits you wear skiing or sledding aren't necessarily appropriate for open lakes or slushy ice. Pay particular attention to your feet. Cold hands might

Ice fishing can be pleasure or pain, depending on how well protected you are against chill winds and subfreezing temperatures.

mean warm heart, but cold feet means cold all over. You and your youngster should wear two pairs of socks, one thick and woolen, the other conventional, inside thick, dry, ankle-high boots. Always bring along spare socks in case melting ice should start seeping through the boots that you could have sworn the man said were waterproof.

Bodies need a layer or two of heavy shirt and pants sandwiched between insulated skivvies on top of regular underwear on the inside, and insulated jacket on the outside. Two lighter layers are preferable to a single heavy one because they trap air, the best insulator of all.

Hats should protect ears as well as head, and gloves should combine warmth with the ability to articulate your fingers enough to play fish. Normally, of course, you'll play fish and bait hooks barehanded, but subzero weather soon freezes alfresco fingers, especially after they've handled damp bait and dripping lines a few times.

When in doubt about whether or not to tote a few more clothes, tote. They won't take up much room in the trunk of your car, and if you should find you need them (as you most likely will), they won't do you or your child any good if they're back home in the bureau drawer.

In recent years science has invaded the outdoors with warmers for hands, feet, and other vulnerable parts. Recently I heard of a new space-age back-pocket installation called "Seat Heat," designed, its promoters claimed, "to combat that draft aft." Well, now, the Fallon keesters get as cold as the next guy's, but, while we don't spurn a little help in keeping hands, feet, nose, and ears warm, we draw the line a few paces this side of Sterno for the stern.

Protection on the ice is provided either by firmly anchored canvas or wooden windbreaks, or by what surely has to be the most inspired example of utilitarian architecture since the two-cylinder privy, the bobhouse. Only ardent anglers should invest in bobhouses. Not that they're terribly difficult or expensive to build: despite some clever conveniences on the inside and distinguishing designs on the outside, most bobhouses represent the ultimate triumph of function over form. Nevertheless, they take time and a truck to transport and install, care to maintain, and attention to ensure that they're removed before spring ice becomes periously thin. The bottom of many a North Country lake is marred by rusting trucks—some with their drivers still behind the wheel—whose owners waited too long.

If buying or building a bobhouse is inappropriate for you, maybe you can rent one. There's always an enterprising up-country resident or two ready to do some dickerin'. If you can rent one at a reasonable price, by all means do. Not just for the physical comfort it can provide, but for the relaxing, reassuring neighborliness a bobhouse always encourages. Keep a coffee pot perking. Its fragrance will attract chilly fishermen like a chumline. Then your child will learn first-hand about one of the outdoors' most delightful dividends—people. Warm, bright, open, honest people whose creed of helping and sharing and caring sometimes seems to be the only salvation for this poor abused planet of ours.

And incidentally, be careful of that fire in your bobhouse stove. Be sure you have an extinguisher handy in case a carelessly placed newspaper or bread wrapper should ignite, and also let in air occasionally. Stoves use up oxygen fast.

Outside, a blazing bonfire can warm hands, cook food . . . and melt ice. In short order a big blaze can eat through a couple of inches. Even if your weight doesn't take you through the rest of the way, you can wind up ankle-deep in ice water, an unpleasant circumstance even when you're wearing heavy boots and thick socks. Jack and I came upon an ideal solution to the problem in the cove of a neighborhood pond where fishermen had built their bonfire on solid ground. Firewood was plentiful and their tip-ups, arrayed in a broad arc before them, were easily monitored while they chatted and ate, and, incidentally, invited us to join them.

Eating as well as heating contributes to angling comfort. This is especially true of children, whose appetites are accustomed to frequent attention. Start their day with bacon and eggs and home-fries, preferably at some diner they've never been to. For children there's something adventurously adult about such breakfasts. (For adults who've been lucky enough to enjoy such meals when they were children, the adventure never wears thin.)

A thermos of hot chocolate or soup will keep juices flowing on a cold day, lemonade or soda on a hot one, but for a real treat in the woods, one to recharge your spirits as well as slake your thirsts, find a cool spring or a clear brook and drink your fill. Don't gulp. Sip and savor. I can see and hear and smell and taste every brook and spring I've ever drunk from: soft trickling sibilations; the rich musty redolence of earth; cool penetrating purity, like liquid diamonds or the distillation of eternal dews.

Cold can plague you during spring and fall as well as winter. Best fishing, with certain understandable exceptions, is found early and late in the season and early and late in the day. On those May mornings that haven't warmed up yet, and those brisk autumn evenings that suddenly succeed sunny afternoons, chills can quickly put your child out of commission. Likewise rain. A downpour can (although not necessarily does) improve fishing, but it also will dampen your youngster's enthusiasm once his teeth start chattering. So bring your foul-weather gear, and before you leave home, patch those rips in his parka and pinholes in his boots. From tiny trickles great torrents grow.

The biggest bane of warm-weather fishing is insects. The best time for fishing is the worst time for bugs, and those relentless swarms of black flies and midges and mosquitos are more than just an irritant; they can put a child in a hospital. The only really effective insect repellent I've found is a smoldering, billowing smudge from the rankest stogie I can find. Next morning I feel like sandblasting the inside of my mouth, but at least I'm assured of a few hours of uninterrupted fishing.

Stogies, though, won't help your youngster, so anoint him—and yourself—liberally on all exposed skin with a reliable potion, either commercial or kitchen variety. Be sure also to button collars and cuffs and to tuck pants inside stockings. Inquire about and experiment with repellents until you find one that works reasonably well for you, but also keep a couple of headnets handy for those all-too-frequent occasions when insects won't stop for anything short of a flamethrower.

Warm, dry, bug-free, and well fed, your youngster now can fish in comfort for as long as his stamina will allow. And for heaven's sake, remember that it won't last as long as yours. Saturation for him is a lot less than surfeit for you. When you see your son slump, pooped, under a tree, and you holler as you continue to cast, "Hey, what're you, a sissy?" his bruised subconscious is going to chalk one up against fishing. From now on, says his subconscious, let's you and me stick with less pain-prone pursuits.

It's just as important, therefore, to keep him psychologically comfortable as it is to keep his body dry, warm, rested, and unhungry. I recall with chagrin the embarrassment I caused Mary Beth when she was a teen-ager by having her waddle past her peers on a crowded beach wearing my mammoth and much-too-masculine waders. I recollect with sympathy a lad on a Cape Cod shore whose inept casting with his father's 9-foot surf rod mortified him unbearably in the presence of my Julie and Margaret.

And now one final suggestion for coping with those minor crises that you can't anticipate but which always seem to happen anyway: bring along matches, flashlight, sunburn lotion, first-aid kit, boot-patching kit, dry socks, a couple of candy bars, and a small pair of wire cutters for snipping off the barbs of hooks that sometimes get themselves imbedded in flesh.

Children tire more easily than adults. When they run out of gas, don't force them to keep fishing. Even a fighting fish doesn't interest the youngster sleeping in the bow of this boat. (Photo: Terry McDonnell)

## DON'T FORCE THEM

Matthew Fallon, sixteen, loves to write, draw, paint, sculpt, cook, dream, act, manufacture paper, decorate cakes, produce movies, reenact Revolutionary War battles, and put on puppet shows at schools and hospitals, but he hates to fish. Through some confusion in our chromosomes, Peg, who loves fishing, and I, who am obsessed by it, have begotten ourselves a genetic sport.

Very early in the game, Matt made it evident that fishing wasn't his cup of cocoa. When a trout rose on a forest stream, launching me and Matt's brothers into an orbit of excitement, Matt would more often than not continue chasing his butterflies or scrutinizing his flowers. Same with the seashore. He would come along gladly, but not for the fishing. One night on the Massachusetts coast I waded from where Matt and Jack sat on a bouldered bank enjoying the star-spangled serenity, cast into the ebony ocean, and caught a striped bass on my first try. Jack was grabbing for the rod before I had beached the bass, but Matt barely moved.

Perhaps, I thought, I just haven't hit on the right brand of angling for Matt. Something intimate and active, I reasoned, yet leaving him enough leeway for enjoying the environment. Jetty fishing, I concluded: ocean on three sides, plenty of opportunity for ruminating between casts, and with the April cod run in full swing, a high probability of latching onto a big fish in challenging waters. We ate well, we dressed properly, and the bright balmy morning was coined for the occasion. Matt observed attentively while I tied on a pair of appropriate-size hooks above a 4-ounce pyramid sinker, baited them with clam necks, and cast about 30 degrees upcurrent with my 7-foot spinning rod. After a pair of practice casts, he was heaving his bait as accurately and as far as my own.

It couldn't have been more than five minutes later when Matt edged up behind me as I arranged our gear on a flat rock.

"Uh, Dad," he said, "is this what we're looking for?"

Ten pounds of bright, bronzed, brawny beauty! On his first cast! If this doesn't make a fisherman out of him, I exulted, nothing will.

It didn't. And nothing will. Ten minutes after his triumph, Matt had slithered down into the jetty's jumbled innards to examine a cluster of barnacles. After that he edged back toward the beach, ambled along the strand, and spent the rest of the morning watching gulls soar and swoop and tumble, pausing occasionally to pat a dog or pick up a shell. A beautiful boy, Matthew Fallon, but not a fisherman.

Since that day Matt and I have had an understanding: if he should want to go fishing, he'll say so; otherwise I won't invite him. This is not just an implied understanding. You can't simply assume when you're dealing with something as sensitive as a son's suspicion that he might be disappointing his Dad. You talk about it. In plain words.

"Matt," I said, "seems to me you're not fond of fishing. Am I right? And please," I added, "don't feel that you'll be disappointing me if you say no."

Since then Matt and I have been spending time together in ways we both enjoy: swimming, an occasional visit to the Concord Bridge, or just lying under our apple tree and counting stars. If your son, like Matt, doesn't enjoy fishing; if you've honestly enabled him to try it in enough different ways with the odds for enjoyment heavily in his favor, and he still sits serenely on his rock when bass are busting, then don't force him. Without a seed of interest, all the fertilizing in the world won't make him flower into a fisherman.

Every child, remember, is delightfully different—in interests, personality, coordination, size, shape, sensitivities, metabolism—and the biggest difference of all (vive!) is between boys and girls. Each is a marvelous mosaic of distinguishing elements, and the balance and emphasis of these elements are altered by age. Today's carefree Huckleberry Finn is tomorrow's busy butcher, baker, and candlestick maker.

Matt and I, we have our own private assortment of memories. Like the morning I tiptoed to his bedside, woke him, and whispered:

"C'mon, get dressed. Let's have an adventure." We drove 30 miles to the Boston airport, boarded a plane, and flew to the New York World's Fair. Jack, Dan, and Mary Beth had visited the fair with their aunt, and Matt's trip was sort of to even things up.

That evening as our plane rose from LaGuardia's runway and banked sharply toward New England, Matt snuggled up close. I like to think he snuggled solely out of affection, but considering that he was almost ten, I suppose I'll have to credit gravity with an assist. Nevertheless, Matt and I at that moment, united by a common contentment, experienced a classic father-and-son closeness.

As Manhattan swung past our window like a cluster of smog-shrouded stalagmites, Matt lifted his head, sighed, and said, "This has been the best day of my whoooole life."

And with this, Matt taught me another of the many lessons I have learned from my children. He taught me that even in my angling-oriented world where there are few experiences more important than fishing with my children, one of these experiences is just plain being with my children.

## START THEM IN GENTLE WATERS
## WITH SIMPLE METHODS

My father, one of the sweetest, swellest, roughest, toughest, softest, tenderest Great Guys in humanity's history, could lick a lion, charm a snake, and coax a smile from the Sphinx. In fact, as a boy I thought there wasn't anything Dad couldn't do. This illusion lasted until it came time for him to tell me about sex.

"Son," he said, "I think it's time we had a talk about, well you know, girls and, well, you know, things like that."

My glib "Okay, Dad, what is it you want to know?" so unnerved the poor guy that he quit right there and called in the reserves. He sent me to our family doctor, who so confused me with talk of sperm and ova and adolescent acne that he set my puberty back a good six months.

A few years later Dad made another stab at letting me know what makes the world go round. By this time I was seventeen, only a few months from the Army Air Corps, and had pretty well mastered the principles if not the practices of the birds and bees. What Dad had in mind, however, was something more advanced: a cram course in homosexuality.

"No son of mine is going to put on a uniform without knowing what's what."

We were weekending in New York City, an annual New Year's rite which we both knew would soon be interrupted by my military service, when Dad brought me to my first night club. Soft lights, cozy couples, patronizing *maître d'*, claustrophobic dance floor—all authenticated the atmosphere of a real live Manhattan bistro, and had these clues left any doubts, the sylphlike beauty of its chorines would have dispelled them.

Then Dad had to go and spoil it by leaning across our table and commenting casually, "They're guys, you know."

My buck-and-a-quarter Coke almost wound up in my lap.

"Yeah," he said, "they're all guys dressed up like girls. Even that one."

"That one" was Eva, the featured performer, an utterly unmasculine assemblage of bumps and bulges, animated by fluttering mascara'd eyes, crowned by a crop of spangled raven curls, and sinuating with a sensuality that would have made the Dance of the Seven Veils seem like close-order drill.

"Sure," Dad repeated as Eva's act concluded, "all guys. Here, let me show you."

"N-n-no thanks," I insisted, but Dad was beckoning to Eva to join us.

"Your act," he said with a wave of his hand and a mincy little wiggle of his shoulders, "was gra-a-and."

"You really think so?" answered Eva—eyebrows up, chest out, breath in. "Well, you know, I'm surprised, really surprised, because well, y'know, last night was New Year's Eve and all I can say tonight is I'm one sick bitch."

You can understand, then, how there were times when I was grateful that Dad didn't fish. Much as I would have enjoyed his company, I shudder to think of the traumatic initiation I might have received: killer whales on dry flies, a canoe trip around Cape Horn.

A lot of incipient anglers have been disenchanted by being expected to handle a job they couldn't cope with. Fathers who would readily acknowledge the absurdity of expecting their sons to backstroke across the English Channel first time they tried swimming don't hesitate to start them fishing for spooky trout with #16 dry flies or for bruiser bluefish in choppy seas. Then they wonder why the lads do a disappearing act next time Daddy comes up the cellar stairs toting his tackle box. They've been embarrassed, that's why, and they've been unfulfilled. Both are mortal sins for the father who would befriend his boy. Both leave lasting scars.

Take bruiser blues (or dolphin or permit or steelhead; whatever fits). Let's say you're trolling alongside a Nantucket Sound shoal: stiff 5-foot rod, star-drag reel, Monel line, 20 feet of 40-pound-test monofilament leader, and a bucktail jig with pork-rind tail. The big leagues, right? Nothing's too good for your youngster.

After years of practice, you can jig at the right rhythm, the right angle, for hours before your arms ache or your fingers cramp, but a boy's biceps can't take more than a few minutes of this punishment. The more tired he gets, the sloppier he operates; the sloppier he operates, the more impatient you become. Your soft tolerant tones start taking on a cutting edge. No, of course you don't notice it, but your son does.

Nor will a little action take care of everything. With bluefish, there's no such thing as a little action. A 10- or 12-pound blue can make a monkey out of most inexperienced men. (They still humble the hell out of me regularly.) With a tempest by the tail and a rolling, pitching boat keeping him off balance, he'll hold on and hope for the best till he dips his rod or reels too slowly, and his line suddenly goes limp. Unless, of course,

Start a boy on fish he can handle in waters he can cope with. He'll have a better chance of taming the big ones if he learns how to handle the smaller ones first.

you "give him a hand," grabbing his rod with a "Here, watch this," and demolish his confidence completely.

And don't delude yourself into thinking that your well-intentioned reassurances ("That's okay, son, you'll get him next time—I lost four blues myself before I boated my first one") will boost his ego. A couple more lost fish and those reassurances will be received as blatant patronizations. They may not be transmitted that way, but that's how the boy will be receiving them. And when you spike these reassurances with impatience— and you will, you will—you'll be lucky to have the lad accept your invitation to an ice-cream factory, let alone accompany you fishing again..

This is about the point where a father quotes Robert Browning: "Man's reach," he reminds himself smugly, "should exceed his grasp."

For adults this is an ennobling exhortation, the second-best formula yet devised for making things better. ("Do unto others..." still leads the list.) Boys, though, are better off building up a backlog of minor victories before they start reaching for the stars.

Much as you might like to brag to the boys at the office about how your youngster tamed a 30-pound striped bass first time he had a rod in his hand, he probably won't. And even if he should, the experience is not likely to help him as either a fisherman or a person. He might well wind up like the nine-year-old whom I met recently on the riprapped edge of the Cape Cod Canal while I was cleaning a 5-pound striper. Now mind you, this was a special fish, my first in five long, hard sessions, and I was proud of it.

"Caught a striper, huh?" said the lad, edging up alongside me.

"Yeah, you like stripers?"

"Oh, I catch big ones," he said, raising his eyebrows a notch. "Me and my dad, we caught a 30-pounder last week."

The rest of that poor kid's fishing is going to be an anticlimax to an imagined achievement. Even worse, he'll probably grow up to be one of those boorish blowhards whose conversation is a continuous round of "Can You Top This?"

Embarrassment is inevitable when you start a boy at too high a rung on the ladder of angling achievement. The deck is stacked against him. He's not strong enough, he's not savvy enough, even more important, he's not committed enough. For him fishing is something that looks like it might be fun. He's glad to give it a try. But until he's committed by a conviction that fishing can charm and challenge and fulfill him like no other recreation, it must compete for his attention with—depending on his age—girls, swimming, cars, girls, TV, stereo, and, of course, girls.

To enjoy fishing, he first must be able to handle the method he's using; in fact, to master it in short order. That's why something simple—perch in a pond, flounder in a cove—is the only way to start.

The second essential for a beginner to enjoy fishing is for him to receive tangible and prompt rewards for his efforts. Behaviorists call it reinforcement. Sure, your sincere pat on the back helps, but mostly his reinforcement has to come from himself. He has to know that he made that cast well, that he played that fish competently.

And don't be impatient about when he's going to get around to those big bluefish. He'll get to them soon enough. Sooner, probably, than you think if you let him climb that ladder a rung at a time and at his own pace. And as he ascends those rungs with you right there alongside him, there never will be any great gulf of ability separating you. By coming closer in competence, you also can come closer in feelings and values and friendship.

A rung at a time and you can take a refresher course in the simple joys, peeling away those insulating layers of artistry and esoterica.

A rung at a time and he will know not just a single scene in the drama of fishing, but all of its fascinating themes and characters, conflicts and climaxes, plots and counterplots.

A rung at a time and every rung, from bluegills to bluefish, from inland creek to open ocean, will give him the enduring satisfaction of knowing that he earned it, that he paid the price of an honorable apprenticeship.

## EQUIP THEM PROPERLY

"What's the best fishing outfit for my boy?" a neighbor once asked me. "I mean the best that money can buy. I've been working day and night for twenty years. Now I've got the world by the whatchamacallit. It's high time my boy and I caught a few—heh, heh—trophies together."

"What kind of fish?" I asked.

"What do you mean, what kind of fish? A fish is a fish."

"Freshwater or salt?"

"Water's water."

"Bait fishing? Fly-fishing? Plug casting?"

Like a man who had suddenly discovered the significance of $E = MC^2$, he shrugged, turned, and walked away.

"Boat fishing, shore fishing, trolling, surf casting?" I continued.

Last I heard, my neighbor had become a pretty fair golfer. His son,

Milt Rosko makes sure his daughter's equipment is suitable for the size and kind of fish she's likely to tie into: stiff enough rod, strong enough line, big enough hook. (Photo: Milt Rosko)

who had been fishing all along with a pal who knew a thing or two about worms and sunfish, frogs and bass, grasshoppers and trout, recently caught his first rainbow on a homemade #12 White Miller.

Since I couldn't prescribe the ideal outfit for my neighbor's son, whose size and strengths and interests I at least knew, I certainly am not going to speculate blindly on your youngster's needs. For now I'll simply offer four fundamental suggestions plus some advice that applies to most any kind of fishing. In later chapters you can learn about which fish and angling methods might interest him most, as well as about the equipment required, what it costs, and how to use it.

1. Start simple: simple waters, simple species, simple methods.

2. Try someone else's tackle before you buy. No, I emphatically do not mean borrow it. (The surest way to torpedo a friendship is to borrow a buddy's money, fishing tackle, or wife.) I mean rent it from a tackle shop or a party boat.

3. Ask advice. Experienced friends and reputable tackle vendors will be happy to steer you in the right direction.

4. Observe carefully. As in all of life's endeavors, you can learn a lot from studying the pleasures and problems of others.

Unless your gear is appropriate, complete, and working, you'll never fish at full efficiency. Gear is appropriate when it matches the occasion: lures that are likely to entice the kind of fish you seek; rod and reel and line that enable you to present your lure properly and play your fish sportingly. Bear in mind that correctness can change with time and place. In May, for example, Cape Cod stripers feed on herring, but in mid-season their menu calls for mackerel; and that fly that entices trout on Montana's Madison might frighten the fins off Texas largemouths.

When fishing with children, concentrate at first on only a few kinds of fish. Otherwise you'll need a truck for a tackle box. Even then if you're not selective you'll need a small trailer to tote all those sure-fire, action-tested, satisfaction-guaranteed, thermonuclear absurdities that are more likely to make fish laugh than bite. Not only are they astronomical in number, they're endless in variety. At last count, one version of the justly famous Finnish Minnow came in five sizes, four colors, four shapes, and three running depths. That's 240 possible variations! My modest mentality already is overtaxed by crush-proof boxes of filter-tip, king-size, mentholated, low-tar-and-nicotine cigarettes.

So which lures should you buy? Eventually experience will spotlight a handful of favorites for you and your boy. Meanwhile, take advantage of experimenting that others already have done. Stick with the old standbys—the Dardevle and Atom, the Mepps and Flatfish, the Muddler and Coachman—and your arsenal will be better than 90 percent adequate. The buying and toting of what it would take to add the other 10 percent would cost you a small fortune and a large hernia, hardly a wise investment. But just so you and your boy don't feel too regimented, leave room for one or two untried mavericks. Otherwise you'll always suspect that maybe that vibrating, oscillating, undulating, supersonic salami sandwich that you didn't buy might have turned the trick.

Complete gear is what you've got so far—doubled. Then when a rod breaks, a reel freezes, a line birdnests, or a lure snaps off, you'll be sure to have a replacement ready. In today's missiles, this built-in backup is known as redundancy—a standby circuit ready to take over when the first one fails—but missiles are paid for by Uncle Sam. On your fishing budget you'll probably have trouble enough affording even one each of the articles you need, let alone two of all you'd like.

Your solution, then, is to play the odds, buying a backup only for those items that are most likely to require replacing. And when you think about it, these are just your lure, your reel, and your line. Since we've already agreed that you'll be concentrating on only a few favorite lures, your investment with them won't be large.

Reels, on the other hand, can be quite expensive, so do your best to ensure proper operation. The battle is half won when you invest in a well-made reel; a cheap one that costs less in dollars always makes up for it in lost time. Having bought a good reel, then take care of it. The gear that binds, the bail that breaks just as that school of fish arrives that you've spent half the night waiting for—these probably wouldn't have malfunctioned if you had spent a few minutes of that half-night cleaning and adjusting and lubricating before you left home. Don't pick up that screwdriver, however, until you've learned what to do with it. Study the drawings that always accompany a good reel so you won't wind up with an extra screw or two after reassembling, and read the instructions so you won't, as I did, rinse your surf reel with religious regularity, only to have the repairman exclaim, "Cold water! That's the worst thing you could use." Once a year also have your reel overhauled by a pro. You and your boy will derive great comfort from the knowledge that you'll be starting a new season with everything in A-1 condition.

Lines probably take a heavier toll of a fisherman's time and temper than any other equipment. When an angler starts snapping and snarling, it's a good bet that his line is doing likewise. While the more philosophical of fishermen might resign themselves to the inevitability of the backlash and the birdnest, the more practical of them, by obeying three common-sense rules, are able not only to reduce the number of tangles but also to minimize their effects. First, they buy better line. Realizing that quantity and quality seldom are synonymous, they spurn those "pound and a half for a buck and a half" bargains in favor of something a little more expensive but a lot less troublesome.

Second, they cast more carefully. Examining every tree and bush and rock and weed, they might take a little longer to get their line out, but it always does get out, even when less deliberate casters have theirs braided into branches behind them. And when their line hits the water, it's working immediately, not wrapping itself around rocks and logs.

And third, they carry an extra spool of line as protection against the innumerable hazards that even good line and careful casting can't avoid. (Ever drop a cigarette ash on 4-pound-test monofilament?) One of the first lessons a youngster should learn about fishing is this: Despite all the legendary lunkers that get away, more lines are broken by fishermen than by fish. A brute of a brown trout in New Hampshire's Connecticut River snapped my 4-pound mono because I ignored a spot of line-fraying rust on my reel. A submarine-size striper (well, okay, maybe only a two-man submarine) severed my 10-pound line with its gill plate because I hadn't taken the time to tie on a 30-pound leader. And many a fisherman's flybooks must contain Gray Ghost streamer flies extracted from the mouths of landlocked salmon that have eluded my net because I tied but didn't tighten knots.

## *MAKE* TIME, *TAKE* TIME

There's a story, probably started by a golfer, about a pair of fishermen casting into a roadside stream when a funeral cortege started passing slowly by on the highway behind them. Reeling in, one of them turned, doffed his battered old fedora, held it over his heart, and stood in reverent silence as the hearse drove by.

Impressed, the other angler commented, "Say, that's nice. That's real nice," to which the first fisherman replied, "It's the least I can do. She was a good wife."

Now let it be known right from the start that I do not contend that fishing should take priority over everything else. Earthquakes, five-alarm fires, and the more critical kinds of coronaries occasionally can preempt fishing. For an hour or two anyway. But one excuse which under no circumstances is acceptable is, "I haven't got time."

Consider what this means. In effect you are saying that you do not have time to fish with your children because you are spending this time on more important things. Like what? Television, maybe? Or sleeping? Or working? Or trimming the hedges? Let's consider them one at a time.

*Television.* Next in-season night you're atrophying your intellect with reruns of "The Beverly Hillbillies," remind yourself that you could just as easily be popping for largemouths, jigging for walleyes, casting for shad, plugging for stripers, dangling for catfish, or fishing for whichever of the many night-feeding species you prefer. If that doesn't pry you loose, phone your undertaker. You're ready for embalming.

*Sleeping.* Sleep might, as Shakespeare says, "knit the ravelled sleeve of care," but it also uses up a lot of prime fishing time. Few of us need all the sleep we get. Eight uninterrupted hours is as habitual as a three-meal day, and as easily adjusted. Six hours in bed plus two in the surf recharges my emotional batteries better than a week-long sauna. Furthermore, most of us don't sleep well in warm weather anyway. For years I tossed and turned, cussing the heat and humidity until it occurred to me that I was counting striped bass, not sheep.

This dad obviously is glad he made time for striper fishing with his son, and his son is, too. (Photo: Larry Green)

*Working.* Even apparently inflexible obligations such as work can sometimes be budged if you want badly enough to fish. I don't mean simply by playing hookey. (Try that a few times and you'll find yourself with all the free time in the world.) By spending a few extra evenings at the office, I have been able, with clear conscience, to beat the Maine-bound Friday-night traffic or to attend New Hampshire's April 1 Opener.

*Trimming the hedges.* Durante sings a song for the angler with shaggy hedges and other such domestic encumbrances: "Didja evah have da feelin' dat ya wanted ta go, and still have da feelin' dat ya wanted ta stay?" Torn between uncaught trout and untrimmed arborvitae, the fisherman usually stays home, loudly lamenting the former, listlessly pursuing the latter, and doing justice to neither.

Some resolve the dilemma by botching chores and growling at children till their wives are glad to get rid of them. But this is no more than an armed truce, hardly conducive to the clear mind and conscience necessary for relaxed fishing. One man I know has an even simpler solution: he just goes, professing to be of callused enough conscience and disciplined enough mind to enjoy every minute of it. As I drop him off after a day's fishing, though, I can see him wince at the prospect of his wife's waiting like a coiled cobra to exact her pound of flesh.

Ironically most wives are quite reasonable about their husband's fishing once they become aware of its therapeutic and rejuvenating qualities. Life, after all, is more enjoyable for them too when hubby is fit to live with. But unless you educate the Little Woman, you'll never get more than a desultory "How nice" when you show her your trophy. What to you is one of God's noblest creations is to unenlightened her just a smelly, slimy, totally inadequate return on the hours and dollars you've invested.

Enlightening her is not hard; you are, after all, promoting an excellent product. Take her to dinner, lubricate your larynx with a swig or two of Old Mattressfeathers, and start with the disarmingly direct "Honey, let me try to explain why fishing is so important to me." If you really believe it, the rest will come easy: eloquent, earnest, and persuasive. My office walls are adorned with two pictures, one of my family, the other of me landing a striped bass. In between is my IN basket. When the basket gets inundated and pressures start pushing things out of perspective, I simply lift my head and everything eases back into focus. Put that into your own words and your wife will understand.

Granted, wives have a legitimate complaint about peeling paint and waiting till July for the storm windows to be taken down, but many chores can be done just as easily off-season, when you spend most of your time rummaging aimlessly through your tackle box anyway. Furthermore, sons, inspired by the prospect of a few hours' fishing, invariably reveal unrealized talents as house painters and hedge trimmers. And finally, those jobs that you can't reasonably reschedule or have someone do for you will go much faster if you set goals for yourself. Not work-seven-straight-hours-type goals or don't-let-up-until-dinnertime-type goals, but go-fishing-as-soon-as-the-north-side-of-the-house-is-finished-type goals.

So okay, you won't plead too little time, but hey, it's raining. You can't take a youngster fishing in the rain, can you? Or can you? Dressed properly, you both can fish in comfort. Furthermore, by patronizing the right places you'll find feeding fish and more than likely have them all to yourselves. Rain, remember, washes food to waiting trout; surging seas drive stripers into sheltered coves; late-season snows fall on salmon and lake trout as they chase smelt schools into the shallows. And ice fishing—well, don't knock it unless you've tried it.

"But," you might protest, snuggling into your armchair for the opening kickoff, "the season's closed. I couldn't take my boy fishing no matter how badly I wanted to." What season? Trout? How about bass, pickerel, walleyes, pike, crappies, catfish, sunfish, yellow perch, white perch . . . ? And what about neighboring states? When trout season expires in New Hampshire in early autumn, enterprising Granite Staters simply drop down to Massachusetts where plenty of big rainbows, browns, and brookies can be caught, often in surprisingly wild settings, right through freeze-up, and even after that through the ice. And, of course, if you're lucky enough to live near the sea, you can enjoy year-round action regardless of latitude. In the teeth of a February blizzard I have seen cod and flounder being caught in Boston Harbor just a couple of casts from where Colonists dumped His Majesty's tea from the decks of *Beaver, Helen,* and *Dartmouth.*

Almost as limp an excuse as "too little time" is "too far to go." If you're seriously interested in accompanying—not taking but accompanying—your son fishing, then a plain old creek or brook or pond or river or bay will suit you both very nicely. Waters like these abound close to home no matter where you live.

In the final analysis, then, fishing, like everything else you do or do not do, from getting out of bed to crossing the street to buying that stock to eating a second helping of pie, is simply a matter of priority. If it's important enough, you'll go; if it isn't, you won't. And one thing for sure if you do go: you probably won't have much trouble persuading your youngster to come along.

# LEARN AS WELL AS TEACH

A country pond on a summer day and two little girls to share it with: what could be nicer? Photographs, that's what! Fifty-dollar-apiece photographs to illustrate an article about fishing with children that an editor was anxious to publish. Two minutes after I had succumbed to Julie's and Margaret's "Can we try it, Daddy?" I regretted letting them row our rented skiff.

Their efforts were more along the lines of Laurel and Hardy than the Harvard crew. Totally unsynchronized, they pushed when they should have pulled, pulled when they should have pushed, caught more crabs than a Russian trawler, and averaged about one complete rotation of the boat for every foot of advance. By the time we reached our destination, a distant cove out of the path of speedsters and water-skiers, they had used up more than a half-hour of fishing time and in the process a lot of paternal patience.

When one of them splashed me for the 832nd time, I grabbed the oars and soon had the girls floating their bobbers alongside a patch of lily pads. Now, I thought, for some photos. Plenty of light, plenty of fish; I should get some corkers.

My blood pressure had returned almost to normal as I checked my camera settings and sighted through the lens. It did not remain normal for long. Whenever a bobber dunked, the sun went in; by the time I had reset my camera, the fish invariably had stopped biting. I could feel my mercury once again approaching the boiling point when Margaret, framed sweet and serene in my lens, punctured my petulance like a pricked balloon: just as I was achieving the right combination of expression, light, composition, camera angle, and lens setting, there bloomed from Margaret's lips a big blue blossom of bubble gum.

The message was clear: cool it, Daddy; keep things in perspective; enjoy these little lassies while you can. And for the rest of the afternoon I sure did: rowing and laughing and splashing, even taking the time to sneak up on a real live turtle basking on a log, and, of course, catching countless colorful perch and sunfish.

Children, bless 'em, have an enviable capacity for enjoyment. Eager, uninhibited, and refreshingly unrefined, they can have fun fishing any time, any place, by any method that happens to be handy. For them, snaring suckers in a cesspool can be an exciting adventure.

Then they grow up. I don't know when it starts, but suddenly worms are dirty, spinning makes it too easy, and all species except native brook trout are trash fish. Lavishly equipped, sartorially resplendent, and flawless of form, they find that the only angling (they never call it fishing any more) compatible with their cultivated tastes and busy schedules is a once-a-week rise on some "members only" aquarium. And then they complain about how little fishing—oops, angling—they're able to squeeze into their cluttered schedules.

Now, there probably are reasonable explanations for this sad phenomenon: psychological (ego craves exclusiveness), social (exclusiveness enhances status), maybe even physiological (something to do with a decelerating metabolism). Still, it's a pity it happens, and I wonder if sometimes we don't build barriers that shut out more than they shut in. As one who, under the guidance of my children, has rediscovered the similarity between stream fishing for trout and surf fishing for striped bass, relearned the fun of catching panfish and mackerel on a flyrod, and even retained my respect for worming so long as it's done skillfully and sportingly, I urge you to observe how your youngsters enjoy their fishing and see if you can't pick up a few of their tricks.

Besides their capacity for enjoyment, children also have a nifty knack for flagging you when your interest starts atrophying into obsession, when your seriousness starts setting into a cement of solemnity. Like last week, when I plugged a soft dawn with Dan and his pal Tim. By working hard—concentrating, casting almost incessantly, moving from rock to rock as the flooding tide formed new rips and backwaters, and continuously recalculating where and how and when to cast—I was able to catch two small stripers and watch perhaps a dozen more chase and swirl and slap at my popping plugs that excited but didn't quite ignite them. Neither Dan nor Tim caught a fish, sharing one "for sure" and one "maybe" hit between them, but by their own unsolicited admissions, they had a great morning. For them, as for me, the ingredients of enjoyment—adventure, beauty, suspense, hard work—had blended in just the right proportions.

Dan and Tim, however, had one element in their enjoyment that I did not, and its absence set me to thinking. The element was—oh, I guess you'd call it frivolity. Not fun, because, Lord knows, I was having fun, but that ancient and honorable American pastime of fooling around: a stone thrown to make the other guy think a fish had swirled; a nudge to topple him from a rock; a cast across his line when he's not watching; and the joshing, endless, affectionate, and predictable. "Hey, seaweed has to be 16 inches before you can keep it." "Wanna borrow a stick of dynamite?" "Where'd you learn to cast, in the Campfire Girls?"

What Dan's and Tim's fooling around set me to thinking about was if maybe I wasn't taking my fishing too seriously. From my three sons and three daughters, as well as from a wife who becomes eleven years old every time she gets a rod in her hand, I receive regular reminders of this sort. They're beneficial and therapeutic.

This tendency to take one's fishing too seriously seems to increase with age and experience. "Maturity" is the label it's usually peddled under, but sometimes it's no more than a hardening of the recreational arteries. Instead of lingering for a few moments on that rock and yelling "Hi, there!" to that big, bright, yellow moon that's gilding the quiet cove from which you've just plucked your first striper in two weeks, you restrain the impulse. Kid stuff, you figure. Somebody might hear me.

Do I bay at the moon that way? You bet your sweet sixpack I do. Also sunrises, sunsets, seagulls, marsh smells, friends, fish that outsmart me, and fish that don't outsmart me.

From children you can learn about fun you've been ignoring, beauty you've been overlooking. From Matt I learned that even though a boy catches a bigger cod than his brothers and his dad, he won't necessarily enjoy fishing.

Lest you get the impression, however, that I don't take my fishing seriously, let me assure you that I've got zeal and zest to spare. It's just that I like a little Huckleberry Finn along with my Ahab.

A few years back on a Gloucester mudflat, Jack cleaved through my excessive seriousness like the USS *Manhattan* cleaves through Arctic ice. For two unproductive hours of a sweltering August afternoon we had cast into a narrow channel as the incoming tide seeped into the marshes behind us. Normally by this time we would have been heading home, but I was mad. I had discovered stripers hanging off the edge of a sandbar, and on three of five casts my white bucktail streamer had been hammered just as I began lifting my flyrod to start another cast. Twice because of my carelessness a fish had snatched my fly and snapped my leader. On the third hit I hooked a fish, but in a single short run and roll, the beast had left me with a limp line and a seething temper.

At this point smoke must surely have been oozing from my ears, flames belching from my mouth. Swinging my rod with all the finesse of a lion tamer, I lurched into the water with a splash that must have spooked every striped bass on Cape Ann.

"Donkey!" I mumbled. "Clown!"

I had narrowed my next step down to a choice between rod smashing and wrist slashing when, from 40 feet to my right, where Jack had been casting from a cluster of rocks, I heard a splash. Jack, having concluded that his favorite sport was becoming too much like work, had decided it was time for a swim ... clothes and all. Jarred back into perspective by his "C'mon in," I joined him—clothes and all—for a perfectly delightful conclusion to what otherwise might have degenerated into a nerve-rasping endurance contest.

Fresh water, with its tighter operating parameters, can present an even tougher test of parental tolerance than salt water, especially when bored boys start spooking fish. I confess that irritation was my initial reaction the time I took Jack, Dan, and four of their friends to a cherished little trout pool on a wild New Hampshire stream only a half-hour's drive from my northern Massachusetts home. It had taken me years to discover this private little paradise, and I confess that I had my doubts about twelve-year-olds being worthy of it. After an hour of relentless insect assaults, I still was totally preoccupied with stalking a rising rainbow on the far side of the pool just below where the stream surged out of an alder-edged run and burbled over a ridge of small rocks. The June sun had long since sunk behind the steep pine-treed slope behind us, and the dwindling light made casting to the edge of a barely discernible bushy shoreline a pretty tricky proposition. Carefully I floated my fly to my left, swinging it slowly toward shore, raising my rod, cocking my wrist in preparation for my next roll cast, when "Whap!"—I got walloped on my bare thigh with a blob of mud.

All action ceased, all noise was stifled. The boys froze in midmotion, their eyes boresighted on my own in anticipation of my reaction. Would it be irritation? Anger? Rage? I am proud to report that without cracking a smile, I leaned forward, scooped up a fistful of muck, and with a war whoop heaved it at my nearest assailant, thereby launching the greatest mud battle since my boyhood along the oozy aromatic banks of the Merrimack River. When we all went skinny-dipping later on to remove the mud, that rainbow must have thought the dam had burst.

No, I never again have brought young children to this pool. Now I make sure that grammar-school fishermen fish grammar-school waters, graduating only after they have passed the tests of patience, proficiency, and appreciation. This pool is an adult environment, where heat and bugs and exertion not only are endured but enjoyed, where fish are few and small and choosy but very very special. A place like this you work up to. Generally it takes a long time.

But having once made my mistake that long-ago June, I'm glad I acted as I did. It's good for youngsters to be aware that when it comes to knowing how to have fun, they have no corner on the market.

## INCLUDE YOUR DAUGHTERS

When girls are young, there's little discernible difference between their "sugar 'n' spice 'n' everything nice" and their brothers' "snips 'n' snails 'n' puppy dogs' tails." What works for one generally will work as well for the other. But when a daughter starts blooming into a young lady, daddies, if they're going to compete successfully for a few hours with fellas and fashions and such, should be ready to make a few concessions.

Girls, for example, are inherently more refined than boys. Even at six and nine, my two rambunctious roughnecks, Margaret and Julie, exhibited more and more frequent flashes of femininity. But it was their older sister, Mary Beth, whose modesty and squeamishness reminded me that ground rules should be modified for girls: that a three-mile walk through the woods can be too high a price even for the pleasure of fishing a pool full of wild trout; that maybe it really is asking too much of a young lady to clean her own catch and handle slimy seaworms that squirm and

When Lerner and Lowe wrote "Thank Heaven for Little Girls" for Maurice Chevalier to sing in *Gigi,* they could have had fishing in mind.

wiggle and nip; that outdoor bathroom arrangements should be planned beforehand.

Girls also tend to tire more easily than boys. This, I suspect, is because they run out of enthusiasm rather than gas. Lord knows, when they get to be housewives they handle monumental workloads in running households and raising families. By tradition, though, physical endurance is a masculine trait, and until Women's Lib establishes its own pantheon of musclebound deities, the enjoyment of little-girl anglers is likely to diminish in direct proportion to how tired they get. It's a rare daughter of twelve or so who wouldn't be repelled by the prospect of an all-night session in the surf that probably would thrill her male counterpart.

If you have any question about little girls' embarrassing easily, I refer you again to my daughter, Mary Beth, and her experience of waddling across a beach in her father's waders before the critical eyes of her bathing-suit-clad contemporaries. For an almost-teen-ager, this must have bordered on the traumatic. But the real embarrassment is mine: I was totally oblivious of her agony. In fact, I used to misinterpret her haste. "Smart," I used to think, "how she hurries instinctively toward that rockpile way up the shore there. Best spot on the beach. A real natural, that girl."

Eventually parties and pretty dresses become more important in your no-longer-little-girls' lives. Mary Beth, as I recall, had just turned sixteen when she revealed to me how much she had dreaded wearing those waders and allowed as how maybe she was becoming a little too grown-up for that kind of stuff. By then, though, she had stored up a stake in the outdoors. Clean air, clear streams, wildlife in balance with its environment—these will be familiar and important to her as an adult and she is not likely to stand idly by and see them destroyed.

Who knows, she might one day be lucky enough to marry a man with whom she can share these values. Then, with this new dimension to her marriage, she and her husband, like her mother and me, can be best friends as well as man and wife.

*... to love, honor, and cherish, in sickness and in health, till death do us part ...*

These phrases were resounding in my ear, nuptial echoes from twenty years before, when Mrs. Fallon couldn't tell a striped bass from a canned salmon. Now here she was on a September dawn perched atop a barnacled boulder in the edge of a surging little tidal rip working her first striped bass of the morning into the shore. "There ought to be something in these marriage vows," I thought, "to make it unlawful for a wife to outfish her husband."

Peg and I had made the hour-and-a-half drive to a remote point on Massachusetts' Plum Island, where we hoped we might run into a school of stripers feeding up for their southward migration. The night was clear and cool, with a brisk easterly breeze at our backs, as we groped our way down the bank of a steep bluff and along the boulder-strewn beach. Street lights from the far shore complemented the stars.

Now, it might be said that wading over slippery rocks into a cold black sea with a current doing its darnedest to capsize you is not the kind of activity that a mother of six would be especially crazy about at three o'clock in the morning, but my particular mother of six rigged her rod, donned her waders, and strode into that ocean as if she owned it.

"Some broad!" I mumbled admiringly as I eased my way to a submerged rock 20 feet upcurrent. For close to two hours, until the ebbing tide had run its course, we cast our swimming plugs continuously into a wind-whipped turbulence that should have been teeming with hungry stripers. If it was, though, you couldn't prove it by us. As dawn oozed across the marshes behind us, I suggested that we adjourn to our coffee-filled thermos in the lee of a gigantic boulder at the base of a tall clay cliff.

Togetherness comes in many forms. There's the intimacy of the intellect, where two people share the same ideas, the same principles; of experience, where enjoyment is reinforced in the reflected joys of sharing; of conviction, where common values are held and adhered to. And there's the classic closeness of a touch, a caress, an embrace. All were in exquisite balance that morning as Peg and I sat sipping our hot black coffee and reflecting on how lucky we were just to be there: dawn colors and marsh smells and bird sounds; the rustle of wavelets whipped by the wind; the unsullied solitude before starter cords are pulled and throttles are gunned.

Then she had to go and spoil it! By now her favorite rock had been uncovered by the ebbing tide. Checking her lure, a black-backed silver swimmer, she rose, turned, and said, "Honey, it's time we stopped fooling around and caught some fish. If you can't do it, I guess I'll have to." Then, wading up to her waist, she climbed to her perch and with a casual competence I didn't know she possessed, proceeded to cast her plug to the outside of a little tidal turbulence and reel it in slowly, deliberately, as it swung from left to right with the now-incoming tide.

At the same time I was skipping a blue-and-white bucktailed popper across a rumbling rip about 30 feet to her right. On my third retrieve, as I pulled the popper out of the turbulence and let it set for a second to tempt any bass that might be following, a swirl appeared in its wake. When a saucer-size tail walloped my popper, I twitched it and let it set and twitched it again, hoping to convince the fish that it had successfully stunned its prey.

The bass didn't return, but my energy did. Here was the first action of the day, the first indication that fish were present and on the prowl, and, in the overly optimistic fashion of most fishermen, I was convinced that this was a prelude to a morning of monumental action. Soon, I assured myself, I'll be putting that cocky spouse of mine in her place.

Fat chance! Within minutes Mrs. Fallon was announcing with all the aplomb and restraint of a sweepstakes winner the first of two stripers she took during the next quarter-hour.

"Honey, honey," she hollered, "I've got one, I've got one. Ooooo, it's a big one, it's getting away, it's pulling out my line."

Classy she ain't, but even with her yelling and bouncing around on that rock as if she had a wasp in her waders, she left no doubt about who was in control. She let the fish run and buck and sulk until it tired, then eased it triumphantly into the shallows, a fine, firm, well-proportioned 6-pounder.

I'll have to give my mate credit, though: she didn't rub my nose in it. Oh, there was an occasional allusion to what a good teacher I am, ostensibly an attempt to let me share in her glory but really a left-handed back-pat, but I have to admit that she wore her laurel wreath with grace and dignity.

Like all good husbands who delude themselves into thinking that they are the stronger and more accomplished of the sexes, I sulked for a day or so, nursing my wounded ego by pointing out how she had had the best spot, the best lure. And like all good wives who know intuitively how to heal their little-boy husband's punctured pride, she kissed my emotional booboo and made everything all right again by removing from the oven as I entered the house the following evening a long oval platter lined with foil and bearing the bass stuffed with mushrooms, onions, grated carrots, and breadcrumbs, and baked to a golden brown.

To further dispel the illusion that fishing with children is strictly a dad-and-the-boys business, I asked several well-known women anglers how they got started and where fishing fits into their lives. Here are their replies.

Jackie Knight is daughter-in-law of the late John Alden Knight, developer of the famous Solunar Tables, an annual forecast of the daily feeding times of fish and game for every day of the year. After Mr. Knight's death in 1966 and her husband's two years later, Jackie took over publication of the tables as well as the writing of their outdoor column for the Register and Tribune Syndicate of Des Moines. In 1972 Jackie joined her husband and father-in-law in the Fishing Hall of Fame. Among her outstanding catches she lists two on 6-pound-test line, one a 53-pound Atlantic sailfish, the other a 64-pound white marlin. Both are International Spin Fishing Association records, and the sail is also listed as a record with the International Game Fishing Association.

I grew up on Long Island, and my maternal grandfather from time to time would take me out on one of the head boats that left from the local docks. At an early age I even inoculated myself by sitting on one of his fishhooks, but I really didn't do much fishing until joining the Knight family.

Obviously the Knight-family situation differed from the usual "family or for-fun" fishing; the results of fishing trips were carefully recorded in conjunction with research for the Solunar Theory. Since that was the business that supported the family, there was more than casual interest in fishing and hunting. At any rate, whether through osmosis or concentrated exposure, I have become fairly adept at the technicalities and techniques of fishing. I make up my own leaders (for all types of fishing); every now and then I tie a fly (my late father-in-law tied beautiful flies and left an extraordinary collection of materials); and I spend a considerable amount of time fishing both fresh and salt water.

Insofar as tackle choice is concerned, I prefer light tackle: fly for both salt and fresh water and light spinning. I've belonged to the International Spin Fishing Association for a number of years and have a pretty good collection of "button fish"—fish at least twice line test in weight.

So far as I know, I am the only woman syndicated in the hunting and fishing field, and believe me, I am not a writer with imagination; I have to get out there and DO to get column material. And I enjoy it.

Edna Perinchief's husband, Pete, runs Bermuda's Fishing Information Bureau, an occupation which enables Edna to spend a lot of time trying to entice her beloved bonefish from Bermuda's beautiful beaches. Not only does she manage to score impressively on bones, but her 26-pound, 12-ounce blackfin tuna has been a woman's world record on 12-pound-test line since 1957. Her greatest thrill, she says, was conquering an 83-pound, 14-ounce amberjack on 20-pound-test line in 1966. This also is a woman's world record.

Wish I could set the stage for a really glamorous beginning into the fishing world, but unfortunately, it was not so. My only experience as a child was fishing with a handline from a pier on one of the North Shore beaches of Massachusetts, catching what I now know was tinker mackerel. It was fun and whether the family cat was the recipient of a fishy meal, I really don't recall.

My introduction into game fishing was much, much later and due entirely to my husband's dedication and enthusiasm.

As so many wives have discovered, if you can't lick 'em, you might as well join 'em, and that's what I did in self-defense.

My first fish on rod and reel was a porgy, not a great prize but good for eating. I remember vividly that I then remarked to Pete that now I was eligible to join the Bermuda Angler's Club.

We entered a club tournament that summer and to my surprise, a wahoo struck my line and proceeded to strip the reel that I had clutched firmly in my tenderfoot hands. The reel froze at the most inopportune moment and the fish was lost. However, I was firmly hooked from that moment on, and the thrill of a singing reel with a fish on is never to be forgotten.

There are lots of big ones out there in the depths off Bermuda, but our greatest love of all is bonefishing along our superb beaches and sandy flats. The biggest thrill, surpassing all else, is the moment of releasing the beautiful silver bonefish to his native habitat after successfully enticing him to hit an artificial lure. The reward of seeing this magnificent fighting fish slowly swimming away after giving his all is something one can experience only by doing it, and we both heartily endorse this method, because after all, he'll be just that much bigger the next time around.

Most fishermen have seen June Rosko's pretty face illustrating books and articles by her husband, Milt. While she has caught more species of fresh- and saltwater gamefish than most anglers ever see, including a 290-pound blue marlin off Chub Cay in the Bahamas, June has lost none of her enthusiasm for fun-fishing the bay bottoms around New Jersey for flatties.

On the subject of how I began fishing, I had to stop and reconstruct it all for a moment, for it goes back to high school days. There was a fishing enthusiast who sat alongside of me in school. At the time, fishing was uppermost in his mind, and often he'd even have lures in his pocket, and all he talked was fish and fishing. During school he was just a school chum, but soon after graduation he called, and we began dating, and then fishing. He was, of course, Milt Rosko, and we married, doing a lot of fishing during our dating days. We even started our marriage off by fishing almost every day of our honeymoon in Florida.

We have two children, Linda, who is now seventeen, and Bob, thirteen, both of whom began fishing with us when they were just three years old, using spin-cast outfits for winter flounders, yellow perch, and other easy-to-catch species. As the family grew, we traveled about the country a great deal, camping, boating, and fishing, and have together visited forty states, Canada and Mexico. Milt and I have visited several foreign fishing grounds too, always enjoying ourselves immensely, experiencing different types of fishing, meeting lots of fine people, and seeing a great deal of this fine country of ours.

I've caught many of the exotics of the tropics, including wahoo, sailfish, the various tunas, king mackerel, and bonefish in the Atlantic. On the Pacific I suspect albacore and salmon were the major species, while along the Gulf the list would include seatrout, redfish, amberjack, and others.

In fresh water I guess the list runs the gamut from brown trout on Montana's Madison River to smallmouth bass on the Delaware, and northern pike, walleyes, largemouths, and a wide variety of panfish too.

Locally, we fish for stripers and blues a great deal, but quite frankly, I enjoy winter flounders in the spring and fluke in the summer. They're fun to catch, and great to eat!

Now that the children are older, Linda has lost some interest in fishing, and I guess that's normal with a girl her age. As for Bob, he's eager to go all the time and never seems to get enough of it, taking after his father.

Well, that's how it all came about, and I suspect fishing has resulted in our doing many other things together that we might not otherwise have done. For the family as a whole I think the experience of camping, traveling, and fishing together was a good one. I'm the first to recommend it to others.

Outdoor writer Charles Waterman dedicated his book *Modern Fresh and Salt Water Fly Fishing* (Winchester Press) "To my wife Debie, who continues to cast while I eat lunch." That, it seems to me, says it all. Here are Debie's comments.

My parents didn't fish much, but I have been hooked since childhood. Charley has fished all of his life and I did get really serious about fishing after we were married. I never took any interest in any kind of fishing contests.

Almost all of my fishing has been some kind of casting. There are some kinds in which a man has definite advantages, especially with heavy tackle such as in the surf or from jetties. On the other hand, women have an advantage in some of the most delicate forms such as light dry fly and nymph fishing for trout. Although some of the very best flytiers are men, it appears to me that women learn flytying more quickly and I tie nearly all of my trout flies—they aren't of true commercial quality but quite satisfactory. Flytying isn't a hobby with me, but I do it just to get the flies, and the same goes for the saltwater bugs I make. Some fishermen call my bugs "Debie poppers" and I make them with very light hooks that don't last long but are extremely easy to cast. They wouldn't do as commercial bugs because the hooks are short-lived.

It's in patience that I have an advantage in spooky trout water, and I study water more than *most* men. Tough trout are more fun than easy ones, and there are some spots where I (and a couple of other women) do consistently better than men. Women are at a disadvantage in heavy wading, and I fall short on steelhead. I don't have the strength needed for the heaviest tarpon rods and streamers in all-day fishing, but when you get down to an 8- or 9-ounce rod, I can throw off all of the line if conditions are ideal and can fish those outfits all day.

I have never liked spinning, as the long reel handles tire me much more than baitcasting tackle. In recent years I have used free-spool plugging reels except for black bass, for which I prefer light tournament-type reels that are not free-spooling. If I had to state my best catches they would have to be a 3¾-pound brown trout on a 6X tippet and #16 fly from a spring creek and some big snook along mangrove shorelines with plugs. None of these are records, but the conditions were tough.

Most women don't pay enough attention to tackle to get the best out of it, generally taking whatever is handed to them. Other rods don't make much difference, but I have bought a lot of fly rods, some of which were poor buys.

My worst shortcoming is that I don't like to practice casting and have learned most of my tackle-handling in actual fishing. When we used to do casting demonstrations I often used tackle I hadn't practiced with at all and the results showed it.

Years ago we used lots of pictures of my fishing, but we decided pictures of women over forty don't have much appeal and we don't shoot much on me any more.

Women fish no better or worse than men in most situations, having advantages in some kinds and disadvantages in some. Their main shortcoming is lack of serious interest and a tendency to do what men tell them to do. Very few women read much about fishing methods. I've had fairly good luck teaching women to fish if they're really interested. Most of them aren't. Some of the best-known women fishermen pay no attention at all to matched tackle.

I sometimes wish men didn't make quite so big a thing about a woman catching her share. Years ago I caught the first "wall fish" (more than four pounds of trout from a stream on a fly) for Dan Bailey's wall. I was proud of the fish all right, but couldn't understand why it was more important than such a fish caught by a man. I could cast and I could select a fly and that's all most of the men could do. The rest was simply sticking with it. In playing fish under touchy circumstances there is no reason why a woman can't be just as careful and a little more patient.

Joan Salvato Wulff has been at fishing's stage center ever since she won the first of her seventeen national casting championships. Although accuracy is her forte, in 1960 she set an unofficial world flycasting record of 161 feet, easily outdistancing her male competitors. Her 4-pound, 2-ounce brook trout on a fly and 4-pound-test leader is an International Women's Fishing Association record. Among her other outstanding catches are a 651-pound bluefin tuna that took almost thirteen hours to tame, and an 84-pound tarpon which she subdued in twenty minutes with a fly rod. With her world-famous fishing husband, Lee, Joan has appeared in three ABC TV's *American Sportsman* programs as well as a Warner Brothers Seven Arts film.

My Dad, Jim Salvato, ran an outdoor store, the Paterson Rod and Gun Store, in Paterson, N.J. So the emphasis at our house was on hunting, fishing, and dogs.

We lived in a suburb of Paterson very near a good-sized pond. I joined the other kids in the neighborhood and dangled worms for sunfish, calico bass, and an occasional trout. When the Paterson Casting Club built a dock on our side of the pond and began holding their sessions there, my interest grew. I don't remember the thinking that led up to it, but one day I asked my mom if I could try flycasting with my father's rod. She said yes and I put it together and tried my hand. It was a disaster! I hadn't put the ferrules together tightly and the tip flew down the line and into the water. It was six or eight feet deep and I knew I couldn't get it out. It seemed the end of the world. I ran home crying. Mom enlisted the aid of the man next door and he accompanied me back to the pond, where he retrieved the tip successfully with a rake, of all things. I was ten years old at the time.

Dad decided I could learn to cast, and I was given help and instruction not only by him, but by the many active casters in the club. In my first state competition I won the Sub-junior dry fly accuracy title, and I was hooked.

I spent more time casting in those teen-age years than I did fishing, but the desire to fish has altered my life more than once since then. I had two brothers, one of whom started to cast before I did (and I was jealous, I think), and we all had a natural affinity for woods and water.

My mother, by the way, sat and watched through all our early years. She also got stuck rowing the boat for my dad when he was bass-bugging, and I remember thinking that it was better to be the fisherman than the rower, after listening to him tell her that her rowing was keeping him too far or too close to the shoreline.

She fishes herself now and her specialty is catching northern pike and walleyes with bait.

## ENJOY THEM WHILE YOU CAN

Time passes. Children grow and go. With few exceptions, little girls who love to fish become young ladies to whom worms are uncouth and waders unfashionable; boys eventually prefer pals to parents.

Oh, Jack and Dan and I still fish together (the family that casts together lasts together), but now more as compatible adult companions than as father and sons. Despite our differences (gray hair—me, faded jeans—them; "Honor thy father and thy mother"—Moses; "Love unearned is spurned" —me again), we fish as affectionate equals. Like cosmic cushions, the sea and the forest tend to dampen most of our differences.

What's left after they've gone is mostly memories. These can be empty recollections of opportunities missed, or bright retrospective dividends of delight. It's up to you, Dad and Mom, to decide which it's going to be. I'm grateful that my memories include Jack's and Dan's supreme achievement of catching from a pure pristine New Hampshire salmon lake a foot and a half of strong, surging, slashing . . . sucker; native trout from a Maine river where a "Beware of the Bears" sign kept them glancing nervously over their shoulders; three days on a harbor houseboat surrounded by cooperative mackerel and flounder; Dan's first surf-caught striped bass on the night of his twelfth birthday; Jack and I plucking sunfish from a neighborhood pond with flies Jack had tied himself.

Jack and Dan fished my waders off on this occasion. Since they'd soon be out of college and on their own, I thought it might be our last trip together, but as defeated champion, I now have the privilege of challenging them to a rematch.

The legacy of these experiences will be mostly memories, yes, but there's this too: the knowledge that my children, like myself, are better and fuller for our having fished together, and that this injured earth always will have them on her side. Perhaps my proudest moment in the outdoors occurred on an autumn evening after Peg and I, with our three sons, had climbed and descended Mt. Monadnock in southern New Hampshire. We picnicked on cold chicken and hot chocolate in a small park at the base of the mountain. After we'd eaten, we packed our gear, tidied up the area, and prepared to go. As we were approaching the parking lot, Dan saw some napkins and paper plates being dumped from the window of a car. Though quiet by nature and even a little reticent about asserting himself, he headed straightaway for that car, picked up the papers, and returned them to the auto's occupants, saying, "Here, you dropped these."

# 2.

# Fishing Tackle

〜〜〜〜〜〜〜〜〜〜〜〜〜〜〜〜〜〜〜〜〜〜〜〜〜〜

Fishing looks more complicated than it really is. Despite the vast variety of techniques and tools for enabling men to outwit fish, the process boils down to three simple steps. First, you have to place something that interests a fish where the fish will see it. Second, you have to give this thing an action and appearance that will induce the fish to strike it. Finally, after the fish has been hooked, you have to prevent it from breaking free before you land it. This fundamental simplicity is what you have to keep in mind when you're outfitting your child in a tackle store that looks like a cross between Santa's workshop and a physics lab. Unless you do, you can go broke, balmy, or both.

Many years ago I visited an exclusive New York City outdoor emporium with a friend. We were about to embark on our first trip to the Maine woods and I had saved $25 to buy additional equipment I felt I would need for bridging the gap between neighborhood bass and native North Country brook trout. In that pre-inflation era, $25 was a pretty fair boodle, and besides, it wasn't as if I were starting from scratch. I already owned an adequate arsenal. All I'd be needing, I assumed, was a few special items. Maybe one of those split-bamboo fly rods with line and reel to match and a good supply of flies and leaders. With what was left over I would replenish my supply of lures and maybe even buy an ultralight spinning outfit to show those Down Easters how easy it is to handle those landlocked salmon they're always raving about.

What I wound up with was a fishing vest and $3 in change. My friend discovered the vest, remembered how I never seemed to have enough room in my pants pockets for all the paraphernalia I toted, and told the clerk to wrap it up for me while I was temporarily mesmerized by the $200 price tags on the fly rods. In the long run the transaction has worked out well. My vest and I have been constant companions over the years. Its roomy pockets always seem to have space for an extra candy bar, and their annual end-of-season emptying-out invariably provides some pleasant memories. On a dollars-per-year basis, it's been a bargain.

Furthermore, if I had been able to afford that $200 fly rod, I probably would have bought the wrong one. At the time, my experience had been much too narrow, too brief to enable me to know the qualities I should be looking for, the criteria I should be applying for so substantial an investment. The clerk would have helped, sure, but only with the mechanics. The all-important "feel" a fisherman seeks in an outfit cannot be calculated according to height and weight and arm length. These are part of it, of course, but equally important are the waters where it will be used, the fish it will be used on, and the methods for which it will be employed. The rod that's right for those little wrist-action roll casts on a small brush-bordered brook won't be satisfactory for those long curling loops you need for reaching that riffle way out in the middle of a wide-open river. The whippy little wand that tames quarter-pound crappies won't be much help when you're trying to put the brakes on a 10-pound landlock. And as I learned years later when finally I was able to afford a finely crafted fly rod, split-cane construction is ideal for delivering a downy dry fly to a quiet stream but too delicate for trolling a streamer for long periods in a rough lake. At the very least you risk developing a curvature in the rod that impairs casting, at the worst you might split it along a seam. I did both.

Recently the fourteen-year-old son of a friend phoned me for advice about buying a fishing outfit. It had been a long while since I had bought equipment for my own children, so I welcomed the opportunity to refresh my memory. Here is how Michael and I went about it.

First, I found out what kind of fishing he planned to do. Michael explained that he was attending school on the shore of Quabbin Reservoir in western Massachusetts, where, during spring semester, fishing becomes as popular as recess.

"We even take courses in it," he said, "and if you catch a big fish the chef will cook it up for you."

I had fished the Quabbin. Four times I had trolled, cast, and still-fished its 25,000 sprawling acres and been blanked on three of them. This poor boy, I figured, will be swearing off fishing within a week.

"What kind of a boat will you be using?" I asked.

"Oh, we fish from shore," said Michael. "One of my teachers might take us out some Saturday if we do real well in class, but all the rest of the time we cast from shore."

Well, that was better than a boat. He might not catch any of the big lakers and salmon for which Quabbin is best known, but I had seen some respectable catches of small rainbows made from shore around the gate where I launched my boat. Maybe Michael would do as well.

"Any of the boys at school catching trout out where you fish?" I asked.

"No, no trout, but one guy the other day was fishing in this little stream that runs into the reservoir and he caught the biggest sucker...."

So things hadn't changed much after all. Michael, like generations before him, was starting at the beginning. Big fish in big waters make nice dreaming, but for now he wanted to catch simple fish by methods he could master easily.

A few more questions revealed that Michael would be doing most of his fishing in a broad shallow bay of the reservoir. Water would be warm here, so he would be seeking pickerel, largemouth bass, and panfish rather than the trout and salmon that would be inhabiting the Quabbin's colder depths. He didn't know this, yet he wasn't disappointed when I explained that odds were overwhelmingly against his catching a glamorous rainbow or salmon or laker. He was satisfied to be assured that there should be plenty of fish in his bay and he was pleased to learn their names.

Most of his chums, he said, liked to cast lures.

"You know, with one of those spinning rods and an open-faced reel. The guys don't like the reels with the covers over them. The line seems to bunch up and tangle, and when they get a tangle they want to be able to see what they're doing."

Michael was proud to be able to use the correct terminology and to talk with authority about the pros and cons of reel design. He had been listening carefully to his more experienced classmates, and I told him so.

"Any of the guys fish worms?" I asked.

He answered in the affirmative, of course; boys always fish with worms. They might graduate more quickly to spinners and plugs and flies these days, with artificials so easy to acquire, but they'll usually have a few worms tucked somewhere in their trousers. Worms are their talisman, their security blanket.

My main reason for asking about worms was to test the tone of Michael's reply. As I suspected, he seemed reluctant to acknowledge that he planned to use them. Even at Michael's age, boys start building up a prejudice against the bait of the bourgeoisie, and peer pressure is a strong influence on young boys, especially in private schools.

"No better bait in the world for the kind of fishing you'll be doing," I assured him. "Worms will work when nothing else will, provided they're used right. There's a lot more to fishing with worms than just hanging one on a hook and waiting for something to happen."

By the time we pulled into the parking lot of the first store Michael had visited while shopping that afternoon, we had concluded that an open-faced spinning outfit would be his best choice. It would enable him to cast lures as well as fish worms beneath a bobber, it was the type of equipment he had used once or twice a few years before in his one brief exposure to fishing, he would be able to use it reasonably well on the brook in which he planned to try for trout before returning to school next morning, and if he should be lucky enough to win an invitation to troll from his teacher's boat, it would be all right there too. But most of all, it was what Michael wanted because "That's what all the guys use."

Michael had $15 to spend. Several hours of bicycling between shopping centers during the afternoon had enabled him to pick out several attractive rods and reels, but their combined price always seemed to exceed his $15 ceiling. When I reminded him that he also would need line, hooks, bobbers, and at least one or two lures, he was crestfallen.

"Our objective, then," I told him, "is to find the best combination we can for the money. For the $12 or $13 you've got to spend on a rod and reel, you can get good ones. Not a great rod or a great reel, but a lot better than what I had when I started. You want a rod and reel that are well made and won't break easily. I can help you find these. But your rod and reel also must feel just right for you. Not too light, not too heavy; enough action in the tip, enough strength in the butt; a handle that's comfortable, a balance that doesn't tire your wrist or your forearm too easily. Only you can make these decisions. The ultimate choice is going to be yours because you're the one who's going to have to live with it."

Our two-hour shopping tour took us to four stores in two cities. For my part I was able to point out imperfections such as windings that would fray easily, ferrules that were attached carelessly or fitted imprecisely, and reel locks that would not hold his reel securely in place. We flexed rods to find a few that blended strength and flexibility in just the right proportions for the kind of fishing Michael would be doing, and we removed reel spools to see how closely gears meshed and how smoothly handles and shafts rotated. Two hours later Michael had narrowed his choice down to three rods and one reel. One rod was eliminated because of price, a second because "Well, this other one just feels better, that's all." The $2.75 balance was just enough for a spool of good-quality 6-pound-test monofilament and a package of freshwater hooks in various sizes. Michael had resurrected a bobber from his earlier fishing experiences, and the two lures I gave him—a red-and-white spoon and an inch-long wobbling minnow—spanned his spectrum from pickerel to perch. When we left the store, Michael carried his rod and reel as if he were Galahad going after a dragon. I wouldn't be surprised if they shared his pillow that night.

There were still a lot of basics for Michael to learn, but not just yet. Tonight he had had enough. Throughout the shopping tour I had been dispensing advice—sharpen hooks, lubricate ferrules, always take the time to tie a strong knot—but now he wore the saturated smile of a boy who was hearing my words but not what they meant. Best thing for Michael would be to fish the brook as he planned to next morning. After that my comments would have more practical meaning. Two weeks later, therefore, I wrote him this letter.

DEAR MICHAEL:

How's fishing? Now that you've been back to school for a while and had a chance to use your new spinning outfit, you must be ready for a few more suggestions. I would have made them last time we were together, but by the time you had selected your equipment, I think you had absorbed all the information you could handle. Besides, what I say will have more meaning now that you've used your rod and reel a few times.

As I recall, the morning after we were together you were planning to fish Stony Brook. Regardless of how many or how few fish you caught, I hope you had a good time. You'll never be a real fisherman unless you're able to come home with a full heart even though you carry an empty creel. The catching of fish is fun. It's the crowning act in an exciting adventure. But it's like jimmies on an ice cream cone: the ice cream is awwwwwful good even without the jimmies.

No doubt you found brook fishing a lot different from fishing the Quabbin. Both are enjoyable and chock full of challenge, yet each is as distinctive as a new day. All forms of fishing are intriguingly different. Try them all. Work out your own set of personal preferences. If you're lucky, as I am, you'll find that there's no form of fishing you don't enjoy, no species of fish you don't admire. Then, no matter where you are, no matter what the season, adventure always will be just around the corner.

This capacity for adventure is a quality that children find easy to acquire. I guess all of us start out as Huckleberry Finns, no matter how civilized our surroundings. Somewhere along the line, though, a lot of us lose our appreciation for birdsong and marsh smell and standing barefoot in a creek bed trying to coax a catfish off the bottom. You know the grownups I'm referring to. They're the ones who aren't much fun to be with. Try always, Michael, to be fun to be with. It will make you a very special person.

Four paragraphs and I've talked more about philosophy than I have about fishing! But this isn't strange, really. Fishing is life in miniature. It's all there: beauty, companionship, achievement, disappointment, delight. Even ugliness is there: in the trash that desecrates the forest; the dam that dooms a species; the willful exploiting of spawning fish; the callused killing of an undersize trout just to save a hook, just to get back into action a second or two sooner. There isn't much that the outdoors can't teach you about life.

What, I wonder, did you like best about brook fishing? Was it the fact that you can enjoy a closeness with a brook that is unattainable with any other kind of water? That's my favorite feature. Brooks are small enough to handle, yet mysterious enough to baffle. You can float a fly or drift a worm through their remotest recesses, yet miss the foot-long trout finning beneath the bank on which you're standing. First time I fished one of my favorite brooks, I caught nothing during two hours of scurrying from hole to hole, then halfheartedly dropped my worm off the edge of a flat rock while I waited for my companion to arrive. Five minutes later, when he climbed the ridge on which I was standing, I casually brought my hand around from behind my back, lifted it to scratch my ear, and exhibited 14 inches of brown trout dangling from my little finger.

That brook, by the way, is right down in Carlisle, only a few minutes from my home and not much farther from yours. I know of another just as good in Westford that you could reach in under an hour on your bike. Despite all the construction that's been carving up our countryside, plenty of trout-rich brooks still lace our wooded lowlands like silver veins. A prospector who knows how to use a topographical map and is willing to brave a little brush will always find one. And when he does, Michael, he will enjoy the exalting knowledge that this is his place, his discovery.

Years ago I crossed an inviting little stream while driving home from New Hampshire. Cars were parked on both sides of the rickety wooden bridge and anglers flocked across a field whose owner had hospitably erected a sign saying, "FISHERMEN WELCOME HERE." Several days later I returned, but not to the bridge. Instead I parked my car a half-mile upstream and headed straight into the woods. Within ten minutes I had come across a footpath that led me to wild stretches that couldn't have differed much from when Indians occupied the land. Over the years I have watched deer drink and beaver swim while I cast to rising trout, all because I was alert and willing to work a little harder than the people who stayed by the bridge. This stream, by the way, is also only about an hour's bike ride from your front door.

But stream fishing is not what you're doing now that you have returned to the Quabbin. Perhaps we can discuss streams during your next vacation. I'm sure you'll be calling for directions to some of the waters I've just described. No, I do not give out this information easily, and never without exacting a promise to leave a place cleaner than you found it, but I'm sure I could be bribed with a slab of your mother's apple pie.

The main difficulty in fishing a big body of water from shore is that it all looks pretty much alike. A few ridges and wrinkles distinguish the shoreline, a patch of weeds here and there breaks up the monotony of the shallows, but beyond that it's all water, and hey, water is water, right? Wrong. Remember how I said last time we talked that until you can see what's going on under that water, you're just a guy who goes fishing? A real fisherman sees sandbars and spring holes and temperature layers as clearly as if a window covers his lake. Sure it takes years to do this well, years of studying and listening and observing, but a few simple tricks can remove you from the ranks of the vast majority of fishermen who just cast blindly and hope for something to happen.

First thing to consider is your shoreline. If it's a steep banking, then its steepness probably continues right into the water. This enables you to reach deep water with an easy cast. A gradually descending banking, on the other hand, probably continues to taper off at about the same angle after it enters the reservoir. From a shore like this you're always fishing in shallow water. Water depth is especially important after summer weather raises surface temperatures. Then trout and salmon, which cannot tolerate warm water, must head deeper, but bass, pickerel, perch, and sunfish inhabit the shallows all summer long.

Since the part of the Quabbin you're fishing is not especially deep, it's unlikely that you'll be tying into any trout or salmon. It's not impossible, however. In the spring while water is still cool, salmon feed on schools of smelt that swim close to shore as they head for the mouths of small brooks. Smelt are long thin silver-and-black minnows that swim up brooks about mid-April to spawn. Salmon especially, but also Quabbin's rainbow, brown, and lake trout, eat them the way you do jelly beans.

By mid to late May, trout and salmon will have headed for cooler water, but you might have just the water they're looking for right under your nose. Did you ever, when you were swimming in front of your school, dive close to bottom and hit a cold area, as if someone had opened a window in the winter? This is a spring. Because its temperature remains about the same throughout the year, it often attracts trout and salmon even when water all around it is too warm for them to tolerate.

Finally, of course, there is that deep water in front of the steep bank I mentioned a few paragraphs back. As you've probably noticed while swimming, water gets cooler as you dive deeper. This water might be cool enough to keep salmon and trout at your doorstep all summer long. On the bottom of a lake, warm-weather water is too cool and stagnant to support fish. They seek an intermediate layer called the thermocline. (Try that on the teacher with the boat.) This layer contains the just-right temperatures between the too-warm of the top and too-cold-and-stagnant of the bottom. Big-league boat fishermen find this layer with a special kind of thermometer, but for you it's enough to know that the thermocline exists. You'll continue to do most of your fishing for bass and pickerel and panfish because that's what your area of the Quabbin is best suited for, but you might want to devote some part of each fishing expedition to wiggling a lure or dragging a worm along the slope of a sandbar where coldwater species and the bait they feed on might be spending a comfortable summer.

And where will you find such a sandbar? The shoreline will tell you, just as it revealed how deep the water in front of you is likely to be. Bars usually are continuations of ridges that begin on land. Cast beyond that rocky point or that narrow peninsula and you'll find a fast-sloping extension.

Most important of all shoreline features is the mouth of a brook. Fish congregate here all the time waiting for food to be washed out to them. To really capitalize on a feeder brook's attraction for fish, float a worm out of its mouth and into the lake during a rainstorm.

Weeds will grow as the weather warms, and so will your aggravation as you keep getting caught in them. Everyone cusses at weeds, but the smart anglers capitalize on them instead of condemning them. Underwater vegetation provides nourishment and protection for minnows, and anywhere you find minnows you'll find bass and pickerel preying on them.

Try catching a few minnows for bait. Nothing beats the real thing properly presented. If you can't come up with a net, try wading outboard of some minnows and splashing them onto dry land. Hook one just under the skin in front of its dorsal fin and cast it, about a foot and a half beneath a bobber, along the inside edge of a sprawl of lily pads. Ordinarily I'd suggest the outside edge during daylight, but with 6-pound-test line, you'd better avoid putting any weeds between you and a fish. You need 10- or 12-pound line when a bass tries to weave itself into the weeds.

No doubt you've heard about plastic worms for largemouth bass. In the right hands one of these can be as devastating as a stick of dynamite. For hands to be right, however, they must be backed up by a supply of patience so large that Job himself would have envied it. After casting a plastic worm into large-mouth territory, let it settle and set for about a minute. When you finally start retrieving, rotate your reel handle at a pace that makes a snail seem jet-propelled. Hardest part is when a bass picks up your worm and starts cruising casually away. With your bail open, you must watch line peeling off your spool until precisely the right moment to strike. With a 6- or 8-inch worm, this can take more than a minute. That, Michael, is patience!

Bass, by the way, will be spawning in shallow water from about mid-May until mid-June. Look closely for the cleared circles of their nests. Often you will see big males standing guard while eggs are incubating and for a short while after the young emerge from their eggs. These big bass are terribly vulnerable at this time. Almost anything dragged through their domain will be snapped up. Some men catch and keep bass under these conditions and boast of their achievement. I prefer to regard this period as a time-out between rounds, when I can kneel quietly on a bank and study the opponent I'll be trading punches with later on in the season. Try this once and I doubt that you'll ever keep a bass you catch on its spawning bed. All of your bass fishing from that moment on will be affected by the sight of that superb fish fulfilling its divinely ordained destiny.

Somehow I can't feel quite so compassionate about pickerel. Bass, I'm sure, eat as many small fish as pickerel do, and in the normal order of things, the eating of small fish by bigger ones, whether they be pickerel or bass, is necessary for keeping their underwater world in balance. Maybe I am less fond of pickerel because of the stealthiness with which they strike or the readiness with which they always seem to quit once my rod starts applying pressure. Also, I'm sure, it's partly a result of my once having made the stupid mistake of sticking a finger into one's mouth to see if those teeth really are as sharp as they look. (They are!) To catch pickerel, pull that red-and-white spoon of yours in short spurts along the edge of lily pads or pickerel weeds. If that doesn't work, cut yourself a long alder sapling, tie about four feet of string to its end, and skip a hooked perch belly across a weed bed.

Finally, Michael, there's something you might as well learn early about fishing: there's never enough time to do all you'd like. If you wait for openings to occur in your tightly scheduled school day, you probably won't find them. Commitments such as classes and meals and study hours take an allotted number of hours and occur in inflexibly prescribed time-slots. What's left over just doesn't do fishing justice, so since you can't take time, what you have to do is *make* it. At daybreak, for example, you can cast to big breakfasting fish for the very modest price of an hour's sleep; after dark, largemouths are pushovers for noisy topwater plugs.

And before I am accused by your teachers of distracting you from your readin', 'ritin', and rithmetic, I'd better wrap this up with one final suggestion: don't just stand there, go fishing!

Please give my regards to your parents, and be sure to call me when you come home on your next vacation.

Your friend,
JACK FALLON

If $15 sounds surprisingly inexpensive for the rod, reel, line, and hooks that Michael bought, it is. Dads bought a lot less for a lot more when they were boys. Nevertheless, it's true. For under $20, you can buy a youngster all the rod, reel, lures, and accessories he needs to get started. His rod won't be tournament quality, his reel might not last more than a year or two, but they'll do the job adequately during his indoctrination. After he's flubbed a few critical casts because his bail balked and missed a few fish because his rod didn't have the heft he thought it had, he'll be better qualified to make a bigger investment in higher-quality equipment. In fact, he might even decide after a year or two of spinning that he prefers to pursue some other method entirely—bait casting, for example, or fly-fishing or surf casting. Meanwhile, thanks to modern science, volume production, mass merchandising, and smart shopping, he will have a serviceable rod and reel to help him learn.

Intelligent shopping is the key to finding the right equipment at a reasonable price. Technology developed during World War II made available the materials for producing low-cost fiberglass rods. Returning servicemen, anxious to renew their love affairs with the outdoors, supplied the demand. Today, seasons are previewed with highly publicized promotions by companies that have to provide efficient, attractive, dependable equipment at prices the average angler can afford; otherwise they don't stay in business. Part of these promotions are pre-season specials, and it was these that enabled Michael to buy what he wanted even within the narrow limits of his bare-bones budget.

We did our shopping in department stores rather than tackle shops. There are advantages to each, but our choice was made for us by Michael's needing his equipment for the following morning's fishing date; when we met at seven p.m. for our shopping tour, only department stores were open. Nevertheless, we probably would have stuck with department stores anyway because of the few dollars that Michael had to spend. Prices normally are lower in chain-store tackle departments than in small independent tackle shops because of the enormous quantities in which the chains can buy their wares. If you know what you're looking for and can find it on your own, as was the case with Michael and me, you probably can buy it for a little less from a chain store.

If you need guidance, however, you're not likely to find it at any of the chain-store tackle departments that I've patronized. These always seem to be attended by clerks who answer all fishing questions the same way: "Well, uh, this isn't my usual counter." Many of these counters,

I'm sure, are manned by employees who are helpful, attentive, and informed. I just haven't run into any. When you get right down to the dollars and cents of it, I suppose it's unreasonable of me to expect expertise along with a chain store's low prices. If they hire too many experts, their prices won't be low any more.

Tackle shops, on the other hand, usually are owned and staffed by people who know and love fishing. They talk the language, they've learned most of the answers, and they realize that the best way to keep you coming back, despite their higher prices, is to give you all the help you need and then some. The dad who doesn't know much about fishing would do well to invest a few extra dollars to make sure his son gets the right guidance.

Another advantage to trading in tackle shops is that they've always got up-to-the-minute information about what's going on in their vicinities. Before I fish any new area, I find out from friends who've been there the best local source of bait and information. Thereafter I always patronize

A tackle-shop owner who will spend a little time fitting out your youngster properly can help him to avoid a lot of awkwardness and frustration when he starts fishing. (Photo: Terry McDonnell)

the same place on the premise that the better they know me, the more accurately they can aim me in the right direction. Occasionally when something spectacular happens—ice-out up north, a bluefish blitz on the coast—I'll receive a collect phone call from an on-the-spot tackle shop announcing it.

Whether your choice is tackle department or tackle store, you're likely to find your best buys just before the season opens. During the three or four weeks preceding the opening of the freshwater season in late April, newspapers throughout the Northeast regularly announce rod-and-reel specials which a generation ago would have been the envy of every boy and girl on the block. As recently as twenty years ago, these outfits simply weren't available at any price. Designed with children in mind, their weight, action, and dimensions are tailored to the size, strength, and interests of fledgling fishermen. They might not be an ideal match for your particular fledgling, but they're certainly worth a look.

Several looks, in fact. Stocks of "specials" are limited, so what one tackle counter might be out of, another might still have in stock. Also, where one store touts a particular manufacturer's wares, a second might offer something even better in another line.

Often you can find attractive buys at end-of-season sales, when merchants traditionally lower their prices to reduce their inventories. The only fault with fall sales is that your youngster has a whole winter during which he might change his interests. Many a young spinning or casting enthusiast has been converted to fly-fishing during the off season by books, movies, brainwashing, or a couple of lessons at a casting clinic.

In-season sales are harder to find, but they're there for the attentive shopper. Closeouts, discontinued models, and product lines that aren't moving well sometimes are sold at startlingly low prices. Occasionally fishing tackle is sold at auction. If you see some advertised, arrive at the auction hall early and examine what's being offered. If there's something there you want, try to persuade the auctioneer to put it up early. If he agrees, you not only will save time, but, because the house will not have filled up yet, competition might be less. When bidding starts, have a top price in mind and stick to it. There's a contagious hysteria about auctions. Clever auctioneers cultivate it with provocative suggestions ("The opportunity of a lifetime!") and implied challenges ("Someone sitting in this hall is going to walk out of here with a real bargain"). First thing you know, you're in a sky's-the-limit competition with other bidders. I've seen equipment sold at auctions for much more than buyers would have had to pay at retail stores, and once I watched a man bid and buy a bilge pump for three times what it was worth, only to realize as the auctioneer's gavel descended that he didn't even own a boat to use it on. Conversely, I recently paid one dollar for an inconspicuous cardboard box which the non-fisherman auctioneer had described as containing "some lures." Indeed it did! An earlier look had revealed to me that there were fifty-five of them, various models and sizes of my favorite stainless-steel design, all in their original packages and each labeled with a price that averaged just under $2. After I had loaded up the Fallon tackle boxes and given several to friends, I sold the balance to a delighted merchant for better than $20.

Mail-order buying, especially through firms that specialize in fishing or outdoor equipment, can save you real money on items such as line, hooks, leaders, swivels, and lightweight lures if you buy them in bulk. So who needs a hundred #5/0 stainless steel O'Shaughnessy hooks or a gross of assorted brass snap swivels? You, your family, and a handful of friends probably can use them over a season or two. On heavier items such as large saltwater sinkers, check postage costs before placing your order. These plus occasional sales taxes sometimes can offset your savings.

I wouldn't hesitate to order a rod or reel for myself through a catalog, but a boy shopping for his first outfit should never buy blind. That first purchase should be made in person and after all the deliberating he darn well feels like doing. Let him look and try and ponder to his heart's content, and when he makes his decision, let him handle the transaction himself. Later, after he has cast enough lures and played enough fish, he will have learned from experience what he wants: a little less whip, a little more length, a different type of reel seat, a more comfortable handle. When he finds a make and model that fills the bill, he ought by all means to look it up in several catalogs and compare prices.

Lures often cost less through a catalog, but you have to wait for delivery. A $2 plug might cost only $1.75 via mail order, but if you need it for next week's opener, the quarter saving is insignificant. But if along about October you should order, say, two dozen such lures as stocking stuffers for Christmas, that's smart shopping.

What about those "bushel of lures for a buck" bargains you often see advertised? A few years back I mailed in my buck—or two, or whatever it was—and more than got my money's worth. The lures were cheaply made, sloppily finished, and imperfectly balanced, but they worked well enough to enable my sons and me to coax several fair bass and pickerel from an underwater forest. By the end of the day most of our lures were decorating submerged branches, but that's what I expected and that's why

I bought the lures. Had I lost an equal number of my first-team fish-foolers, I would have been out a great many more dollars.

Quantity also is more important than quality while your child is in his kindergarten stage of casting. Until he gets a season or two under his belt, his lure losses are likely to be high. Fortunately this stage coincides with the period during which all lures look pretty much alike to him— BEAUUUUTIFUL!—and a bulging tackle box is a mark of distinction. Later, like generations before him, he will come to prefer the old standbys such as Mepps, Dardevle, Flatfish, Atom, Hula Popper, and any others which by then will have wiggled their way into immortality. He will learn to appreciate features such as precise and invariable weight, dependable balance, and authentic action that have been designed and refined into old favorites and enabled them to pass the test of time. Meanwhile a few colorful clunkers will serve the dual purpose of saving money and enabling him by contrast to see what it is that makes a good lure good.

Some lures would be more at home in a joke store than a tackle counter. Recently a friend gave me a contraption called the Kitchen Sink Spinner. Touted as the lure to use when you've thrown everything at the fish but the kitchen sink, it consists of a small rotating blade on a thin steel shaft to which there also is attached a piece of plastic pressed in the shape of . . . that's right, a kitchen sink. I presume that its manufacturer meant it more as a conversation piece than a fish-catcher, but I'd use it in preference to some of the silly creations I've seen offered for sale.

A boy can become bewildered awfully fast by a seemingly endless assortment of lures; lures for every species, every season, every condition of weather and water. Only in the greeting-card business, where I expect before long to be able to choose from a selection of illustrated odes celebrating the successful removal of a bunion from the big toe of my Aunt Matilda's left foot, has specialization been carried to a comparable extreme. That's why it's important that the lad start simple: simple fish, uncomplicated methods, easy waters. And that's why it's important that he be reminded occasionally that a lure is only as good as the man who uses it; that its appearance is less important than how it is presented and how it is retrieved. An able fisherman can make a bad lure look good, but no lure can make a good fisherman look bad.

Here's a checklist you might want to run through before buying that outfit for your youngster. Remember, though, that this is his purchase. His intuition has to play as big a part in the decision as dimensions and dollars. If this checklist suggests to you some feature he might not be giving enough thought to, by all means let him know. If he still wants a rod because in spite of an inadequacy or two it has that special "feel," that's the one he should buy. He's the one who will be living with it, inadequacies and all. Remember, too, that expert advice is better by far than a checkoff list. Try to persuade a fisherman friend who is also an accomplished parent to come along.

# TACKLE SELECTION

### ROD

*Is it comfortable?*

1. Does his arm tire easily when he holds the rod straight out in front of him for a few minutes?

2. Does it respond smoothly when he raises and lowers it at various speeds with his elbow held at his side?

3. Does the shape of the handle feel natural in his hand?

4. Does it balance with the reel he'll be using?

*Is it appropriate?*

1. Is it right for the locale he'll be fishing in? Is it too long, for example, for frequent treks through thick brush?

2. Does it match the kind of fishing he'll be doing? Deepwater trolling is best done with a rod that's much shorter and sturdier then one that's ideal for casting quarter-ounce lures.

3. Is it right for the species he'll be seeking? Despite his desire to catch as many different kinds of fish as possible, that ultralight wand he fell in love with won't help him worth a hoot on a 30-pound codfish. Better that he make his choice beforehand.

4. Will its metal parts stand up to salt water as well as fresh if he plans to use it in both?

*Is it well made?*

1. Are windings even, more than one layer deep, and covered with a protective coating of plastic or varnish?

2. Are metal ferrules tight and secure? Do they fit together easily and stay together while the rod is being flexed? Can they be pulled apart by your boy without undue strain?

3. Does the reel fit snugly on the reel seat? Does the locking ring look as though it will keep the reel in place?

4. Do all guides line up with one another as well as with the reel? Incredible as it sounds, I once discovered eight boat rods on display in a store which had their line guides on the side opposite from where the reel would be installed.

5. Is the rod joined solidly and neatly to the handle, or is it likely to work loose? If it does, by the way, you can bank on its happening right in the middle of your boy's playing a big fish.

## REEL

1. Is the handle tight and secure, with no unnecessary play in any direction?

2. Are all screws tight and flush?

3. Are there any rubbing or grinding noises as you rotate the handle?

4. Does it fit snugly and balance comfortably on the rod you will be using?

5. Does the handle rotate only in a forward direction with the anti-reverse on and clicking? Does it rotate in both directions when it is not?

6. Are all metal parts corrosion-resistant?

7. Are replacement parts conveniently available?

8. Does the drag operate smoothly? You'll have to wind some line on the spool to find out, but demonstration models should be available.

The open-face spinning reel permits long casts even with lightweight lures. The trick is to release your index finger at precisely the right moment in your forward cast. Children learn how quickly. (Photo: Terry McDonnell)

9. On an open-face spinning reel, pay particular attention to the bail. Does it flip easily and stay in position until tripped back by the rotating of the reel? Does the bail spring push it back solidly into position? Also check the spool carefully. If there is too much clearance between it and its housing, line may slip in without your noticing and become hopelessly snarled on shaft and gears. With the spool removed, examine shaft, gears, and other visible moving parts. Do they fit snugly with no noticeable play?

10. On a rotating-spool reel, make sure there is no noticeable friction when it is operated in free-spool. If it is a level-wind design, does the pair of parallel bars through which the line is fed ride smoothly on their track and reverse direction immediately after reaching the end of a run?

Whereas the open-face spinning reel is mounted on the bottom of the rod, the closed-face spin-casting reel is mounted on the top. (Note how this boy's is mounted slightly off level, a trick that he and his dad have worked out for better casting control.) Closed-face reels inherently have less slack line, which means fewer tangles. (Photo: Terry McDonnell)

LINE

1. Monofilament line should blend limpness, strength, thinness, stretch, and uniformity of composition and diameter. You'll get no bargain from a line that is thick, coarse, and stiff no matter how low its price. All monofilament has memory—that is, a springlike tendency to return to its original coiled condition. In good line this is not a problem, but a line that recoils too readily will cast poorly and tend to tangle.

2. Check the line spool for powder. This is evidence of deterioration, either from age or careless storage.

3. Pull a few feet through your fingers. Does it feel rough? This might indicate deterioration or poor workmanship.

## ACCESSORIES

*Tackle box.* A tackle box is as indispensable for the young angler as an attaché case is for the young executive, but make sure it's more nearly the size of a shoe carton than a steamer trunk. Remember, you're going to have to do most of the filling. If it has hinged drawers that swing out when the top is opened, do these drawers swing smoothly on strong corrosion-resistant hinges? Does its top close easily and stay closed? Even when the lock on the front is not snapped, can it be picked up without the top's opening and the box's contents spilling out?

*Boots.* Boots or waders are essential when fishing stream or surf. And don't delude yourself into thinking that your youngster will be careful and not get wet. Water is for walking in. It's the pathway to that big fish that always lurks just a few steps farther out. Along tropical shores, pants and sneakers are preferable to waders when walking near coral clumps or sharp shells.

*Landing net.* Because fish usually put on a final furious flurry of action when you have them alongside your feet or your boat, a landing net will save you a lot of disappointments.

*Nail clipper.* This is an invaluable implement for trimming loose ends of knots. Not only is it more efficient than teeth, but it also cuts down on dental bills.

*Fishing knife.* A fishing knife has a hundred uses, from cleaning your catch to spreading peanut butter on luncheon sandwiches. Keep yours sharp.

*Scaler.* An aluminum scaler that can be bought for about 20¢ is much easier to use than a knife when removing stubborn scales.

*Stringer.* Fish can be kept fresh in a cooler, but one of these might take up more room in your boat than you can afford. An easier way to ensure freshness is to keep your catch alive by hanging it over the side on a stringer. Be sure, however, to tether each fish through both lips, otherwise they might drown from water being forced through their mouths while your boat is in motion. When moving at high speed between locations, haul the stringer of fish into your boat. I've seen entire catches torn off by anglers anxious to get back to camp and show their buddies how well they had done.

*Tape measure.* Always have a tape measure handy to answer the inevitable question, "How big do you think it is, Dad?" If weights of fish are important—some locations limit daily catches to so many pounds—a scale/tape measure combination registers pounds as well as inches. These rust easily, so keep them dry.

## TACKLE MAINTENANCE

Even the best equipment won't last long if it's abused or neglected. Here are a few suggestions for keeping yours and your child's operating the way it should.

### ROD

Carry it, move it, store it carefully. A bump on a rock, a snag on a tree can bend or even break a guide. Once after carrying my spinning rod clear across the continent and halfway up the California coast, I climbed a rocky bluff on the Russian River, uncorked a cast, and broke my rod in two. It had been nipped in the car door while I was disembarking. Recently, with fly-fishing in full swing, I had to mail my favorite fly rod back to the factory because I had broken its tip on a branch the night before while wading a shad stream.

Be sure to secure your rod when you lay it down in a boat. One of the loveliest fly-fishing outfits I ever owned rests on the bottom of Maine's Attean Lake because I didn't notice it slide over the side while I was netting a fish being played by my neighbor, Vernon Merrill. Vern outdid me a year later in salt water when, after leaning his rod against the gunwale of his 16-footer to go forward and check the anchor line, he turned just in time to see it being pulled over the stern by the striped bass he'd been trying all afternoon to tie into. Not all such incidents end so sadly. While drifting seaworms across a mud-bottomed bay, my friend Frank Sheehan watched one of the two rods he was using slingshot off the amidships seat and out of the boat courtesy of a 6-pound weakfish. As we watched it disappear astern, my rod tip dunked with what turned out to be the catch of the day: Frank's rod and reel with his weakfish still on the hook. Frank credited me with an assist on this catch.

Rust ruins a rod by corroding metal parts. Even a thin film of rust on the inside of line guides can abrade line and reduce casting distance. A rod that is to be used in salt water should have at least an anti-corrosion finish on its metal parts. Even better is corrosion-resistant metal such as stainless steel. Ask the man from whom you're buying the rod about this. Most corrosion problems can be minimized for the occasional saltwater angler by spraying metal parts with a thin film of silicone. Rinsing with fresh water also is a must, but be sure to do it immediately after coming off the water. Don't wait until after the drive home.

Metal ferrules and line guides, especially the tip-top guide, should be checked regularly for looseness. Way off in the woods with trout rising all along a wilderness stream is no time to discover that a rod cannot be assembled because last time it was taken apart, the male ferrule stayed inside the female.

### REEL

Lubricate! A regular anointment with a few drops of reel oil not only eliminates problems such as seizing of gears and binding of drag, but also improves casting. Doses should be frequent rather than heavy. Just a few drops usually does the trick. Ever since I've been toting a 29¢ tube of reel lubricant in my tackle box, my casting problems have almost disappeared.

Check screws to make sure they're tight and flush. I've had an inoperative saltwater fly reel for almost two years because I let a screw fall out and haven't been able to find one small enough to replace it.

As soon as you detect sand beneath the spool of a spinning reel, wipe it out. Just a grain or two blown in when you lay your rod on the beach can make it sound like a cement mixer.

When parts start to wear noticeably, replace them right away. Don't wait for a chain reaction in which one malfunctioning part makes another wear out, and that in its turn makes another, etc.

Check your reel immediately after it's been dropped or bumped. The bail on an open-face spinning reel is especially vulnerable to bending.

The problem that most persistently plagues the new user of monofilament is tangles. If it's cast too casually: tangles. If it's retrieved too jerkily: tangles. Tangles also result when it's wound loosely, unevenly, or too high on a spinning spool. Better than half of all tangles can be eliminated by buying good line and winding it well. Monofilament cartons often have illustrated directions showing how line should come off the supply spool in the same direction as the pickup bail turns, but best winding is done by machine. Most tackle shops offer this service. It's free, fast, flawlessly efficient, and can save you money because you buy only as much line as you need. But the big savings are realized in the replenishments you avoid. As an example, I filled one of my reels with moderately good line six times in one season for about $3 a load. Next year I had it filled once—same reel, same kind and frequency of fishing. It cost me only $5 and as an added bonus the line was of much better quality.

Trolling twists lines so that when slackened, they spring together like Brillo pads. Anti-twist swivels reduce twisting when trolling or casting, but weeds and wild fish always seem to contribute their share. One of the most valuable tips I ever received was to trail my line behind a boat with everything removed—hooks, swivels, leaders, everything. A minute or two of this at a fairly fast speed, and every troublesome twist is removed.

Fishing around rocks, pilings, stumps, coral, gravel, and shell beds can fray lines to the point where a hit from a good fish will snap them. Fortunately, fraying usually occurs in the first few feet of line, so when rubbing reveals roughness, snip off the first 4 or 5 feet.

## TACKLE REPAIR

Even with the best care, you'll get occasional breakdowns: windings fray, screws fall out, bail springs break. By learning to make minor repairs yourself, you can save money, but even better, you won't have to sit out any trips while someone is doing the work for you. Here are a few repairs you and your youngsters might want to try.

### ROD

Rewrapping is tedious and time-consuming without a machine to lay on the threads for you. With a lot of hours and patience you can make a winter project out of rewrapping, but your results probably will look less than professional. If you enjoy it, fine. If you don't mind working for the equivalent of a few cents an hour, great. Me, I'd rather share winter evenings with my son at meetings of clubs where we can watch fishing movies, reminisce with friends, and lay the foundation for next season's fishing. When wrappings start unfurling, I dab them back in place temporarily with several coats of clear fingernail polish. Comes the winter, I drop them off for an annual overhauling with instructions to have them ready in plenty of time for opening day.

Broken line guides can be taped back in place to enable you or your boy to complete your day of fishing. For this purpose I always carry a couple of spools of narrow plastic tape in my tackle box. Permanent replacement of guides, however, requires rewrapping, so I have it done by a pro. If you're a regular patron, a shop owner often will do a small job like this while you wait.

Normally the foremost guide, or tip-top, can be replaced without rewrapping. In case you lose yours, keep a spare handy along with a stick of ferrule cement. This is melted with a match, and dripped onto the rod tip. After the tip-top is worked into place, the cement is allowed to harden for a few minutes, and presto, you're back in business.

Metal ferrules also are replaced the same way. With ferrules, though, be careful when pulling them off your rod. You might want to remove and recement a loose one that rotates but doesn't slide off easily. If you use pliers and squeeze too hard, you might misshape it so that it no longer fits snugly with the other ferrule.

## REEL

Well-made reels usually are packaged with spare parts and a tube of lubricant. Also included in the carton is a set of instructions keyed to an exploded diagram with all parts carefully labeled and numbered for easy reordering. A good investment for you and your youngster would be to spend an hour or two disassembling and reassembling your reels. Learn how they operate, as well as where the spare parts are used and how each of them functions. Carry pliers and a screwdriver in your tackle box so you can make on-the-spot adjustments and repairs, and use a plastic bag to protect these tools against moisture.

For major repairs, you can either bring your reel to a local authorized dealer or send it to the manufacturer's factory repair facility. I used to return all my reels to the factory for an annual overhaul. Work invariably was expertly done, prompt as long as I didn't wait till the last minute, and economical even with postage costs included. I still send them to the factory for major work, but routine refurbishing is done by the same shop that rewraps my rods.

## TERMINAL TACKLE

Common to all methods of fishing are those items known collectively as terminal tackle. Back in the days when tobacco companies were allowed to sell cigarettes on television, viewers were relentlessly reminded that "It's what's up front that counts." As anyone who has tried to catch a bluefish without a wire leader or a flounder on a hook too big to fit into its tiny mouth knows, this reminder also applies to fishing. My friend Bill Stone tells of a man with whom he fished for bluefin tuna out of Bailey's Island, Maine. This man had invested almost $200 in a mechanical marvel of a reel. His rod, custom-built for the occasion, cost him close to another $100. After almost two days of trolling, a mammoth tuna finally struck his string of mackerel, providing the man with a chance at last to fulfill his lifelong dream, but he lost the fish after only a few seconds because a cheap swivel gave way under the strain.

"He sure pulled out all the stops when it came to buying equipment," said Bill later. "All told, he must have invested nearly $1,000 in that one chance, yet he muffed it because of a 10-cent swivel. It was like trying to run a Rolls Royce on kerosene."

Similar incidents occur all the time. Remember that lunker largemouth your youngster lost because it wrapped his line in the weeds? It might be adorning his mantle if you had had him use a little heavier leader. Your family might have enjoyed a much bigger feed of weakfish if you had taken the trouble to sharpen your youngster's hooks. Rainbows might have been attracted instead of repelled by his spinner if you had noticed the bend in the shaft on which its blade rotated.

Terminal tackle, then, is everything that is attached to the forward end of your line, and consists of swivels, leaders, bobbers, spinners, sinkers, hooks, and lures. Although knots technically are not terminal tackle, I am going to include a few comments on them too.

### SWIVELS

To connect a line to a leader or a leader to a lure, you can use a device consisting of two metal eyes joined by a pin. This device, called

## FRESH WATER SERIES

General usage: nos. 1 and 2, light spin fishing; no. 2, casting also; no. 3, spinning, casting and trolling; no. 4, casting and trolling; no. 5, heavy casting and trolling; no. 6, extra heavy trolling. The pound designation figure below each number indicates swivel test.

## SALT WATER SERIES

Designed for use in all types of salt water fishing. Different riggings are available for local fishing requirements and preferences. **Salt water rings are made of brazed monel.** The pound designation figure below each number indicates swivel test.

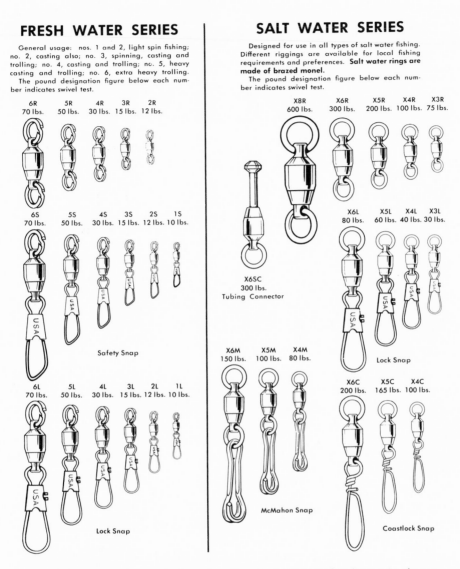

| 6R | 5R | 4R | 3R | 2R |
|---|---|---|---|---|
| 70 lbs. | 50 lbs. | 30 lbs. | 15 lbs. | 12 lbs. |

| X8R | X6R | X5R | X4R | X3R |
|---|---|---|---|---|
| 600 lbs. | 300 lbs. | 200 lbs. | 100 lbs. | 75 lbs. |

| 6S | 5S | 4S | 3S | 2S | 1S |
|---|---|---|---|---|---|
| 70 lbs. | 50 lbs. | 30 lbs. | 15 lbs. | 12 lbs. | 10 lbs. |

Safety Snap

| X6L | X5L | X4L | X3L |
|---|---|---|---|
| 80 lbs. | 60 lbs. | 40 lbs. | 30 lbs. |

X6SC
300 lbs.
Tubing Connector

| X6M | X5M | X4M |
|---|---|---|
| 150 lbs. | 100 lbs. | 80 lbs. |

Lock Snap

| 6L | 5L | 4L | 3L | 2L | 1L |
|---|---|---|---|---|---|
| 70 lbs. | 50 lbs. | 30 lbs. | 15 lbs. | 12 lbs. | 10 lbs. |

Lock Snap

McMahon Snap

| X6C | X5C | X4C |
|---|---|---|
| 200 lbs. | 165 lbs. | 100 lbs. |

Coastlock Snap

Ball-bearing swivels from a single maker, Sampo. A swivel makes it easy to change lures and will prevent the line from twisting.

a swivel, is made in such a way that a rotating lure or bait cannot transmit its twist to your line.

There are two basic kinds of swivels: barrel and snap. In the barrel swivel, both eyes are permanently closed, while in the snap, one can be opened like a safety pin to slip on a lure. Another type, popular among ocean bait fishermen, is the three-way swivel. As the name suggests, this design has three rotatable rings assembled around the periphery of a circular central band. The line is tied to one ring, while leaders from hook and sinker are tied to the other two.

Many swivels are made of brass and steel, but black and brown finishes are more practical in salt water, where school fish such as mackerel often will strike a shiny swivel in preference to your lure. Small accumulations of salt can impair a swivel's rotation, so make sure that yours moves freely and smoothly. To ensure smooth rotation throughout prolonged trolling, you might want to invest a few extra cents in precision-built ball-bearing models.

While snap swivels are convenient for making quick lure changes, their presence can spook wary fish in low clear water. When spinning a shallow stream for trout, for example, I never use a swivel, even though my line sometimes twists because of it. When casting moving lures for bass, pickerel, and panfish, I use a swivel unless my lure is a lightweight floating model such as a popper. This lure is designed to float at a pre-scribed angle so that when it is pulled, the force of the water against its face produces a noise that is attractive to fish. The weight of a swivel can alter this angle enough to impair the lure's action.

In salt water it's always advisable to use a swivel. Aggressive ocean fish are not easily spooked by one's presence, and tides and winds increase a line's tendency to twist.

## LEADERS

A leader is a length of wire or synthetic material such as nylon attached to the end of a line. In fly-fishing, its purpose is to make the connection between heavy flyline and fly as nearly invisible as possible, and fly-fishing leaders are tapered to fine diameters for this purpose. In freshwater and saltwater casting with monofilament line, the line is unobtrusive enough, so a leader is used principally to prevent breaking by sharp-toothed rough-scaled fish and abrading on underwater obstacles. When casting with braided line instead of monofilament, it is customary to use about 6 feet of 10-pound-test monofilament leader to reduce visibility. These can be bought with a loop tied in one end or simply snipped off a spool of monofilament and connected to the braided line with a barrel swivel or a blood knot.

Wire leaders are desirable in fresh water only when casting for large pike, muskies, and walleyes, although a few feet of 30-pound-test monofilament should provide ample protection against their sharp teeth. Even pickerel rarely get by a swivel. When fishing for these species with bait, though, about 4 to 6 inches of wire leader is desirable because bait usually is swallowed deep before the hook is set. Just be sure to use a wire that is fine and flexible enough to let your bait move naturally, yet strong enough to stand up to these species' sharp teeth.

## BOBBERS

The term "bobber" denotes any float used in still-fishing whose bobbing motion indicates when a fish bites the bait dangling beneath it. As a boy I used twigs and matchsticks successfully on panfish; more recently, when my plastic bobber broke while I was floating live mackerel for striped bass, I improvised with an empty plastic oil bottle and the stripers didn't seem to mind at all.

Today's bobber market has pretty well been taken over by hard plastic spheres with spring-loaded clips for securing line. Mass-produced by the millions in sizes ranging from marble to tennis ball, they're as inexpensive as they are convenient. The bright colors—usually red and white hemispheres—make modern bobbers easy to see, although small ones can be lost sight of easily in choppy water or the sun's glare. Long pencil-type bobbers that tilt upright when a fish bites are more practical when water is rough.

## SPINNERS

Spinners are rotating blades that attract fish through flash, motion, and vibration. Even in murky water they are effective because of sound waves from their vibrations. They can be used alone as hooked lures or as attractors for other lures. An example of the former is the Colorado Spinner, with a treble hook behind its single broad blade; an example of the latter is the Cape Cod Spinner, with which a seaworm is trolled behind two willowleaf blades in series.

Spinner arrangements range from the single small blade to a string of "cow bells" simulating a school of baitfish. The latter are trolled deep and slowly ahead of an artificial lure or sewed-on bait for low-level species such as lake trout.

A spinner's size and shape determines its action, but a pull through the water is needed for rotation. This pull is imparted by trolling, retrieving, or hanging in a current. Always check a spinner's action before you use it by pulling it through the water with about the same force it will receive when in use. If its action is slow or erratic, see if there is a bend or a nick in the shaft or ring on which the spinner's blade rotates.

## SINKERS

Sinkers are metal weights for securing or moving baits at desired depths. Usually they are made of lead because of this metal's high ratio of weight to volume and because its dull color does not distract fish. Sinkers come in literally hundreds of shapes and in sizes all the way from split shot not much bigger than bird shot to the three-pound cannonballs used in trolling for Pacific Coast salmon.

Most designs are variations on the sharp-edged pyramid and the smooth-contoured dipsey. Stone sinkers much like our bank type have been uncovered in ancient South American tombs, and in emergencies I too have used stones, as well as nuts, bolts, and in one desperate instance a pair of rusty pliers.

Sinkers come in a bewildering variety of sizes and shapes, but only a few types will suffice for most fishing.

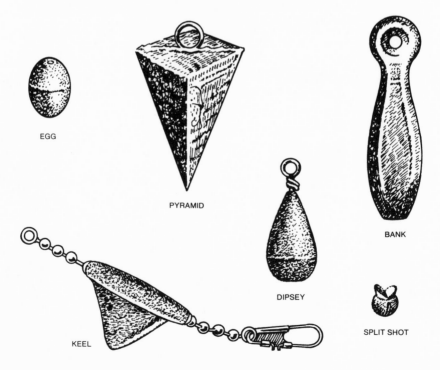

EGG

PYRAMID

BANK

DIPSEY

SPLIT SHOT

KEEL

Most of a boy's freshwater-sinker needs can be filled by a compart-mented package of split shot that comes in various sizes and with tabs which enable individual shot to be reused. When wading streams, where pocket space is at a premium, a matchbook-type package of thin lead strips is uniquely convenient. These strips are simply torn off, wrapped around line, and twisted tight. For fishing bait on the bottom, an egg sinker is excellent because a fish can pick up and run with bait without having to tow the sinker along with it. To keep an egg sinker from sliding down on your youngster's hook, slip his line through the sinker and tie it to one ring of a barrel swivel, then tie his hooked leader to the swivel's other ring.

In salt water a pyramid sinker will hold your boy's bait close to a mud or sand bottom, while a bank sinker is better on rock or coral. A bank also is a good choice for bottom-fishing bait from an anchored boat. Sinker weight is determined by the combined pull of wind and current.

For drifting small baits such as mudworms through a tideway, split shot are ideal. Pinch as many on in series as you think necessary to bring your bait to the level where you feel that fish might be found. For trolling, special streamlined designs such as the keel sinker are available for cutting down water resistance, minimizing air bubbles, and reducing line twists.

## KNOTS

Knots always remind me of a long-ago spring morning on a New Hampshire lake. . . .

It wasn't so much the solidity as the suddenness of the salmon's strike. Lulled almost into lethargy by hours of unproductive trolling, my thoughts were on other things: the beauty of the day, the compatibility of my companion, a warm sun, a cool beer. Mesmerized, my mind didn't register immediately. So rapidly was action followed by acrobatics that my first reaction to seeing the landlock leaping behind my wake was not "Hey, I'm on!" but "Hey, look at that landlock leaping behind my wake!" Relationship between fish and fishing did not register immediately.

But it didn't take long. Suddenly, indisputably, from the buzzing of my reel and the bucking of my rod, and from the tidal wave of adrenaline that surged into my system, I was aware that at last, at long last, I was doing battle with one of those famous Lake Winnipesaukee warriors. Not my first salmon, not even my first Winnipesaukee salmon, but my first one with real heft and size and authority. When it ran I let it run, satisfied just to be able to keep it on; retaining, not restraining was my goal. And when it leaped—correction, not leaped, soared—I marveled at its grace and strength and fight. And at its size. Here, I thought, with the presumptuousness of a farmer counting unhatched chickens, is a fish worthy of mounting, an adversary whose classic and courageous combat has earned it the immortality of a taxidermist's touch.

I had just about made the mental transfer from frying pan to fireplace wall when—you guessed it—I found myself with a line as limp as a strand of spent spaghetti. My salmon had gotten away.

As I reeled in my line, I felt a faint foreboding of what I would find on the bitter end. When I got it in, I felt the sickening futility of self-recrimination when I saw that my suspicion had been correct: the telltale curl on the end confirmed that my fish had gotten away because the knot with which I had tied on my fly had come loose.

Sound familiar? It certainly is to me. Despite my many hours on the business end of a fishing rod, I still lose fish occasionally because I have been careless or impatient about tying on terminal tackle. Lord knows it's hard enough to hook a good fish in the first place and hazardous enough to land it without adding to the obstacles. And I'm well aware of how easy it is to forget that final loop or that test tug when rising rainbows or swirling stripers have your heart pounding and your hands shaking so badly you're lucky even to be able to hold onto your rod. But I also have a lot of memories to remind me of how costly such carelessness and impatience can be.

A few summers ago, for example, I lost two stripers that I really wanted to catch, first because they were exceptionally fine fish, second because I was using a fly rod, and third because I was standing only a few yards away from son Jack, whose attitude about his father's artistry with a fly rod falls several levels below adulation. I was using a Platinum Blonde streamer, tied, incidentally, by Jack to make the victory of which I was confident just that much sweeter. Furthermore, I did everything right, tying the fly to my 8-pound-test leader with a five-twist clinch knot, adding the special safety factor of an extra loop, clipping the excess leader closely, and yanking hook against leader to be sure it could take a solid wallop.

Unfortunately I didn't do everything well enough. Because the hook had an especially thick body, from which a knot could work loose, I should have test-pulled harder and longer before casting. This would have revealed that the closely clipped leader end would slip loose with prolonged pressure, and sure enough, the first fish to apply this pressure caused precisely that. Next time around I did everything wrong, omitting in my excitement the safety loop, the test yank, plus a glance at my supercilious son who had come closer to watch his old man make a fool of himself. Daddy didn't disappoint him. Within, oh, two minutes, I had hooked myself by the seat of the waders, entangled my feet in flyline, and lost another fish, this one sucking the loosely tied fly from my line with the ease of a kid inhaling an ice cream soda.

"Having trouble, Dad?" asked Jack.

I didn't answer.

As if losing face and fish aren't penalty enough to pay for poorly tied knots, you also lose lures. At a dollar or two apiece, that extra second it takes to make sure your knot is secure is a good investment.

Finally, remember that one feature common to all well-executed knots is unobtrusiveness. When properly tied, they are small, solid, and compact enough to offer no obstacle to the smooth flow of line from your reel. Loose ends always should be trimmed flush with the body of the knot. A fingernail clipper is ideal for doing this.

In the beginning, two knots will take care of most of your youngster's needs. With the improved clinch knot he will tie on hooks, lures, and swivels; with the blood knot he will connect two strands of line that have equal or similar diameters.

## LURES

Cheese, bread, boiled potatoes, corn, hotdogs, marshmallows: a good menu for a camping trip. It's as good, in fact, for catching fish as it is for feeding campers. Processed cheese, kernel corn, and mini-marshmallows are so readily eaten by trout that they have been made illegal in some places. Boiled potatoes, especially when garnished with licorice or dipped in oil of anise, is a traditional catfish favorite; sunfish are pushovers for bits of damp bread squeezed onto the barb of a small hook; and hunks of hotdog have saved many a fishing trip after the worm supply has run out.

All of these are lures if you subscribe to the definition of a lure as a hooked device whose appearance and movement induce a fish to bite it. A distinction in terminology sometimes is made between natural bait and artificial lures, but I prefer to combine them under a single heading, lures both natural and artificial. Seems to me this arrangement is just as clear, and in its own small way it aids the cause of simplicity in its futile fight against formalization.

Natural lures, then, include all baits that are fished substantially as they are found in nature. (The "substantially" qualifies the licorice and marshmallows.) These can be live—worms, crawfish, crickets, hellgrammites, crabs, eels, mullet, menhaden, minnows, etc.—or they can be dead—whole herring floated in a tideway, clam necks anchored on the bottom, perch bellies skittered across a weed patch. Artificial lures are manufactured in more shapes, sizes, and materials than the 25,000 or so of the world's fish species that they're designed to catch. Except for a few mavericks, which I shall conveniently file under "miscellaneous," most of them are either spinners, spoons, plugs, or flies. The mavericks include the surgical tubing that accounts for so many saltwater scrappers and the rubber and plastic worms which, since first patented back in the mid-1800s, have been the downfall of so many largemouth bass.

Most spinners are attractors, used for calling a fish's attention to a lure behind it, but a few are armed with hooks of their own. These hooks can be fished bare or baited, but if you should plan to spice a spinner with a little something extra such as a small worm, make sure that the spinner's action is not impaired by the bait. The Colorado Spinner, for example, works best with its treble hook unbaited, while the Cape Cod and Rangeley spinners are designed to be trolled ahead of bait. A spoon is much like a spinner, but instead of rotating while being trolled or retrieved, it wobbles and flutters like a wounded fish. Bait rarely is used with a spoon because it seriously dampens its action. One notable exception is where the wiggle of a porkrind strip hung on the hook of a weedless spoon more than makes up for the reduction in the spoon's wobble.

Plugs are made of wood, plastic, or metal in size-shape-color combinations that correspond to baitfish. A few are made to resemble other forms of fish food, such as frogs and mice. Popping plugs, because of the concave contours of their faces, gurgle when jerked through the water, attracting fish by their sound as well as their motion. Other noisemaking plugs employ fore-and-aft propellers to kick up a commotion. Darting plugs are long and slender with grooved heads, and as their name suggests they are designed to be fished in a dive-dart-stop-float sequence. Swimming plugs submerge and wobble from side to side when retrieved or trolled because of pressure on a faceplate under their chins. Depth is determined by current, retrieve speed, and the angles at which the faceplate tilts downward and the tie-on eye tilts upward. Sinking plugs swim much like swimmers, but do not float when their motion is stopped. An experienced angler can cover a lot of water with a sinking plug, but a beginner will get many more hangups than hookups.

Flies are either dry or wet, depending on whether they are fished on or under the water. Nymphs and streamers are types of wet flies. Dries are floated on the surface in imitation of an insect that has just hatched from or alighted on the water. Wets and nymphs imitate insects under the water, a wet fly representing one that already has hatched, a nymph one that has not yet hatched. Streamer flies are not supposed to look like flies at all, but rather like small fish. Special flies are tied to imitate shrimp, frogs, mice, and crawfish. (More "miscellaneous.")

How lures got their start is shrouded in the mists of time. We do know that Polynesians have been catching fish for centuries with make-believe bait made from mother-of-pearl. In the second *Book of Saint Albans,* published in 1496, the author of *A Treatyse of Fysshynge wyth an Angle,* now generally agreed to have been a legendary nun and sports-woman named Dame Juliana Berners, described dressings for the first modern trout flies. The records of ancient Rome, Egypt, and China reveal hints of how fish were lured to their doom in those days, and I suspect that even cavemen knew a thing or two about how to con fish. Surely Og of the sloping shoulders and woolly-mammoth body shirt must have noticed one day when he dropped a twig off a flat rock that a prehistoric perch came up to investigate. Next time it came up, Og klonked the poor creature with his club, and that's how it all began.

## HOOKS

An arcing cast dropped the plug two feet beyond a gnarled tree trunk that angled out from a swampy shore. A gentle twitch suggested to the bass finning in the tree's shaded shelter that here was an easy meal; a cripple, stunned and struggling. Another twitch followed by the start of a slow wobbling retrieve convinced the bass that it was now or never. With a swing of its broad tail, it streaked upward, smashing its victim so suddenly that the plug was almost wholly in its mouth before it realized its mistake. Veering back toward the tree trunk, the bass shook its head to expel the strange lifeless object, when suddenly it was pulled out by some external force. The only sensation the fish felt was a slight stinging from the object's hard metallic tail.

It couldn't have been the plug, thought the disappointed caster. A half-ounce of streamlined plastic, its colors were as bright and its action as realistic as they had been the year before. It couldn't have been the fish. Largemouths like this had pulverized this same plug throughout the previous season, and, as many delicious midwinter dinners had attested, more often than not they'd gotten themselves caught in the process.

The angler's problem, of course, was his hook. Whenever a fish is lost, chances are very high that it is because of a hook that is too dull, too weak, or simply not the right design for the job. Ironically, in proportion to the importance of the part they play in catching fish, hooks are given less attention than any other item of terminal tackle.

Fundamentally a fish hook is a length of metal wire curved back on itself with a point at one end and an eye at the other. The fish hook is descended from the prehistoric gorge, a short rod made of bone, stone, horn, or shell, and pointed at both ends. Tied to a line and imbedded in a bait lengthwise, the gorge's line was pulled when a fish swallowed the bait, causing the gorge to become stuck crosswise in the fish's throat.

Copper hooks were among man's first metal tools. Along with the Bronze and Iron Ages came the development of barbed hooks with flattened ends in which holes were made for securing line. Modern fish-hook manufacturing began in London during the seventeenth century as an adjunct to the production of needles. Today Norway is the world's center of hook making, with Oslo's O. Mustad and Son the best-known firm. Most freshwater hooks are made of carbon steel. Those used in salt water require a corrosion-resistant metal such as stainless steel, or at least an anti-corrosion plating such as nickel, tin, or cadmium.

A hook's size and strength are influenced most strongly by the size, strength, and habits of the fish being sought. For delivering bits of seaworm to the minuscule mouths of one- and two-pound flounder, a long, narrow, fine-wire Viking design is ideal, but big muscle-mawed codfish are more easily caught and controlled with a couple of clam necks adorning a broad thick O'Shaughnessy. A rule to remember is that a short barb is imbedded quickly but easily thrown, a long barb less easily thrown but more difficult to drive through a fish's hard bony mouth. The tarpon, an acrobatic head-shaker with a mouth like leather, requires a carefully selected compromise. So does the weakfish, an underwater battler whose membranous mouth tears easily.

How a fish feeds and how it fights also should influence hook selection. For a careful shallow-water bottom-feeder such as the bonefish, I would use a long, sturdy but narrow hook that I could camouflage inside or alongside my shrimp bait. For brawling bluefish that seem to be able to throw anything that offers even the slightest leverage, I normally troll with a single-hook jig in preference to a plug with trebles.

Hook care is as important as hook selection. Check regularly to see if your barbs have been bent or your points blunted when you've snagged a rock. In salt water especially, oxidation quickly takes its toll. Even a thin coating of oxide can dull a point to where your normal setting of your hook won't be enough to drive its point home. To be on the safe side, invest a few seconds before you start fishing in sharpening the points on all the hooks you'll be depending on. A sharpening stone sells for only a few cents; fish dinners are a lot more expensive than that.

Besides the many hook types, of which Kirby, Carlisle, Siwash, Limerick, Viking, Chestertown, and O'Shaughnessy are perhaps the best known, many hooks are manufactured for special applications. In cork- and wood-bodied lures such as bass bugs, shanks sometimes are bent or humped to ensure that their lures' bodies will not turn on their hooks. Bait fishermen often use hooks such as the Eagle Claw with points offset from the line of the shaft, as well as with barbs on their shafts for holding bait securely. Trout fishermen occasionally use barbless hooks to increase their sport. When casting or trolling in weedy water, anglers commonly employ weedless designs. These have thin flexible arms leading from eye to point which guide grass and weeds away from the hook's bend. Treble hooks are used on the majority of casting and trolling lures, as well as by many marine anglers who fish with live herring, mackerel, or menhaden for striped bass.

Lest you think that the days of innovation in hook design are over, two live-lining friends of mine came up recently with a new twist that they estimate has added another 20 percent to their striper catches. Trebles, they found, were being detected by the bass, which spit them out before they swallowed my friends' mackerels. Single hooks were unobtrusive enough, but they often would not sink into the bass's flesh. Ideally, my friends concluded, there should be two hooks back to back. In that way there always would be one barb within setting distance of either the roof or floor of a bass's mouth. Their two hooks, #3/0 and #5/0 in size, are soldered together back to back with their eyes coinciding. When they haul back on their lines to set this combination, either the upper or lower hook always snags their fish.

For every job, therefore, there is a right hook. Next time you're tempted to buy that "whole season's supply for a dollar" special, make sure that they're strong enough and properly designed for the size and species of fish you'll be seeking. A cent-and-a-half hook on the end of an outfit that's right in every other respect is a poor investment.

# 3.

# Fishing Techniques

~~~~~~~~~~~~~~~~~~~~~~~~~~~~~~~~~~~~~~~~~~~~~~~~~~~~~~~~~~~~~~~~~~~~~~~~~~

So much for buying, caring for, and repairing equipment. Now let's look at the various types of tackle and techniques as well as some of their accessories that your youngster should know about. These are bait casting, spinning, spin casting, surf casting, and fly-fishing. Each has a near-infinity of adaptations to suit a particular locale, species, or collection of colloquial prejudices, and in time your child might find that one of these fits him perfectly, but for now he should stick to the fundamentals that he needs to build on.

## BAIT CASTING

Bait-casting tackle isn't for bait casting. Not any more. That was its purpose when it was introduced back in the nineteenth century, but today it is used almost exclusively for propelling artificial lures or heavy sinkers. Today, in fact, the term "plug casting" is gradually eclipsing "bait casting" as a name for the technique, and in keeping with the trend, I shall use the more modern term.

Plug casting is not as easy to learn as spinning or spin casting. Nevertheless, because of the unique combination of accuracy, comfort, and control that can be achieved with practice, it still has plenty of enthusiasts. The technique is especially popular with tournament casters who appreciate the challenge of controlling their casts by direct pressure from their thumbs on the rotating spools of their reels.

Thumb pressure slows a rotating spool as a lure approaches its target and stops the spool when the plug lands. This is done to avoid the birdnest snarls caused by backlash, a condition which occurs when the spool spins faster than it is being pulled by a cast lure or a running fish. Anti-backlash and level-winding features reduce the risk of backlash, but thumb control still is essential, especially when strong winds interfere with the normal trajectory of a lure.

Besides braking a fish and feathering a spool, the thumb can be used to keep line tight during the retrieve. This is done by holding the reel in the palm of the left hand (just the opposite for lefties) and running the line between the thumb of the left hand and the forward grip, located immediately in front of the reel.

A plug-casting reel is installed on the top of the rod. Its handle is on the right side for right-handed casters, and the rod is held in the right hand for casting, the left for retrieving.

Freshwater plug-casting rods are short, usually around five feet unless big pike or muskies are the prey. The snap from a whippy tip propels the lure. This whipping action, once derived from a steady taper between butt and tip, has been improved by reinforcing rod butts and designing most of a rod's taper around its center. Now even light lures can be cast reasonable distances with plug-casting rods that are tapered in this fashion.

Bait-casting rod and reel. Since a revolving spool is used, the line can backlash if the spool is not braked properly with the thumb at the end of the case—which takes some practice. (Courtesy South Bend Co.)

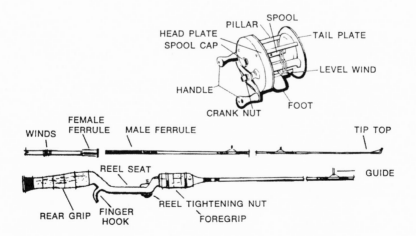

Braided line has long been a favorite of plug casters because of its lack of stretch and its thinness in relation to its strength. Continuous improvement in monofilament, however, has made it almost as satisfactory. Since a monofilament leader probably will be required in clear fresh water anyway, your boy might as well make it mono all the way. Ten-pound-test is strong enough to survive most snags, yet light enough to avoid overburdening fish of, say, a pound and a half or better.

Plug casting begins with the rod aimed at where the plug is supposed to land. Facing in the direction in which he will be casting, your youngster should rotate a quarter-turn to his left, moving his left foot behind his right and distributing his weight any way that comes out comfortable. He should hold the rod grip firmly but not forcefully in his right hand, with his index finger on the trigger. Placing his thumb on the left side of his spool, he should turn his hand so that his palm faces down and his reel handle is up. With his elbow almost touching his body, his rod tip should be on target.

Action is initiated by lifting his rod until his reel reaches eye level. Lifting should be done mostly with the forearm, using the elbow as a pivot. Very little wrist action is required.

He should stop the rod's backward motion just about at the vertical. The lure will continue aft, bending the rod's tip. By immediately starting his downstroke with a smooth forward thrust of his wrist, he will send his lure on its way. When the rod is about halfway to horizontal, the lure will start spooling off line. This is when thumb pressure must be eased off.

Thumb pressure is increased as the lure approaches target, with full pressure stopping the spool as the lure hits the water. With the rod halted in its original position, the casting cycle is completed.

The thumb obviously is the key to successful plug casting, and practice, practice, practice is the only way to determine proper pressure. Most youngsters will prefer to start with easier-to-learn spinning and spin casting, but if your boy should show an interest in plug casting, give him a chance. He may just find some special satisfaction in meeting the challenge of a more difficult technique. If he's interested, he'll pick it up quickly. In no time he'll be backhanding around obstructions and side-arming under branches.

Adults generally tend to underestimate a youngster's ability to learn. As a result, we often either patronize him by explaining too much and demonstrating in an A-B-C detail that bores him, or we administer instructions with all the warmth and rapport of a drill sergeant. The result in either case is canned casting, leaving a lad little room for cultivating his own style.

And there is plenty of latitude for style in all forms of casting. Fundamentals don't differ—aim, lift, thrust, brake, retrieve—but a great many personalized factors influence how these are achieved. A child's bone structure, for example, might make a minor redistribution of weight more comfortable, or his muscle development might make it advisable for him to start his forward cast sooner. If casting were merely a matter of muscles, a slender shapely Joan Salvato Wulff would not have been able to leave her muscular competitors in the dust back in 1960 when she cast her fly a phenomenal 161 feet.

Fundamentals, then, are all a youngster needs. He can learn them himself with the aid of a few diagrams and directions, but it's best done with the help of an informed adult with enough sense and sensitivity to know how to steer without stifling. Many communities and organizations these days have clinics for aspiring anglers. One I heard of recently, sponsored by a marina in suburban Los Angeles, offers a nine-session course on Saturday mornings in which parents and children are given a capsule course in angling basics which they top off with a final exam aboard a party boat. According to a friend who attended, the fun alone is worth the $20 tuition.

Within an easy drive of my home are several organizations, such as the Lowell (Massachusetts) Flyfishers and the United Fly Tyers (Boston), whose members are delighted to share their knowledge with newcomers. Sportsmen's shows, of course, provide opportunities galore to try any kind of casting under the helpful scrutiny of some of the world's top pros, and in recent years several tackle manufacturers have been sponsoring casting schools throughout the country. Prices for these seminars might be a little lofty for the beginner, with meals and accommodations for from three days to a week running well up into the three figures, but because they're held at prime fishing locations, they attract a lot of anglers who want to combine recreation with education.

Plug casting, by the way, is an authentically American form of fishing. It began back in the early 1800s when a group of Kentucky watchmakers designed and developed the multiplying-spool reel. Prior to this time, reel spools revolved only once for every turn of the reel handle, but with the new design, the spool revolved more than once, the multiple depending on the gears used. In this way the pace of plug casting—or more accurately bait casting, since the first plug wouldn't be showing up for almost a century—was speeded up. Water could be covered more quickly and more thoroughly, and a greater variety of movements could be imparted to retrieved lures.

## SPINNING

The technique of spinning was conceived in Europe when an angler designed a reel from which line could be pulled in the same way in which he saw thread being pulled from spindles in a linen mill. The reel was refined in England and France, and in 1935 it was introduced into the United States. Regarded initially as just another novelty, its popularity was starting to gain momentum by 1938, when World War II cut off the American distributor's source of supply. It was not until the late forties, therefore, that spinning really got underway in America.

Its quick acceptance influenced some reel manufacturers to overpromote their products. When their spinning reels failed to perform as promised, some anglers became temporarily disenchanted. Spinning's convenience, versatility, and economy didn't mean much if their reels were in the repair shop most of the time. Reputable manufacturers eventually put things back into perspective by producing dependable reels at reasonable prices. Today it is estimated that more fishermen use spinning gear than all other types combined.

My first spinning reel was a prime clunker. Foreign-made, probably

Spinning rod and reel. The reel, mounted on the underside of the rod, has a fixed spool, eliminating backlashes and making long casts easy even for beginners. (Courtesy South Bend Co.)

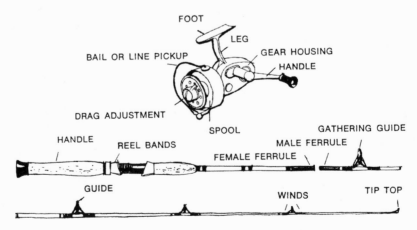

from an old mess kit salvaged from some Pacific atoll, it cranked like a coffee grinder and malfunctioned every time a catchable fish came within casting range. As for replacement parts, they would have been easier to find for the *Monitor* and the *Merrimac*. The five dollars I paid for it seemed like small potatoes considering the inflated prices we pay today for everything from beefsteak to bubble gum, yet for five dollars last week I bought a sturdy, attractive, dependable ultralight spinning reel and had enough change left over for two saltwater swimming plugs. Viva free enterprise!

The main advantage of spinning is that it enables your youngster to cast very light lures long distances. This is possible because its fine monofilament line flows from the face rather than the side of the reel spool, with the spool remaining stationary instead of rotating, as it does on the plug-casting reel. Since the spool's inertia needn't be overcome before the lure can be cast, a light lure has no initial resistance to overcome. Resistance increases, however, as line gets lower on the spool and has to run against the spool's edge, so keep spools filled to within a quarter to an eighth of an inch of the flange on the face of the spool.

The fixed spool also eliminates the plague of all plugcasters, the backlash. Thus, casting can be learned quickly. An hour or two invariably has been enough to enable my children to cast with acceptable accuracy and distance.

Another attraction of the spinning reel is its simple drag adjustment. With a twist-of-the-wrist rotation of a screw adjustment on the spool's face, your child can set the resistance against which a fish must pull to take out line. A few rotations in the opposite direction and the line spool can be removed. This is an invaluable asset when you want to switch quickly to a different-test line or when your line snarls just as fish start biting. The spinning reel's economy results from the less precise tolerances of parts used in fixed-spool as opposed to revolving-spool operation.

The only significant disadvantage to spinning is the ease with which lines tangle. The problem was serious in the early days of spinning when coarse kinky lines were the only ones available, but today's strong limp monofilament has made tangles only a minor irritation for spin fishermen who invest in good-grade line, wind it carefully, and avoid twisting. Troublesome twists occur when the handle is turned but no line is being brought onto the reel. When a fish is taking out line against a set drag, therefore, it should be allowed to play itself out; reeling will not restrain it. For the same reason a firmly snagged lure should be worked, not cranked, loose.

The most noticeable differences between spinning and plug casting are in the location of the reel under the rod, and the much larger sizes of line guides. Balance requires that the reel be installed beneath the grip. Also, if it were not, line leaving the spool would be pulled down slightly by gravity. This would cause it to slap the rod and would make directing of the line into the first line guide difficult. Even with the reel under the rod, large-diameter line guides are necessary because of the broad loops in which line leaves the spool.

With the reel beneath the rod, cranking must be done with the left hand (right for a southpaw). This will seem awkward for your son at first, especially if he has done some plug casting, but in short order it will become second nature. If he should try to eliminate the initial awkwardness by holding his reel above his rod and cranking right-handed, discourage the practice. Not only will it brand him as a beginner, but it will require that he switch his rod from his right to his left hand before starting his retrieve.

As in plug casting—and indeed all casting—individual steps should be blended into a single smooth sequence. Timing, not strength, is the key. To start his cast, your boy should hold the rod handle with his thumb on top and the reel foot between his second and third fingers. Then with his left hand, he cocks the pickup bail while he lightly restrains his line with his right index finger. Stance is the same as for plug casting: right shoulder pointed toward target, with left foot behind right.

The standard overhead cast commences with his rod tip at eye level and his rod on target. He lifts his hand to just below eye level by pivoting his forearm on his elbow. This brings his rod to slightly beyond vertical, where he halts its backward motion. The lure will continue to pull the tip back, flexing it into a bend that will propel the lure forward when he brings his forearm forward and down in a snappy chopping motion.

Line is released from the index finger as the rod nears its starting position. Until experience teaches him when to release his line, a beginner's lures often travel some crazy trajectories, from straight up when he releases too soon to a few feet off the end of his rod when he lets go too late. Once he develops his touch and timing as well as the confidence that goes with them, he will learn to prevent overshooting by applying pressure on the uncoiling line with his index finger while the lure is in flight.

The key to trouble-free spinning is line tension. Loose line will cause loops and tangles as surely when casting and retrieving as when coiling it on the spool in the first place. Before casting, tension is applied by the line pickup, through which line is fed onto the spool. In most spinning outfits this is a metal-hoop bail which closes automatically as cranking is begun, but a few reels incorporate automatic or manually operated pickup arms.

When the bail is flipped back preparatory to casting, tension is transferred to the index finger. When the finger is released part way through the forward cast, the lure takes up the tension. Because tension is reduced by high arcing casts, especially into strong winds, make sure your youngster keeps his casts low. Just prior to reeling, have him increase tension by raising his rod tip.

## SPIN CASTING

A blend of spinning and bait casting, known as spin casting, uses a reel whose face is enclosed in a removable cone-shaped cover. As with the open-face reel, line spirals off the front of a stationary drum; in the spin-casting reel, however, it passes out of the cone through a hole in its apex. As with the revolving-spool reel, casting is controlled by thumb pressure; in the spin-casting reel, however, this pressure is applied via a pushbutton rather than through direct contact with the spool.

Closed-face reels are of two types. One is mounted below the rod in the same way as an open-face spinning reel. With some of these reels, line is passed under the index finger and the reel handle is backed off

Spin-casting rod and reel. The reel has a fixed spool, like the spinning reel, but is mounted on top of the rod, like a bait-casting reel. Such a rig is virtually trouble-free. (Courtesy South Bend Co.)

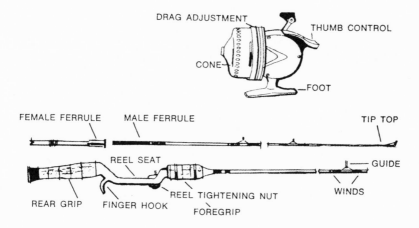

a half-turn to disengage line preparatory to casting; in others, line is released with a pushbutton.

The second kind of closed-face reel is mounted on top of the rod. Normally this rod is a plug-casting type with an offset reel seat.

Many youngsters initially shy away from closed-face reels because they fear that snarls will develop under the hood, which wouldn't occur if they could watch what's going on. They also want to avoid the inconvenience of having to remove the hood to get at the source of trouble.

While it's true that tangles are more troublesome inside the hood of a closed-face reel, it also is true that they are less likely to occur. This is because opportunities for slack line, which is where most tangles start, are fewer than in open-face reels. When tangles do occur, they usually are caused by line bunching up at the exit hole. Braided line or too limp a monofilament tends to pile up this way.

Spin casting, then, is like plug casting, but without the backlash; like spinning, but with far fewer tangles. Its only design deficiency is in the friction on the line as it passes through the exit hole. The distance loss is so small, however, that your youngster won't even notice its effect in normal use except possibly when he is trying to cast ultralight lures.

An inherently trouble-free operation combined with its many other attributes—economy, accuracy, simplicity—make the closed-face spin-casting reel a worthy candidate for your son's consideration. If initially he should vote against it because "Gee, Dad, I don't want to have to take off that hood every time I get a tangle," take the trouble to explain—or better yet, demonstrate—why this reel, by maintaining a more uniform tension than its open-face counterpart, cuts down on the cause of tangles.

## SURF CASTING

Today the term "surf caster" suggests a man in an outdoor clothing catalog. Well-groomed, clean-shaven, and dressed in calculatedly casual attire, he gazes commandingly across the dunes to a sun-gilded sea. Behind him looms his luxurious dune buggy, the chrome and plastic of its well-appointed interior glistening through the doorway in which he is framed. Alongside him, like the scepter of a king, leans his trusty fresh-from-the-factory rod. Before him is a tackle box teeming with angling accouterments that most self-respecting surf casters wouldn't touch with a 10-foot, 8½-ounce, medium-action pole.

In reality, today's surf caster—as well as yesterday's and, pollution and commercial exploitation permitting, tomorrow's too—is a tough, tire-

Surf casters use either open-face spinning reels or bait-casting reels, with distance experts generally opting for the latter.

less, hardy, dedicated, ingenious individual who cares little about comfort, food, sleep, dress, or much else for that matter unless it influences his ability to catch fish. Normally these are striped bass, channel bass, bluefish, and weakfish, whose fighting qualities and close-to-shore feeding habits gave surf casting much of its early impetus. Today, however, any species within casting distance of shore is fair game. My children and I have beached cod, flounder, mackerel, pollock, jacks, and sharks by methods that include ultralight spinning and flycasting. So popular has fly-fishing the ocean's edge become that it now boasts its own excellent organization (Salt Water Flyrodders of America International, Box 304, Cape May Courthouse, New Jersey 08210) as well as its own special set of records.

Plugging the high surf has a natural attraction for a youngster. In it he sees the primal pitting of man against the elements. What he doesn't see are the long exhausting hours that he simply isn't up to enduring no matter how much he yearns to try. I think often of a wild October night when tall cresting combers were uncoiling out of the darkness as I tried to reach a rock from which I could cast to the foamy edge of a sandy ridge. Waiting till a wave had broken on the beach, I hustled toward the rock, arriving just as a wall of water crashed over my head, tumbling me 20 feet back onto the beach and leaving me soaked and sprawling on the sand. By timing the troughs more carefully next time, I was able to get a head start, but I had neglected to consider the braking effect of the water in my waders. I had heaved myself halfway onto the rock when the next wave caught me chin high. My third try was aborted when I slipped halfway to the rock and stumbled head first into the foam. But on my fourth attempt I made it. Drenched and shivering, I leaned into the wind, twisted about 20 degrees to my left to compensate for the wind's left-to-right vector, wound up for my cast, and took a walloping wave flush behind the knees. I remember thinking as I was about to enter the water for my fourth and final washing-machining of the night, "This is no place for a middle-aged man."

It's less a place for a young inexperienced child. Not only will waves and weather be against him, but most of his casts will fall far short of the barrier bars and offshore rips where adults will be concentrating their casts. Sure, he might pick up a decent fish close in from time to time, but the bruisers usually are caught well offshore where the pockets are deep enough for channel bass to hole up in and the currents are confusing enough to make tumbling baitfish easy meals for stripers and blues. That's why seasoned surf casters really he-e-e-eave their heavy metal; that's why surf rods are built more for propelling lures than for fighting fish.

This does not mean, however, that your child has to be denied the challenge of fishing a sea beach. Not all of the ocean's edge is pulverized by powerful breakers. On bays and creeks and leeward beaches, where the shore is patted by gentle swells, a youngster can learn the ropes of surf casting while he develops the sense of rhythm and balance he will need later when he's ready to take on the ocean in its front yard. Fish won't be as big, but they'll probably be more plentiful, more predictable, and easier to outsmart.

Another advantage to starting your youngster on more easily managed shores is that you probably won't have to stake him to a whole new outfit. In the soft suds some of your heavy freshwater or light saltwater tackle might suit him perfectly. My daughter Julie was only in the third grade when she beached her first striper with my 7-foot popping rod.

Surf casting is a two-handed version of what your child does one-handed in fresh water. Almost without exception today's rods are fiberglass, and most of today's lines are single nylon filaments. Reels can be either open-face spinning or conventional revolving-spool types. Spinning is more popular with today's generation of surf casters who have been brought up on the technique, but the pioneers who had to depend on their thumbs to tame the tides have pretty much spurned spinning. Cast alongside one and you'll understand why. With rare exceptions, an all-out cast with a revolving-spool reel will be longer than an equivalent one—same lure, line, rod length, and action—by an equally competent caster using a spinning reel. The difference can be explained in mechanical terms by comparing frictional resistances: with a rotating spool, once inertia has been overcome, resistance remains very low; with a fixed spool, there is no inertia to overcome, since the spool doesn't have to be set in motion, but friction increases as line gets lower on the spool and rubs harder against its rim. There are those who claim that the differences pretty well average out and the longer casts always are made by the more talented casters. Maybe so. Maybe I've just been casting in the wrong company. As far as your youngster is concerned, let him use the kind of reel he's accustomed to, but if some overbearing spinning virtuoso has been burning your ear about his prowess and you'd like to see him brought down a peg or two, book him for a tide alongside the Cape Cod Canal, or at Wasque Point on Martha's Vineyard when birds are diving over bluefish way out on the tail end of the rip. I'll bet a season's supply of sixpacks that next time he sloshes up to you in the surf he'll be wearing egg on his face and casting with a conventional reel.

Dry waders are essential in a cold surf. They're expensive—twenty dollars is about the least you can expect to spend for a pair that will endure a couple of seasons of hard saltwater employment—but don't try to avoid the expense by deluding yourself into thinking that hip boots will do. Every child quickly succumbs to the temptation to wade just one step farther. Once that icy brine inundates his undies, he will have had it for the day.

Waders, by the way, also are a good investment in safety. Air trapped inside a pair that is tied around your child's chest with a tightly drawn drawstring will help to keep him afloat if he should stumble on a rock or be bowled over by a breaker. A lot of stumbling and slipping can be avoided if you stake your youngster to a set of replaceable spiked soles for when he's wading among weedy rocks or walking a spray-slicked jetty. These can be ice creepers, or sandals that are spiked like golf shoes. Felt soles that are satisfactory in fresh water won't work well enough in the ocean. Not only will shells and barnacles shred them, but after a few minutes of squashing seaweed underfoot, your son will feel as though he's sliding on ice.

A lightweight hooded slicker completes cold-weather outerwear. See if you can find one with a plastic rather than a metal zipper. Not only are they corrosion-free, but they seem to operate much more smoothly, a big advantage when spume is spraying your youngster's face and he doesn't want to waste precious seconds getting his plug into the fish swirling in front of him. Undergarments can be as many or as few insulating layers as the weather warrants, but always bring more than you expect to need. If you should have to use them, they'll be there; if not, well, they're not all that much trouble to tote along.

Casters who wade warm Southern waters are more concerned about injuries than chilblains. Long khaki pants will protect your child's legs against jellyfish stings; basketball sneakers will shield his feet and ankles against abrasions from coral clusters and the stinging stabs of sea urchins. Trouser bottoms should be tucked inside socks.

Your child's shirt is a compromise between comfort and how much sun he can take. If you're not sure, always settle for more clothing and less sunburn. A wide-brim hat makes a handy sun shield for head, face, and neck, and by shading his eyes it also enables him to spot fish. One of the old man's old fedoras will do the job nicely. Adorned with a couple of well-chewed streamer flies, it will be worn like a jeweled crown.

On clear shallow beaches and ponds with sunlight glinting off the water, dark polarized sunglasses are better than sonar for seeking fish. The five dollars you pay for his pair will be returned with interest first time he starts getting discouraged because there doesn't seem to be a fish within miles, and then suddenly he spots that dark form finning alongside the rock he's casting from.

Accessories for surf casting include sheath knife, pliers, chain stringer, waterproof light, and a shoulder-strap plug bag to carry them in. A foot-long priest, or billy club, is a handy helper for when a big fish is beached. Gaffs, too, are nice to have, but when plugging an aggressive surf, I've always found them more trouble than they're worth. I used to tether one to my waist on a stretchable cord, enduring the inevitable ventilation of my waders so that when that big bass finally hit, I'd be ready. When it happened—a 20-pounder in a rip-snorting tideway on a black August night—I worked it out of the fast water, through a sprawl of weeds, across a mussel bed, and onto the gravel shore without once thinking of using my gaff. Even if I had thought about it, I wouldn't have used it, first because I wanted to enjoy every exquisite instant of this all-to-rare occasion, and second because it was just as easy to plane the pooped fish onto shore courtesy of a convenient wave.

Gaffs with folding or retractable points eliminate the perforation problem, but I still consider them excess baggage. When working a beach, walking from slough to rockpile to sandbar in search of fish, it's best to keep your cargo to a minimum. When fishing bait from a stationary location, however, by all means keep a gaff handy. Lying there in the lantern light, it's readily available for you to grab and run out to your son if he should tie into a fish big and untamable enough to require gaffing. If, may heaven someday permit, you and he should both be playing bruisers side by side, well, you'll just have to make the waves work for you.

## FLY-FISHING

Buying a fly-fishing outfit is regarded by many who are awed by fly-fishing's mysteries as an ordeal falling somewhere between the patronizing unpleasantness of applying for a bank loan and the intimidating inquisition of an income-tax audit. The script goes something like this.

Fly-fishing rod and reel. This is really the simplest part of fly-fishing tackle—it is the leader, line, and flies that are complicated. (Courtesy South Bend Co.)

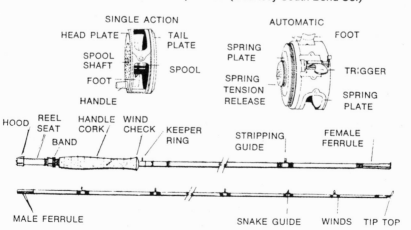

Good morning, sir. May I help you?

Yes. Good morning. I'd like to buy a flyline.

May I inquire, sir, have you done much fly-fishing before?

Well, no, not exactly. What happened is, my wife gave me a fly rod for my birthday and I understand I need some special kind of line for it. I've, ah, done plenty of fishing before, mind you, but I'm no Lee, uh, what's his name? Saw him on television. Lee, ah, Lion? No, ah, Wulff, that's it, Wulff. Lee Wulff. I'm not exactly in his league, but I've caught my share of fish in my time, and I guess there's not much difference taking 'em on flies.

You're perfectly right, sir. A little knowledge, a little practice, and you can lay it out there with the best of them. Heh, heh. Now, the first thing I have to know is, will it be for fresh or salt water?

Why fresh water, I guess. I didn't know they made a distinction.

Oh yes. Composition, specific gravity, coefficient of buoyancy, and all that.

Uh sure, sure, I should have known.

And the color, sir. Would you like green, brown, yellow, or white, or perhaps our new off-mauve that blends so well with the effluence in our local rivers?

Is that what the color's for? To match the water?

Yes. We musn't spook the wary trout, you know. You see, what happens is . . .

Never mind, never mind. I know all about spooking. Just make it green. Most water around here is green.

Fine. Will that be light, medium, or dark green?

Green, dammit, just green! Good grief, do I have to be an interior decorator to pick out a flyline?

Oh well now, sir, it's not quite that bad. Actually it's very simple. You want a medium-green freshwater flyline, right? Now all we need to know is weight, shape, and how you plan to use it. Will you be fishing it dry or wet?

Pardon?

Dry or wet? Will you be fishing dry flies or wet flies? With the former you will want a floating line to enable your fly to remain on top of the water. With the latter you will want a line that gets your fly under the surface.

Oh, of course. It's all very clear when you explain it. I'll take a sinking line. After all, ha, ha, that's where the fish hang out, under the water, not on top of it, right?

Spoken like a real pro, if I may say so, sir. Good sound common sense like that is what makes for success in fly-fishing.

Well, that's very nice of you. Thank you. And now as you said, all you need to know is the shape and weight of the line I want.

That's right, sir. The weight, of course, is to balance with your rod, thereby enabling you to make your casts as far and as accurately as you would like.

Sounds reasonable.

The shape—single taper, double taper, shooting head, or level?

How's that?

Single taper, double . . . oh, of course. I can see how that might be a bit confusing. Let me see if I can explain it this way. If you had an HDH, as opposed to a GAAF, or, in the language of the new flyline code, a DT-5-F versus a WF-9-F— What's that, sir?

I said forget it.

Forget it, sir?

Yeah, forget it. Wipe it out. Cancel my order. Here's what you do instead. See that twine down there? Give me a spool of it. And a handful of those hooks, and a can of worms. I want to go fishing!

Selecting a fly-fishing outfit should have been infinitely easier a few generations ago when rods were made only of hardwoods, lines were of silk and unvarying diameters, leaders could simply be plucked from the tail of a convenient horse, and flies fell into just a handful of patterns and sizes. It should have been, but I doubt that it was. Much of the fun in fly-fishing is matching the outfit to your own personality, and I'm sure our fly-fishing forefathers were just as finicky and fastidious when comparing the virtues of greenheart and hickory as we are with fiberglass and cane. Although they didn't have anywhere near today's variations of length, weight, and material, I'm sure they managed to complicate matters sufficiently to have plenty to argue about over their mulled wine on winter evenings. It's a trait of the breed, this striving for some small superiority of selection. Today's debates about line tapers and rod actions had their origin in arguments over whose horse's hindquarters produced the limpest leaders.

While I don't subscribe to all of fly-fishing's mystique, I do consider it a special kind of fishing. It demands a great deal of its conscientious practitioners, but it always returns more than it takes.

Before taking up fly-fishing, a child ought to cast for a season or two with spinning, spin-casting, or plug-casting equipment. Flycasting requires patience and coordination beyond what a young boy can reasonably be expected to have developed. In the beginning he's not sure he'll even enjoy fishing, let alone one specialized form of it. He'd like to find out, but not if it means enduring a lot of hours of listening and learning and practicing. Those are school stuff. Fishing, that's recess stuff.

A boy is ready to take up fly-fishing when he

... has watched a few good flycasters at work

... has learned by trying it himself a few times that their long, smooth, accurate deliveries are not as easy to execute as they make them appear

... possesses plenty of persistence and attention to detail along with the patience and coordination already mentioned

... shows the necessary interest for a long-term commitment by, say, reading books, asking questions, or tying flies.

Fly-fishing has a special appeal, whether on the classic quiet trout stream or in a saltwater tide rip. Saltwater fly-fishing is a relatively new but increasingly popular sport.

The long-term commitment is necessary because of the substantial investment that fly-fishing requires. No need to be boggled, as I was, Dad, by the $200 price tags on those split-cane rods. These will come later, when your boy's tastes will have refined along with his technique (and, hopefully, his sources of income). But even though very good fiberglass rods can be bought for a lot less than those crafted of Tonkin cane, fly-fishing also requires a special reel, line, leader, and lure. As for accessories, these can range all the way from sprays for making flies float better to creams for enabling lines to slip more smoothly through guides.

Rods, reels, leaders, lines, and flies—how to pick, price, appreciate, and employ them: this is what the next few pages is about. Perhaps they can help to guide you and your youngster through what at times can look to the uninitiated and the undedicated like a bewildering jargonized jungle.

## ROD

Only two types of fly rods are commonly used today, fiberglass and bamboo. The bamboo is not the common canepole variety, but a precision instrument fashioned from six heat-sealed plastic-impregnated strips of split cane. Orvis, Leonard, and Hardy are familiar names among the hierarchy of handcrafted rods. Fiberglass rods, despite an inauspicious introduction after World War II, when materials often were marginal and workmanship faulty, now can be bought in almost any size, weight, and action for a reasonable price.

A fly rod should be limber enough to whip out a well-matched line, yet stiff enough to handle any fish the caster is likely to encounter. Length, weight, and action, of course, should be tailored to your boy's build and coordination. Small wands, such as Lee Wulff's famous 6-footer with which he tames those enormous Atlantic salmon, are used by lesser mortals mostly for stunt fishing, while 9-footers and above are used to subdue big saltwater warriors. You can buy your boy a very good glass rod, one that with careful use and maintenance will last him many years, for around $20.

## REEL

Reels you don't have to be so fussy about. Since a reel's sole function is to store line, a melodious click and a 14-karat finish add nothing to its operation.

Make your child's first fly reel manually operated with an adjustable drag and a one-to-one ratio. By this I mean that it should retrieve line as a result of his turning its handle rather than by his pressing a spring-loaded latch that sucks in line with all the artistry and intimacy of a vacuum pump; it should have a simple adjustment for making it harder for the big fish to peel off line; and one turn of the handle should retrieve one turn of line. Multiple-ratio retrieves are available but are necessary—and in fact desirable—only on big battling bruisers such as tarpon and sailfish, where an extra turn or two on the spool at the right time can turn your fish before it reaches a rock or runs you out of backing.

One final feature: a replaceable spool. Be absolutely sure that your child's reel possesses that inspired feature which will enable him quickly to slip off one line-filled spool and replace it with another. The few seconds he can save in swapping spools instead of reels can be invaluable when he's fishing wet flies with a sinking line and a hatch requiring dry flies and a floating line occurs. A sturdy durable reel with all of these features can be bought for about $10.

## LEADER

Leaders are the foremost part of a line, bridging the gap between flyline and fly. The fly is not tied directly to the flyline, which, of course, is too visible to the fish and too heavy to land gently on the water. Instead, a length of light limp line, usually nylon monofilament, is tied to the forward end of your flyline. Best way to make this connection is by tying the leader's butt end to a tiny metal eye, available in most tackle stores for only a few pennies, whose shaft is inserted into the end of the flyline. Barbs on the shaft prevent its being pulled out. They also make it hard to stick into the line in the first place unless the way is paved with a needle.

When a flyline is laid out over the water, its leader follows its path, but being much lighter, it settles more slowly to the surface, delivering the fly with the delicacy of the nearly weightless insect it's supposed to represent.

While leaders can be of uniform thickness—just a few feet of mono-filament line—casts will be smoother and delivery softer if they taper to a fine tippet. You and your son can make your own tapered leaders, tying together monofilament sections of decreasing size terminating in the diameter and breaking strength you desire. Indeed, that used to be the only way to get them, but today excellent leaders are available in many sizes, with prices ranging from about 25¢ for freshwater 7-footers to 75¢ for more formidable saltwater designs.

Leader length depends as much on personal preference as on fish and fishing conditions. Just make sure that your child's leader is longer than his rod so that its butt end will be outside his tip-top rod guide when he's tying on a fly. Also, remind him that every time he snips off a piece of leader when changing flies, he shortens its length and increases its tippet's diameter.

Leader diameters, for assessing underwater visibility and breaking strength, are shown in the accompanying table.

| Size | Diameter (in.) | Breaking strength, approx. (lbs.) |
| --- | --- | --- |
| 6X | 0.005 | 0.75 |
| 5X | 0.006 | 1.0 |
| 4X | 0.007 | 1.5 |
| 3X | 0.008 | 2.0 |
| 2X | 0.009 | 3.0 |
| 1X | 0.010 | 4.5 |
| 0X | 0.011 | 6.0 |

Choosing the right leader requires about equal measures of common sense and experience. After your youngster has been frustrated a few times by casting too-heavy leaders to spooky fish in low clear pools, or a few big fish have snapped his too-light leader-tippet on underwater snags, he'll learn to discriminate.

LINE

When someone tells me he is confused by flylines, I am sympathetic. There are by my rough calculation 324 possible combinations of line weight, shape, use, and composition, and I've purposely excluded special tapers, colors, coatings, and line lengths. As if that weren't bewildering enough, there are two—not just one—flyline codes that appear to the uninitiated to possess all the clarity of a pre-schooler's composition exercise.

Ironically, it's all very simple, very logical. If you're familiar with a few fundamentals, the mystery is immediately dispelled and facts fall neatly into place.

First consider how you and your youngster want to fish: beneath the water or on it. When fish are feeding on floating insects you'll need floating lines to keep your flies topside. When they're feeding below the surface, sinking lines will bring your flies to them. I recommend a floater for your boy's first line, because dry-fly fishing (I can hear the controversy now) is easier and more fun. It is easier because he will not be fishing blind as in wet-fly fishing, depending for success on a sensitive touch that comes only with experience; he will see his fly and he will see his fish. It is more fun because when his fish strikes, he will experience not merely a tug against his wrist but a cataclysmic disruption of his whole metabolism: adrenaline will spurt, his pulse will accelerate, eyes pop, hands shake, knees knock. It will be a carnival of the senses. He will feel more delicately, see more clearly, hear more distinctly than under any other circumstances this side of jungle warfare. Which, by the way, is a pretty good description of how fishing ought to affect a fisherman.

A floating line it is, then. Now, how about shape? His line can be level (uniform diameter throughout), or tapered at the ends for easier casting. It can even be tapered in special ways, from thick to narrow and back to semi-thick, to enable him to cast heavier bug-type flies, to cast farther, and to cast into the wind. This shape goes by several names: torpedo head, bug taper, rocket taper, and weight-forward.

Special tapers are by far the most expensive, level lines the least. A reasonable compromise is the double taper. A great advantage to this design is that when line frays or breaks, destroying the taper at one end, it can be reversed on the reel, placing a brand-new taper at the forward end.

Line cost is strongly influenced by the material it's made of—silk, nylon, or Dacron—and the kind of finish it's given to make it float or sink. Here especially I recommend that you seek the advice of experienced fly-fishermen, and be prepared to pay $10 or $12 for your double-tapered floater. If you must pinch pennies, don't do it on your youngster's line, the heart of his fly-fishing outfit.

One final characteristic—weight—will tell you which double-tapered floater best fits your boy's rod. Too heavy a line will overpower it, too light a line will not respond to it.

Lines are cataloged by code. Prior to 1962, diameter was the determining factor. An HCH line, for example, tapered from a center section (C) of 0.050 inch to 0.025 inch (H) at both ends. Such a line was double-tapered. GBF, on the other hand, represented a forward taper from 0.030 inch (G) to 0.055 inch (B) to 0.035 inch (F).

The new code was adopted by the American Fishing Tackle Manufacturers Association because new coatings varied line thickness, thereby making diameter an undependable designator. Weight is used instead. A number representing the grams in 30 feet, exclusive of taper, is preceded by L (level), DT (double taper), or WF (weight forward) and followed by F (floating), S (sinking), or I (intermediate). My sixteen-year-old son cast comfortably and competently with a DT-6-F line on his 7½-foot, 4⅜-ounce fiberglass rod.

## FLIES

Cataloged in the American Museum of Natural History are 10 million—count 'em, 10 million—insects. As for the number of chubs and minnows and smelt and sand eels and other forage fish on which gamefish feed, I wouldn't even hazard a guess. Yet it must seem to the aspiring fly-fisherman trying to figure out which flies he ought to start with that every bug from ant to spider, and every baitfish from alewife to sparling, is simulated by at least one pattern, and some by several representing regional variations and life-cycle phases. When you add to these the thousands of individual creations, most of them transitory, a few enduring, which have less relationship to insect or fish life than to the artistry of the tier, and consider that each can be tied on a variety of hook styles and sizes, it's easy to understand why worms remain so popular.

Recently I received my spring catalog from the Orvis Company in Manchester, Vermont. Long renowned as makers of fine cane flyrods, Orvis also sells flies. Its handsome catalog contains several full-color pages as well as a front cover that fairly buzz with beautiful, sturdy, durable make-believe insects, all conceived and crafted in the sincere conviction that they will entice wary fish who can just as easily eat the real thing. Listen to some of their names: Tup's Indispensable, Natural Irresistible, Humpy, Blue Charm, Hot Orange, Rusty Rat, Tellico, Lady Beaverkill, and Zug Bug.

Amazingly, all of these exotic creations, whose appearances in many cases are as wild as their names, *will* catch fish. Often, though, this is less because they are consistently effective food-simulators or fish-exciters than because they happen to land on the water when fish are ready to wallop anything short of a feather duster.

Also amazing is that there are only two classes of flies: every one of these impostors is either a wet fly or a dry fly. The dry imitates hatched insects such as mayflies, mosquitoes, spiders, gnats, and dragonflies that have settled on the water's surface. The wet imitates one of three things: an unhatched insect such as the larva stage of the mayfly (this is called a nymph); a hatched insect that has drowned or otherwise been engulfed (a wet fly); or a small baitfish (a streamer). The dry fly's wings and hackles face forward and outward, enabling it to float, while the wet's feathers face aft, enabling it to submerge quickly. Floatability of flies can be enhanced with sprays and dips sold for this purpose.

Choice of flies depends on so many different factors—kind and size of fish being sought, type of water, time of year and day, kind of weather, geographic location—that for me to suggest flies for anyone but the Fallons would be like a doctor's prescribing medication without first making a diagnosis. Still, I hate hedging as much as readers hate to find holes in the books they buy, so here goes with Dr. Fallon's selection for a starter set. Since every fly can cost you close to a dollar—and reasonably so considering the effort and ingenuity that go into making them—my recommendations are based as much on avoiding bankruptcy as on catching fish.

For dries I suggest the following patterns:

Royal Coachman (Fanwing) (#12)
Black Gnat (#18)
Quill Gordon (#12)
Brown Spider (#14)
White Wulff (#12)

For wets (all #12):

Royal Coachman
Hornberg
Quill Gordon
Black Wooly Worm

Add Blacknosed Dace, Mickey Finn, and Muddler Minnow streamers in #6 3X long size, and you'll be ready for all the trout, salmon, bass, pickerel, and panfish you and your youngster are likely to encounter. Never mind the nymphs for now; they'll come later, when you and he have acquired a little more knowledge and experience. If you want to try salt water, get a few blue and white bucktails, preferably tied in the popular blond patterns.

CASTING

Experts traditionally offer three reminders to fledgling fly-fishermen. First is that dry flies should be floated from upstream down with no line drag to identify them as fakes. Second is that you're casting a line, not a lure, so the weight you are trying to send out over the water, instead of being concentrated a few inches from your rod tip, is distributed more or less evenly along the entire length of your line. And third is that to impart the greatest velocity to your line, you must have it extended all the way out behind you before starting your forward movement, and you must apply this forward force in a straight line.

This is valuable advice. I wish I had received these reminders when I was starting. Not only would they have put a few more trout in my creel, but they would have saved me several expensive flies, snapped off when I bullwhipped my line forward before completing my backcast. They also would have saved my sons from a few frayed nerves as a result of my loud line-snapping reports that sounded more appropriate to lion's cages than quiet woodland streams.

To these sound suggestions I would add two more. First is, practice before you fish. Spend several sessions in your back yard getting the feel of flycasting: its graceful rhythm; its precise timing; its movements, patterned and predictable as an infantry drill yet as personalized as a thumbprint.

Second is, stay loose. In fly-fishing as in all activities, it's easy to become so preoccupied by detail that recreation quickly degenerates into drudgery. There's nothing wrong with aspiring to make the longest or the most graceful or the most accurate casts, but that's not fly-fishing, that's tournament casting. And there's nothing wrong with listening to all the well-meaning experts who will offer you advice, but in the long pull, you and your youngster will be better off if you master a few fundamentals and build your own style upon them.

Start your cast by stripping about 30 feet of line from your reel, and laying it out in front of you on the water (or the lawn if that's where you're practicing). With the rod handle in your right hand and loose line in your left, point your rod tip about 15 degrees above horizontal. Next, raise your rod tip quickly, lifting your line and flipping it high and to the rear.

As your rod approaches the vertical, slow it down and let your line slide through the rod guides, straightening out high and parallel to the surface behind you. Stop your rod at about one o'clock to avoid letting your line drop too low.

At precisely when your line straightens out behind you (look over your shoulder to check), start your forward cast. Aim two or three feet above the water so your line will uncurl straight out before your fly settles on the surface.

Conclude your cast with your rod back where it started, about 15 degrees above horizontal, letting the loose line slide through your left hand and out through the guides.

After you've tried casting a few times, you'll start to catch on quickly, lengthening your casts and cultivating a few personal stylistic touches. But stick with the short line and the standard routine for a dozen or so hours before you start getting adventurous. Casts of under 40 feet can cover a lot of fish. Furthermore, nothing short of leaky waders discourages a beginner more quickly than consistently piling up line behind or in front of him because his timing or his motion or his aim is off.

How sacred are the directions I've just given you? Not inviolable, of course. You'll note that I preceded "30 feet" and "15 degrees" and "one o'clock" with a qualifying "about." You can modify these and any other directions slightly to suit your own physique and feel, but they won't tolerate much tampering. More than any other kind of casting, flycasting is an exercise involving weights and levers and fulcrums. If you examine it in the cold scientific light of a problem in mechanics, you'll find that these figures are pretty much as they should be.

Arm position and wrist action are the areas where you can do all the experimenting you want. And all the arguing, too, for that matter. Advice from veterans will range all the way from "Strap your arm to your side for the first hundred hours" to "Do it the way that feels best, so long as you know the basics and what you're trying to accomplish." I subscribe to the latter school because it's in line with my fishing-is-supposed-to-be-fun philosophy. We're fettered enough already by regulations and restrictions and admonishments about the when and where and what of fishing without also hobbling the how. My wise companion Charlie Pelletier once said it just right when, after a totally unproductive morning of trolling Maine's Pierce Pond, he noticed my frustration starting to show. "Jackson," he said, handing me a beer, "I thought that fishing is supposed to prevent ulcers, not cause them."

There are, of course, many other kinds of casts besides the one I've described. Recently I came across a volume dedicated solely to describing different ways of casting a fly. There were, I think, thirty-seven of them! Casts were tailored to topography, geography, kinds of water, classes of fish, and weather conditions, among other things. All are valid and, I trust, effective, but all are hardly necessary to the ordinary kind of fly-fishing that you and your youngster are likely to be doing for a while at least.

Nevertheless, your repertoire should include, along with the basic back cast, the roll cast, for when trees or brush or rocks make a backcast impossible. A very simple way of laying your line out over the water, the roll cast is done much like rolling a hoop with a stick. Start with about (that word again) 15 feet of line in the water plus another 10 or so feet stripped from your reel. With the rod pointed forward, raise its tip until your hand reaches almost to your ear and the rod is slightly aft of vertical. The belly of the line will then be just behind your elbow. Then hammer your rod sharply downward as if you were driving a nail, looping your line out over the water, and the leader and fly will follow.

Professional assistance while learning to cast is available from many sources, most of them unexploited. I've already mentioned clinics and clubs as possibilities. A few reference books also will be helpful.

What you need when starting is something simple, brief, easy to understand and to follow. Of the scores of volumes on fly-fishing, few fulfill these requirements, most of them concentrating on philosophy and sophistication well beyond the novice's ken or concern. Buy just one book as a starter, Roderick Haig-Brown's lovely and learned *A Primer of Fly Fishing*. Then send 50¢ to Scientific Anglers, Midland, Michigan 48640 for their valuable little volume *To Cast a Fly*, and 25¢ to Cortland Line Company, Cortland, New York 13045 for their practical little pamphlet *Fly Rod Fishing Made Easy*.

# 4.

# Fish and How to Fool Them

〜〜〜〜〜〜〜〜〜〜〜〜〜〜〜〜〜〜〜〜〜〜〜〜〜〜〜〜〜〜〜〜〜〜〜〜〜〜〜

What do you see when you look at a body of water? That pond, is it just a liquid barrier between you and the fish you're trying to catch? That ocean, is it merely a mysterious mass into which you drop your bait and wait hopefully but passively for something to happen?

The quality which most clearly marks the seasoned angler is his ability to visualize what it's like down there: the shape and composition of the bottom; the level at which fish are likely to be found; if and how and on what they're likely to be feeding. Dangling worms on a pond can be enjoyable, sure. At the very least, it's a relaxing respite from the occupational cacophony of jangling telephones and clamoring creditors. But for an eager, anxious, active child, the inherent passivity of this form of fishing can quickly become as dull as a haircut. Later he may learn, as millions of others have done, that sitting pondside monitoring a bobber is his kind of fishing, but first he'll want to try the high-voltage excitement of seeking out fish in their own element and applying his knowledge and skills to outwitting them. If you're an experienced angler, what better way to reflect on past pleasures than by retracing your steps in the company of a child? If you're as new at it as he is, where can you find a more compatible schoolmate?

One of the awesome mysteries to the neophyte is why so few of the world's fishermen almost always catch so many of the fish. It's not a mystery at all. These people—young as well as old, female as well as male—succeed principally because they do three things right: they locate fish, they attract their attention, and they provoke them into striking. This is the essence of successful angling. There's more to it, of course. Tackle, patience, teamwork, and a host of other factors have to click before that hooked trophy can be hung triumphantly from your son's stringer. But first he's got to find that trophy, stimulate its interest, and provoke it to strike.

Locating fish is a matter of knowing their habits: when and where and how they migrate; whether they live high or low in the water or somewhere in between; what they feed on; hours and seasons and conditions when they are most active. A knowledge of their senses is necessary for attracting their attention. How far and in which directions can they see? Which colors do they see best? Which sights and sounds and smells and tastes interest them, excite them, repel them? To provoke a fish into striking, you have to know its personality. Is it guileless or suspicious? Is it apathetic or aggressive? Is it bloodthirsty or benign?

Much of what your youngster needs to know is in this book. Much, but not all. One reason for these omissions is that I don't know all the answers. In fact, after the better part of a middle-aged lifetime of trying to outwit fish, I know only a small percentage of the questions. Young anglers might as well acknowledge early what they will conclude eventually: there are few gamefish which in their own environments are not smarter than the people trying to catch them. A little humility should be one of the first implements in an angler's personal tackle box.

I also might overlook or underemphasize an occasional point because I am trying to avoid making this volume read like a textbook. Fishing according to formula is a contradiction; except, of course, in the commercial sense, where a man is trying merely to earn a living, not *live* a living. Fishing for sport is an arcane art in which rigid rules soon are obscured in mists of mystery. How does one codify a battered, rumpled, smelly old hat? What influence does a man's foul fedora have on whether fish will see and strike his lure? None, of course ... and yet, remember that time you left your hat at home and nothing, but nothing, seemed to go right all day long? Logical people such as wives and golfers could explain your empty stringer by reminding you that without your hat, the sun was in your eyes.

"With that sun beating down on your head like that all day long," they would say, "it's a wonder you didn't get sunstroke. How can you expect to catch fish when your head's throbbing and you can't even see what you're doing?"

But it was overcast that day.

The charms, the fetishes, the incantations—all are essential to successful fishing, and every angler must conjure up the contents of his own amulet. No laboratory has yet turned out a lure that couldn't be improved by a little spitting on, a little talking to.

Children learn best by observing and by doing. When allowed to acquire information at their own pace and according to their own capacities for absorbing it, they learn faster and retain longer. If the process can be catalyzed by an interest in the subject they're studying, you've got yourself a straight-A student.

Little wonder, then, that there are more than 60 million active recreational anglers in America today and that the number continues to grow. The underwater world is an ubiquitous classroom where the savage saga of survival goes on much the same as in prehistoric times. Dinosaurs have disappeared, but sharks and rays endure unchanged. For a boy to beach a barndoor skate or boat a spiny dogfish is, with a little imagination on his part and a little encouragement on yours, closely akin to his whipping one of those weird winged pterodactyls he sees in schoolbooks.

## BASIC BEHAVIOR OF FISH
## AND FISHERMEN

The more your youngster knows about how fish behave, the more successful he will be in catching them. He can learn a lot just by lying on the end of a dock and watching sunfish guard the clear solitary circles of their nests, but even more valuable is for him to be aware that for about a month in the spring, landlocked salmon chase smelt as they school along the edges of northern lakes. He can infer from the experience of unsuccessfully floating fly after fly down the middle of a shallow, sluggish, sunbathed stream that trout don't like this kind of water, yet how much more helpful it is for him to know that comfort and protection compel them to hang out in deep pools and beneath undercut banks.

Trout in a hatchery taught my sons to fish the shadows. On several visits they had noticed that when the sun was high, the trout were congregated along one edge of their deep pens. The edge varied from visit to visit, but on any given visit all fish in all bins were clustered along the same edge. It was, of course, the shaded edge, and over the years this knowledge has added many trout to their creels.

Another observation in the hatchery that paid off was that rainbows seemed to favor the bubbling turbulence where water entered their pens. Originally, the attendant explained, rainbows came from the streams of our Western mountains. Out there the water runs fast and its oxygen content is high.

Mealtime in aquariums affords another excellent opportunity for you and your child to study the feeding habits of species you want to fish for. Does a catfish swim to the surface when dinner is dispensed, or does it wait for the food to sink to the bottom? Does a pike pounce on its prey immediately, or does it stalk it first? And that bluefish—does it always strike a menhaden from behind?

One September evening, my friend Bill Stone and I could have saved ourselves a lot of grief if we had known about the bluefish's tendency to attack menhaden from astern. When a menhaden school moved like a dusky cloud across the quiet water of Woods Hole on the southside of Cape Cod, it wouldn't even have interested us except for an occasional swirl from a scurrying fish. Maybe, we thought, blues are moving along beneath these fish. Maybe the swirls are caused by menhaden trying to evade their attacks.

Reasoning that predators are partial to injured victims, Bill and I tied on short braided-steel leaders and treble hooks weighted with small sinkers crimped just up our lines from the hooks' eyes. The leaders were protection against the blues' sharp teeth and the trebles were for snagging menhaden. By casting across the school and letting our hooks sink for a few seconds, we had only to reel and jerk a few times before our hooks found menhaden. Slowed by the weight of the hook and struggling to get rid of it, the snagged menhaden made a vulnerable target.

The bluefish responded. Time after time they grabbed our struggling baits, but always from behind. Because, for some reason, our trebles always seemed to hit the menhaden up forward, Bill and I invariably wound up with half a menhaden—the front half.

More available than big institutional aquariums are the home tanks that have made the care and feeding of tropical fish one of America's booming industries. These tanks are inexpensive, require little care, and provide an always-open window on a 24-hour-a-day drama that's as enlightening as it is entertaining.

In the room where I'm writing these words is a 10-gallon tank containing the customary gravel, shells, weeds, and bubbles. Seven small fish inhabit this tabletop block of lake bottom. Four are gray, big-bellied bullies with lateral red bands and broad tails; two are slender and orange with black tails; the seventh is a bewhiskered old bird who spends most of his time foraging about the bottom for scraps that his more aggressive tankmates have allowed to fall.

The orange pair are newcomers. A little over a week ago they were introduced to provide some sort of ecological balance, but the four muscle-men have made them about as welcome as sharks in a bathtub. So far, the orange pair have been devoting most of their time to avoiding collisions, and I'm sure that what I've learned from watching their evasive maneuvers will come in handy some day.

You can even populate home aquariums with certain types of game fish, as long as you're careful about selecting compatible species. A friend of mine was not. He installed a tank in his living-room wall in which he planned to raise sunfish and perch that he could observe, photograph, and experiment with. After netting several inch-long samples of each species, he was well on his way to having his own built-in Jacques Cousteau Special.

For several weeks the fish flourished. All survived the transplant, and, with one exception, they grew slowly but steadily. The exception was a dark, sullen sunfish that always grabbed more than its share of food and grew as if it had an overactive pituitary. Then my friend went on a business trip for several days. When he returned, his tank was empty except for—you guessed it—one big, bloated black bass, which, my friend said, "if I didn't know better, I'd have sworn was smiling at me."

Another friend, after studying, experimenting, and continually asking questions of people more experienced than he in raising fish in aquariums, has managed to achieve the right balance of size and species in his tank. Now he is able to observe the reactions of largemouths as he feeds them insects and worms and minnows.

Recently on a visit to this friend's home I dropped two June bugs and a large ant into the tank. The suddenness of the bass's strike was startling. I had no idea a bass could move so fast.

The readiness and speed with which I saw this bass attack is going to make me cover more territory in the bass ponds I fish this season. If I get no strike from two or three careful casts over a given territory, I'll figure it's reasonable to assume that there isn't a bass in residence, or, if there is, it isn't in a striking mood.

My friend has had several misconceptions cleared up by observing his fish in action.

"Worms," he says, "always were high on my list as bass bait, yet I've never seen one taken readily by this largemouth. Eventually, yes, but only after it examines and nudges and toys with the worm first. Worms, especially artificial ones, have to be presented a lot more deliberately than I thought.

"Minnows are another bait that I've changed my thinking about," he says. "Bass love them all right, this I knew, but they always swallow them head first. Because for years I had assumed that bass turned minnows around in their mouths before swallowing, to avoid having their dorsal fins stick in their throats, I hooked my minnows just forward of their dorsal. Now I'm going to do more lip hooking."

Even more educational for my friend has been the activities in a second smaller tank in which he raises bait.

"Watching minnows," he says, "enables me to tie streamer flies more authentically. Observing crawfish as they scuttle backward into the shadow enables me to retrieve their imitators more accurately."

If you should find that raising gamefish in a tank is illegal in your state, you might consider doing it in a backyard pond. State and federal governments often will give you a hand with everything from suggestions for digging to fish for stocking, provided you reside in a reasonably rural area, own a few acres of elbow room, and have satisfactory soil and drainage. Your cool spring-fed pond, if it maintains a good season-long flow of water, might rate a generous stocking of trout free of charge, although usually you will have to open government-stocked trout ponds to public fishing. Easier-to-raise bass and panfish also are available in some states. Byron Dalrymple, one of outdoor writing's outstanding authorities on largemouth bass, tests out many of his theories in his own backyard laboratory.

Best way of all to learn about fish is to dive right down and become one of them. Scuba tanks aren't necessary. They enable you to go deeper and stay longer, sure, but I've found all the fascination I could handle in less than 20 feet of water by using mask, flippers, and snorkel. This $10 investment, by the way, has been paid back a dozen times in the lures and terminal tackle I've salvaged.

Once many years ago, I donned mask, snorkel, and flippers to explore the lips of a tidal river into which I had watched casters heave plugs and spoons for hours on end without ever seeing one of them connect. Stripers, I knew, had to be in there; they were in the surf both north and south, and the river itself was rich with bait. The bait, as usual, held the answer. I found that instead of chasing fast-swimming sand eels in midstream where there was plenty of room for evasive action, the stripers were moving slowly upriver with the tide, less than a rod's length away from the shore from which the frustrated anglers were casting. Flowing in with the bass was a steady stream of small fish and crabs from a cluster of boulders at the river's mouth. When I swam ashore and started fishing, a strike on my first cast with a small bucktail jig bounced along the sloping bank almost under the other casters' noses was all it took to persuade them to shorten their range.

With this inexpensive diving outfit I have rubbed elbows with bluefish, engaged in boxing matches with lobsters, and watched flounder disappear before my eyes as they assumed the exact color and shading of the sand or mud into which they had glided. In fresh water I have swum almost nose-to-nose close to bass, trailed trout to their lairs, and let sunfish nibble on my fingers.

Hatcheries, then, and aquariums, tabletop tanks, private ponds, and diving expeditions—all can enable fledgling fishermen to learn about fish by observing them in action. But before they start trying to catch them, they also should learn a few basics about the behavior of fish in general and about the peculiarities of the species they seek. It is because these species have responded properly over the ages that they have managed to survive; that, in other words, they have absorbed enough oxygen, eaten enough nourishment, spawned enough young, and avoided enough killers. To the observant angler, each of these requirements for survival reveals ways of outwitting fish.

When fishing for landlocked salmon, for example, your youngster will troll high when a brisk spring chop churns oxygen into a lake's cool surface, but deeper after summer has made the surface intolerably warm. In the spring, when pockets of melting snow still linger in the woods, he will look for trout in sunny shallows, but later, when streams are lower and warmer, he will concentrate on deep pools and shaded stretches. A sampling of insect life from under the rocks of his stream will enable him to duplicate or imitate what his trout are accustomed to eating, but when the rains start he will move to the mouths of small feeder brooks because he knows that trout will be waiting there for terrestrial insects to wash down. If his state's trout season has not closed by late fall, he will seek his speckled trout in the small brooks up which they swim to spawn, and always he will approach his trout in a crouch and on tiptoe, knowing that shadow and noise will spook them.

Shallow warm-water ponds is where he will seek largemouth bass, because he knows that this species prefers higher temperatures than trout. Instead of the mayfly imitations he uses on trout, he will simulate or duplicate the frogs, minnows, crawfish, hellgrammites, and big insects that largemouths prefer. In the spring he will work these baits along shallow shorelines where largemouths do their spawning, but later he will look for them in the weeds and lily pads and under the submerged logs where they seek protection.

He also will schedule his striper fishing according to water temperature. If he's an enterprising New Englander, he might start his season a couple of weeks early by heading for where the Gulf Stream edges in close to Nantucket Island. He might even add several weeks to the tail end of his season by concentrating near the warm-water discharges of power plants. Herring or their imitators will be his choice of lure in springtime, mackerel in summer, eels at night, worms over mudflats, shiny spoons in a murky surf, and clams on a beach following an onshore storm. For a crack at spawning stripers he will head in early spring for the upper Hudson River or for rivers such as the Roanoke that lace the lowlands along the upper Chesapeake. And when wading a shallow creek, he will tread softly and try to keep his shadow off the water.

Comfort, hunger, procreation, survival—these are the urges that fish respond to; these are the keys to catching them.

Walleyes in the winter? Position your tip-ups over that springhole that you discovered while diving last summer. Then, you'll remember, it was cooler than the water around it; now it's warmer.

Weakfish? When the tide starts ebbing across that grassy marsh where you saw all those shrimp scurrying as you waded at low water, the weaks will be waiting.

Late-season lake trout? They might still be sticking to their customary deep cold domain, but if the day is gray and winter has been inching in early, lakers might already have moved onto shallow ledges to spawn.

Mackerel? Your favorite spot, of course: Number Two buoy, just a half-mile offshore, where there's always a supply of sand eels . . . unless, of course, the bluefish have moved in. Then macks are more likely to be in closer seeking the sanctuary of rocky shores.

As your child learns by observing, by inquiring, by listening, and as he applies what he learns to the situations in which he fishes, he will be able to visualize more clearly, more accurately what's going on under the water. Gradually its surface will become more lens than curtain; ultimately his imagination will put polarized glasses on his mind.

But it will take time, and children are impatient. That's where parents come in: a little aiming in the right direction; an occasional dusting off after he's stumbled; a reassuring reminder on those days when fish outsmart him that there's always a reason. Always. Make sure he doesn't bite off more than his mental metabolism is ready to digest. Make sure he progresses species by species, method by method, a grade at a time ... with, of course, an occasional double promotion for beating the old man's buttons off.

And this is as appropriate a place as any to field that most frequently asked of all fishing questions: When is the best time to go? Answer: Now. Cancel that meeting. Stow that lawnmower. Delay that beddy-bye. There are streams to be waded and beaches to be plugged. Every brook and pond and creek and bay is an antidote to your tensions, and your youngster knows just the right dosage.

But it's raining! So it is, and so it was on Vermont's upper Connecticut River that early autumn morning when a friend and I caught a skilletful of rainbows from a long narrow stretch that suddenly had come alive when bugs were washed from bushes at the head of the run.

But it's windy! It was windy, too, during that hurricane last fall when Mrs. Fallon and I caught striper after striper from a lee shore.

But it's the middle of the night! Correct, and if you'll listen carefully, you might be able to hear the splashes of those largemouth bass as they chase bait into the shallows of that pond down the road.

No, I'm not advocating that a father should simply chuck everything and fish when he and his children feel like it. That's irresponsible. But no less irresponsible is not fishing at all. Recently three of my friends, all in their early forties, had heart attacks. One died, the other two must now live out their lives with their brakes on. All of these three men enjoyed fishing, but somehow they never seemed to be able to fit it into the pressure-cookers they were living in. One of the great contemporary ironies is that we live in a world of time-saving wonders, yet seem to have so little time.

But although any time is good fishing time, any time is not necessarily good fish-catching time, and the difference often is determined by rain, wind, pressure, time, temperature, and tide.

One of the earliest axioms I recall hearing about fishing is that fish bite best when it rains. After what must by now add up to thousands of hours of fishing in everything from drizzles to downpours, I guess I've enjoyed about equal measures of success and failure. (Yes, indeed, I have *enjoyed* my failures, too.) Usually I have been successful in fresh water when I have consciously imitated the insects which rain was washing into a stream. I've caught landlocked salmon by capitalizing on the knowledge that high fast water following a rainstorm summons them up the rivers of northern Maine, but I've also been skunked trying the same trick on a shallow shad creek that became unmanageably high in a matter of hours.

Sometimes I've scored for no apparent reason other than that I've been there when other anglers have run for cover. On these occasions I know that there is a sound scientific explanation for my success, but while I keep searching for logical answers, I like to think that maybe the fish cooperated because, well, because they appreciated my sticking around.

Absurd?

Of course.

But beautiful?

You betcha!

Wind has both a direct and indirect influence on fishing. Obviously more bugs are blown onto the water when it's windy. Whitecaps whip more oxygen into the water, drawing landlocks to the top, and they push minnows toward a lee shore. In the ocean a classic condition for catching striped bass and bluefish is where wind collides with a tidal current to tumble baitfish out of control. Indirectly, wind is a harbinger of weather. Depending on where you live and time of year, its direction can signal storm or calm.

Closely related to wind and rain is atmospheric pressure. This is the "twenty-nine point nine two and rising" that your TV forecaster includes in his summary. The numbers represent inches of mercury, which happen to be the units in which atmospheric pressure is measured on an instrument called a barometer. The "rising" simply means that the column of mercury in the forecaster's barometer is going up.

High barometer readings indicate pleasant weather and generally good fishing, low readings just the opposite. When the barometer is rising, you can fish optimistically. When it's tumbling, well, you'll just have to fish a little harder and a little smarter. There may not be as much action, but what there is probably will be all yours.

Atmospheric pressure or wind or rain by themselves can fake you out of some good fishing. Don't cancel a trip with your son simply because it's raining. Phone the weather bureau or catch the radio or TV report. Even when it's raining, if the barometer is on the way up, you're likely to be launching your boat into a calm sea under a sunny sky.

Because weather plays such an important part in fishing, your youngster should be alert for signs that will enable him to confirm or contradict these forecasts. Insects, plants, and birds all offer hints of weather in the offing.

Say, for example, a spider has spun its web outside your back door in midafternoon and you notice that the web has been abandoned six hours later when you're loading gear into your car. Smile. You can expect good weather. Normally a spider changes webs about every twenty-four hours. A change in under eight hours or in the morning means that the spider is confident enough of dry weather that it is willing to undertake the spinning of a new home. Before a rain, though, spiders crawl out on their webs.

Bees forecast rain when they return to their hives and do not leave. They abhor wet wings, and over the centuries they have learned to sense the subtle pressure changes that predict precipitation.

Crickets broadcast temperature by the frequency of their chirps. Have your child count the number of chirps made by a nearby cricket in 15 seconds, add 37, and see if it doesn't coincide with the reading on his thermometer.

Most plants predict fair weather when they unfold, foul weather when they close. Mushrooms and toadstools springing up during the night also are supposed to indicate inclement weather. Dew on the grass, because it normally forms when the earth cools quickly, is a traditional forecaster of fair weather.

Perching birds, on the other hand, are harbingers of storms. They perch because it's harder to fly in the low-pressure air that normally precedes a storm. A storm also is likely to be on the way when insect-eating birds feed close to the ground. The reason: bugs become active in the high humidity that precedes wet weather.

Is there any truth to this old nautical verse?

> Red sky at night,
> Sailors delight.
> Red sky in the morning,
> Sailors take warning.

In northern latitudes, yes. Also true is that high clouds never produce rain (what little moisture they contain is in the form of ice), that chimney smoke rising straight up means fair weather (winds are calm in the fair-weather centers of high-pressure areas), that . . . well, why don't you and your youngster sharpen up your senses and learn together how to read the rest of Nature's weather reports?

There's no question about the overall validity of the axiom which says that early and late in the season and early and late in the day are best fishing times. There are, however, a great many exceptions. Brown trout are a good bet for springtime action, but not while melting snow keeps the water so cold that browns might just as well be in their winter comas. Largemouths feeding up for a long lean winter can provide a fall ball, but not on the same frog-simulating poppers that were so effective in midsummer. One of the main reasons that fish are active at morning and evening twilights is because they see best at short range, and in moderate brightness. Many species such as brown trout, largemouth bass, catfish, walleyes, shad, weakfish, whiting, and striped bass are well known nighttime feeders. Not so well known, by the way, are smallmouths, rainbows, crappies, cod, flounder, and bluefish, all of which have brightened up many a dark night for my children and me.

Air temperature influences fishing in proportion to how it affects water temperature. Even a beginner soon comes to the conclusion that fish are sluggish during the dog days of August just as they are when winter cold slows down their metabolisms. Few fishermen, however, consider how air temperature divides most lakes and ponds into three distinct layers, the middle one of which is where the majority of gamefish are found throughout most of the season.

The technical names for these layers, starting at the top, are epilimnion, thermocline, and hypolimnion. No need to remember them, although you might want to tuck "thermocline" on your back burner in case your youngster should come across it in an outdoor magazine and try to trip you up. This is the layer in which water temperature changes rapidly. The three-layer phenomenon occurs because for some reason shrouded in the mysteries of high school physics, water is heaviest at 39° Fahrenheit. Immediately after ice-out in the spring, surface water starts warming. When it reaches 39°, it sinks and is replaced by colder water, which also sinks when it reaches 39°. There is, in other words, a continuous turning over until the whole pond is 39°. Then turnover ceases. After this, surface water gets warmer and warmer, producing a deeper and deeper layer of high-temperature water. Meanwhile, water on the bottom remains at 39°. Because of its higher density it does not move; because air and sun do not reach it, it becomes stagnant.

Most fish shun the upper layer because it is too warm, the bottom because it lacks oxygen. How then to locate the middle layer, the thermocline? You can hang a thermometer over the side of your boat, recording temperatures every 10 feet or so until suddenly you notice them plummeting downward by at least 6 degrees for about every 10 feet of descent. Then check the depth of your thermometer and fish close to bottom at that general level.

"Hold it, hold it," said the last person I explained thermoclines to. "How can I fish close to bottom and still be in the thermocline? You're contradicting yourself."

But I'm not. Lake bottoms are not level. Their thermoclines can be penetrated at many places by peaks and bars and ridges, and of course a lake's shoreline drops off gradually through the entire thermocline layer. Since food is abundant near the bottom, what better bet on a lake in midsummer than where thermocline and bottom coincide?

If this smacks too much of the laboratory for you, just keep fishing at different depths until you score. Thereafter, if you keep your lure in the same neighborhood, you should do as well as the guys with the thermometers. It might take a little longer for you to get into action, but you also might have more fun along the way.

It's easy to see how the continuous in-and-out tidal flow of oceans affects saltwater fishing: flooding across mudflats and weedy marshes, it expands the area in which fish can seek their food; ebbing, it sweeps food along to waiting fish. Timing and intensity of tides are determined by the gravitational attraction of moon and sun. As these bodies move, they literally pull the oceans along with them in a great surging wave. Because the sun is more influential than the moon on mid-Pacific tides, low tide around Tahiti always is at sunrise and sunset, high at noon and midnight, but in most of the world, tides can occur at any time of the night or day. A given tide occurs about an hour later each day, with monthly tidal flow ranging from highest at the time of the full moon to lowest twenty-eight days later at the dark of the moon. Highest tides are called spring tides, lowest are called neap tides.

Everything from werewolf activity to the filling of inside straights is attributed to the moon's mysterious influence, so it's little wonder that a minor religion has been built up around the effect of tides on fishing. And this applies to fresh water as well as salt. Before you scoff, though, consider that there are more falling barometers and bad weather during full-moon tides, and that lower tidal ranges mean that bait is concentrated in a smaller volume of water, and that ... well, suffice it to say that a convincing case can be made for why fishing should be better at times of lowest tidal activity.

John Alden Knight, a gentleman wise in the ways of the outdoors, was so convinced of this relationship that he tabulated what would correspond to periods of low tide for all of North America in his now famous Solunar Tables, a forecast of the daily feeding times of fish and game for every day of the year. Today, several years after his death, these still are compiled by his daughter-in-law, Jackie Knight, and published in newspapers and magazines for the benefit of the thousands of anglers who swear by their predictions. Even those who swear *at* them have to acknowledge the fundamental validity of the premise on which they are based. These scoffers just want to add an "all other things being equal" qualification. "And," they emphasize, "all other things rarely are equal. The effects of sun and moon can be ideal for fishing, but if water's too high or low or warm or cold or clear or dirty or a thousand other things, you're not going to catch fish."

To which I reply, "Let's stop arguing and go fishing. Right now, somewhere, regardless of celestial circumstances or wind direction or the ache in your big toe, fish are feeding. Let's try to pick the right species, head for the right spot, and offer them something that will interest them."

Consciously or unconsciously, directly or implicitly, we all employ Solunar Tables. I regularly check Mrs. Knight's published version along with tide tables, fishing regulations, hot tips, seat-of-the-pants feelings, carefully compiled logs of past expeditions, and a lifetime's accumulation of lore about how fish behave. I have to confess, though, that the only time I feel really confident about catching fish is when the phone rings just as I'm about to leave and an excited voice announces, "Mayflies, clouds of 'em, all along the Squanocook. Get there an hour before sunset just below that fast water behind the airport. And remember," the voice always admonishes as I visualize my caller looking up the phone number of the next friend to whom he's going to reveal this exclusive secret, "don't tell another soul."

With a basic appreciation of fishes' habits and how they are influenced by environment and weather, you and your youngster can appreciably improve your chances of catching fish. You won't, for example, make the mistake of the New Jersey resident who read an article I had written about how my son Jack and I had caught cod from the Plum Island surf in northern Massachusetts and drove 300 miles in midwinter to get in on the action. Stopping off at a boarded-up baitshop, he learned from an incredulous shopowner who hadn't seen a surf caster since the previous fall that cod wouldn't be moving inshore for another three months.

What you and your son *might* do, though, is float a grasshopper to August trout when you discover a grassy field alongside a shaded pool; or choose a warm May midnight to fish the headwaters of a tidal stream because you know that water temperatures in the low 60s will have spawning shad blasting the night apart. Then, with a little more knowledge about how fish hear and see and smell and taste, you can improve your chances even further by choosing the right lures, by presenting them properly, and by employing tricks such as carpeting the deck of your aluminum pram so you can sneak up silently on spooky largemouth bass.

Largemouth, like most species, have a highly developed sense of hearing, although only for low-frequency sounds such as those made by splashes and motors. Not only do fish have ears inside their heads, but an array of nerves along their lateral lines also responds to sound waves. Furthermore, because water is denser than air, it is an even better conductor of the vibrations caused by rattling oarlocks, wading anglers, and carelessly cast lures.

Noise can be a help as well as a hindrance. While it's always a good idea to be careful about casting and wading and rowing and dropping anchor, some noises actually attract fish. With many North Country guides, it's standard operating procedure to troll one of their lures right in their propwash. Nosy landlocked salmon often are caught when they swim by to see what's causing the commotion. Off Florida's Key Largo, a pet grouper answers the call of young Sandy Pidgeon when he dives down to feed it. Even a traditionally wary brown trout was successfully conditioned to respond to splashes from the end of a dock on a small Cape Cod pond. Each evening it was fed fresh liver until it attained a weight of about four pounds. Then its patron, as ugly an individual as ever desecrated the outdoors with his presence, slammed the unsuspecting beast with a paddle and exhibited its carcass at the neighborhood bar as evidence of his angling prowess.

No, son, the Great Outdoors is not invariably great.

Consider what suggestive sounds a fish is likely to hear in its underwater world. On a quiet pond the swimming of a frog can kick up quite a fuss. Capitalizing on this, lure designers have come up with countless froglike creations. In salt water a struggling fish signals an easy meal to hungry predators; hence the popping plug, whose concave face complements a splashing retrieve with a tantalizing "blup" that can toll in fish like a dinner gong. One night in a shallow tidal creek I made a valuable discovery about noise by stumbling over a submerged log. The pool in which I was fishing had abruptly fallen quiet as a crypt following a half-hour of wild splashing courtship by dozens of big shad. After hit-a-minute action, not one of the three of us in the pool could coax a tumble from these suddenly turned-off fish. But when I stumbled, I splashed, and immediately the shad resumed their wild ritual. Apparently what had happened is, one male shad had darted away from me, causing others to think he was trying to make time with a ripe young maiden. Jealousy incited her other suitors to get in on the act, and presto, we were back in business. Today I often activate sluggish shad by slapping my rod on the water.

Competition also can ignite a feeding orgy. In salt water, in particular, schools of prey and predator occasionally can be found side by side, cruising in what appears to be cozy compatibility until suddenly the big ones start attacking the little ones. Hunger can pull the trigger, sure, although I've caught too many feeding fish with bulging bellies to consider a craving for food the prime cause of such carnage. More likely what happens is, one big fish chases one little fish—or even gives the impression of doing so—and right away the other big fish follow suit.

Most gamefish always have a pent-up violence. Their potential for destruction is only temporarily—and tentatively—suppressed by a full stomach. Make them mad, make them jealous, even make them inquisitive enough and you will provoke them to strike. The scent of blood will do it with sharks, a few scraps of meat with bluefish. Barracuda respond to small flashy objects, and the smallmouth that may ignore the spinner your boy retrieves a mere 6 inches over its head will savagely attack the crawfish or hellgrammite which he works slowly across the gravel of the nest the bass is guarding.

Consider what a well-placed plug might do in the case of those two side-by-side schools. Assume that they're striped bass and mackerel and that you've cut your motor and glided alongside the striper school. The mackerel are on the far side of the stripers, about a full cast away.

"Try to lay your plug just inside the striper school," you tell your son, and he drops it accurately, about two feet inside the school's outboard edge. The splash startles several stripers and they scoot for a few feet in several directions. As you predicted, one or two of them scoot toward the mackerel. Other stripers interpret their action as the signal to attack, and suddenly the water is boiling with battle. Awed, your son watches entranced, immobile, but not for long. Like the stripers near his plug, he too has been startled. His reaction is to jump, to jerk slightly. When he does, he yanks his rod. His plug, right in the midst of the melee, twitches. A striper streaking toward the fray notices it behind, above, and to its right. To the striper it is a crippled mackerel: stunned, recovering, attempting to escape. Reshaping its body in an instantaneous interaction of muscles and fins, the bass veers to starboard, strikes the plug, and . . . well, let's let the lad finish the story.

It's unlikely that this striper heard the small splash produced by your son's plug; not with all that other commotion nearby. It struck because it *saw* your son's plug; or, more tactically important, it saw the plug move. Despite the plug's location, above the fish and off its starboard quarter, this striper was able to see it almost as clearly as if it had been in front and at eye level.

Examine a fish's eyes and you will see why. Their location at the sides rather than the front of its head greatly expands the fish's field of vision. Most fish, in fact, can see clearly all around them except for a narrow cone directly to their rear. When a trout fisherman works upstream rather than down, floating flies to fish he knows will be heading into the current, he is exploiting this blank spot in their vision. Through evolutionary refinement a fish's sight has become adapted to the environment it inhabits. Species that live close to the surface or in shallow water have large eyes and see well over great distances. Dolphin, trout, and bonefish are typical. The eyes of bottom dwellers such as catfish and eels are small, but good old Mother Nature has compensated by providing these species with better-developed senses of smell and taste.

But it's motion rather than *com*motion that plays the larger part in persuading a fish to strike. A plug that plops and floats alongside a patch of lily pads is just an inanimate blob to a largemouth while it just seems to lie there. Scared away briefly by the plug's splash, the bass will investigate but probably won't attack. Twitch it gently, though, and only the wiliest of bass will be able to resist the temptation to pounce.

In salt water, the same approach works well on wary fish: cast, wait, twitch, pause, twitch again; then retrieve, pausing and twitching occasionally along the way. True, your lure will drift with the tide, but a fish on the prowl will follow it waiting for some slight sign of life.

As a rule, a saltwater retrieve should be fast, a freshwater one slow, but experiment freely with all sorts of erratic actions. Fish respond best to sudden dramatic differences of sensation. One such sudden sensation that makes fish respond readily but not favorably for a fisherman is a shadow on the water. To a fish that always has to be primed to protect itself if it is to survive, a shadow means a bird or an animal or a bigger fish with mayhem on its mind. The fish's natural reaction is to run for cover. If no cover is available, as on a flat beach, it will head for deeper water. Always be conscious, therefore, of where the sun is located. If possible, approach shallow-water fish facing into the sun. If you must approach with the sun at your back, stay low and try not to make any sudden moves. At night point flashlights away from the water, and avoid crossing between a steady light and the water in which you're fishing.

Be careful also of the color of your clothing. Sunlight bounces off white teeshirts as if they were mirrors. When an experienced angler tells you to keep your shirt on, he's referring to how you're dressed before the fish hits as well as to how you behave after it starts ripping line off your reel.

Yes, Virginia, fish can see colors. Some species, in fact, can see colors at the violet end of the spectrum that are invisible to humans. What is important to the angler, though, is to match color and brightness to environment. The big flashy lure that frightens fish in a small pond can be dazzlingly effective in a bright choppy sea. A brown fly will blend into invisibility in a murky beaver pond, but a yellow one will beam like a beacon. In remote lakes where few fish have felt the sting of a hook, most anything that moves, whether bright or dull, light or dark, might induce a strike. Not so with that lunker largemouth that hangs out around the pilings of the town dock with a half-dozen hooks dangling from its lips. Anything less than live bait or a flawlessly authentic imitation is not likely to break through that bass's barrier of suspicion. (If you insist on artificials, by the way, try red and yellow; a Mickey Finn streamer fly for example. Largemouths are especially fond of this color combination.)

At about this point in any discussion of how fish respond to colors, someone always seems to say, "Yeah, but I caught a largemouth bass on a brass shoehorn with purple polkadots. How do you explain that?"

I don't. If you want to fish with shoehorns or beer caps or clam shells, go right ahead. Odd objects are found regularly in fishes' stomachs. A lot of trout, in fact, are dying because they eat and cannot digest beer caps and filter tips from cigarettes, but I haven't seen any trout fishermen replacing their Royal Coachmans with cellulose cylinders.

The odds, that's what you must emphasize to your youngster. Every case is a turn of the wheel. If he learns and plays the odds—color, brightness, size, shape, season, locality, presentation; yes, even texture and taste and odor—then his number will come up more often.

The importance of texture becomes obvious to a boy after he has missed several trout or sunfish in a row because he set his hook a split second after they had spit out his fly. With moving lures, texture is not as important, because fish normally are hooked in the process of striking, but consider those plastic worms that are so devastatingly effective on largemouth bass. These are picked up and carried by bass, sometimes for long distances, before the hook is set. If these worms were hard and stiff instead of soft and supple, it's unlikely that bass would keep them in their mouths long enough to be caught.

Plastic, of course, doesn't seem to taste or smell like anything from a bass's standard menu. But on the other hand, maybe it tastes just like the leeches that bass love to eat. (Any volunteers for finding out?) Or maybe black bass as a group don't have well-developed taste buds. Or possibly largemouths don't demand good flavor; just the absence of bad is enough.

And what is a bad flavor to fish? Bug spray, I presume, repels fish almost as effectively as it does insects, yet how careful are you to avoid transferring it from your hands to your lures? The gasoline and motor oil which we wipe off but rarely remove completely from our hands probably are equally repulsive to fish. Even the odor from your skin can send fish scurrying for cover. Experiments on a Western salmon stream showed that the mere immersion of a man's hand made fish react like the downwind guy on a halitosis commercial. According to Dr. Clarence Idyll of the University of Miami's Division of Marine Sciences, "If a quart of water in which a human hand or the paw of a bear has been dipped for a minute is poured into a stream, it can cause migrating salmon to stop climbing a fish ladder a hundred yards away." Maybe this experiment applied only to those particular fish at that particular time on that particular stream. Or maybe all the hands used in the experiment had a bad case of manual B.O. But just in case the findings apply to my hands and my fish and my water as well, I usually start a session of fishing by squishing a few handfuls of mud or sand from the bottom, just to be on the safe side.

What is good flavor to a fish? Catfish, with their perverse palates, are partial to the ripest, raunchiest concoctions you can hang on a hook. The juice of minnows simmered for weeks in a mid-summer sun forms the base for stink bait formulas that catfishermen guard with a care normally accorded bank vault combinations. And before trout fishermen start getting snooty about the refined tastes of their chosen species, let me point out that plain old cheese balls catch so many trout that in some areas their use has been outlawed.

I suppose that as reasonable a rule to follow as any is that whatever is suggestive to a fish of what it normally eats is likely to activate its appetite. Remember how those hatchery trout started swirling when pellets were sprinkled into their pens? And how those tropical fish headed topside in your tabletop tank when you started doling out those fragrant flakes? Small wonder! From the label on a can of fish food, I find that $1.45 plus 3 percent sales tax has purchased for my piscine pets a blue-plate special of fish meal, dried shrimp, roe, milt, egg yolk, fly eggs, cod liver oil, wheat germ oil, and assorted other delicacies.

Anyone who's fished from a party boat has observed how effectively fish can be attracted by a chumline of ground bait. On North Carolina beaches imaginative anglers have adapted this technique to surf fishing by heaving small perforated containers of ground fish out where they're planning to drop their bait. This adaptation I classify as clever. The one devised by a secretive old Yankee surfcaster who consistently hauls striped bass from the suds while anglers on either side of him are getting skunked, I classify as ingenious. Sneaky, but ingenious. This rascal always fishes mackerel chunks on the bottom at high tide. What his frustrated competitors don't realize is that when the tide is low, he tiptoes out and pounds pieces of mackerel into the sand a cast out from where he'll be standing when the tide becomes high.

As your knowledge of fishes' behavior expands, you and your youngster will want to start experimenting with new ways of outwitting them. Most of your ideas will be duds, but occasionally one will succeed. And even those that fizzle will be worthwhile reminders that those fish out there are a little smarter than you gave them credit for being.

The longer you spend in the outdoors the more you inevitably must come to appreciate what extraordinary creatures fish are. Every one, from sucker to sailfish, is a miracle of evolutionary achievement. To your child, you can give no grander gift than an appreciation of their marvels and mysteries.

Examine your son's next big fish closely. See if you and he can detect its thin skin, the glands in which secrete that slimy film that covers its skin and scales. See if he can guess that this film has three functions: to reduce water friction and thus increase the fish's speed; to enable it to slip away more easily from enemies; and to prevent disease-bearing organisms from penetrating its skin. Once he becomes aware of this film's importance to a fish, he will handle his catches more carefully.

When you bring this fish home, remove a scale and examine it under a microscope. Observe its annular rings, like the growth rings on a tree. Have your child count them and learn how old his fish is. Have him try to figure out that these rings occur because of differences in growth rate between summers, when a fish is active and eats a lot, and winters, when it eats and moves about much less. See if he can pick out which were lean years for his fish and which were fat.

Then, look in the fish's mouth together. Does it have teeth? (Bottom-feeders such as suckers and carp do not.) Are its teeth on its jaws? On the roof of its mouth? On its tongue? Are they flat for crushing or sharp for ripping. You may be sure that after a close look at the dental weaponry of a barracuda, bluefish, musky, or shark, your youngster will think twice before inserting his finger into any fish's mouth.

To truly appreciate fish—and, incidentally, acquire real proficiency in catching them—it's necessary for your child to know them personally. Just as his friends are not merely people, but Bills and Franks and Marys and Ruths, fish are not merely aquatic creatures, but codfish and flounder and pickerel and perch. The remainder of this chapter, therefore, is devoted to describing a few of my favorites.

## YELLOW PERCH

*Perca flavescens*

Unmistakable with its vertical olive and yellow-gold bands, and light-to-bright-orange belly. . . . A favorite of panfishermen because of its wide distribution, large numbers, voracious appetite, and delicious flavor. . . . Spawns during spring in cool waters, usually at night and near brush and weeds. . . . Often travels in schools, with males and females schooled separately. . . . Preference for large cool lakes enables yellow perch to save the day when trout and salmon are uncooperative.

In southwestern New Hampshire is a perfect little jewel of a pond called Spoonwood. On a spring evening you can tote your boat across a narrow portage from Spoonwood's larger neighbor, Nubanusit, and cast to rising trout without another soul in sight, without another sound save the wind's purring in the pines. One evening after Spoonwood trout had spurned everything I had offered them for better than two hours, I passed close aboard an anchored pram as I paddled back disconsolately toward the portage. Hunched in its stern was an overalled old-timer monitoring a yellow-and-red pencil bobber tethered to an antiquated rod.

"How're you doing?" I asked.

"Good," he said, "real good."

Another case of the natives knowing that secret something about local trout tactics, I figured, shrugging my shoulders and turning to go. Then his bobber started dancing and, beaming like a buttercup, he played and landed a plump yellow perch.

"Nice 'un, huh?" he said, and I had to admit that it was bigger by a good couple of inches than the average Spoonwood trout and darn near as scrappy. And, as I learned later, yellow perch caught in Spoonwood-cool water blends the sweet pure flavor of trout with a bassy kind of richness. Much as I enjoy eating trout and smallmouth bass and white perch, I have to acknowledge that as freshwater fare, only the walleye gives the yellow perch competition.

She's also an impressive scrapper. Few other freshwater species surpass her readiness to tangle with virtually any kind of lure in any type of water. Send a minnow after spring-spawning walleyes and there's a good chance it will be snapped up by a big-bellied perch. Float a fly on a trout pond and odds are high that a perch will pounce on it. Wiggle a small wobbler past pickerel weed and the likelihood is high that you will be seeing some more of those gorgeous yellow-and-green stripes. I have caught yellow perch while trolling for lake trout during a snowstorm, while casting to river-run landlocked salmon in midsummer, while popping

Filleted and fried over an open fire, yellow perch are hard to beat. These gave Matthew and Mary Beth all the action they needed during a weekend of camping in New Hampshire.

for panfish against a backdrop of incandescent autumn foliage, and while jigging for crappies through two feet of ice. The yellow perch truly is a fish for all seasons.

In fact it's the yellow perch's very commonness that makes most adults and a few prematurely unappreciative children scorn them. In quest of other species, we receive a strong strike followed by a scurrying scrap. We're excited and impressed until we see that familiar brightly barred back.

"Ahhh," we sneer, "just another perch."

For children afflicted with this fun-destroying cynicism, I prescribe this three-part remedy. First, spend one day concentrating mainly on perch. Pick a perch-rich pond (an easy assignment) and try catching them with everything from live shiners to dry flies. Second, let every hooked fish fight itself out. No overpowering, no horsing in so you can hurry up and catch another. Study its moves, its maneuvers, the power of its runs, the strength of its struggle. And third, look closely at the first perch you catch, its colors aflame, its dorsal unfurled.

The remedy I prescribe for unappreciative adults has only one part: join your children.

# BLUEGILL

## *Lepomis macrochirus*

Most widely sought of the sunfishes. . . . Called bream in Southeast. . . . 6-8 vertical bands, but basic color can vary according to clarity of water. . . . Small but scrappy, superb sport on flyrod. . . . Spawns in shallows during spring, when round nests are easily spotted. . . . Can be caught through ice on jigs, worms, grubs. . . . Prodigiously productive, should be harvested to avoid stunting and decline of other gamefish. . . . Be careful of sharp spines when removing from hook.

There's a danger in bluegills, and in fact, in sunfish of all kinds, and a child should learn early to avoid it. The danger is in his getting so swept up in the incessant action that sunnies always seem to provide that he just keeps catching and killing until at last it occurs to him that he has caught so many fish he doesn't know what to do with them. Unless he's reminded by a responsible adult about the wondrous beauty of these animated little jewels, he'll regard them as toys whose only destiny is to provide him with pleasure. The shore will be littered with his callous

Catch a lot of bluegills and you will enable the rest of the fish to grow bigger on a pond's fixed food supply. But never ignore the bluegill's beauty, and never waste them.

carnage, and Lord knows there's too much of it already. You've seen it: dried rotting carcasses of creatures that endured a thousand dangers only to wind up scorched, foul, and repugnant.

Not that there's anything wrong with catching and keeping a lot of sunfish. The more of them you and your youngster take, the less competition there will be for the pond's fixed food supply. Sunnies, like most panfish, spawn prodigiously. When there are too many fish for the food available, they become stunted. Every time you take home a stringer full of sunnies, you improve the food-per-fish ratio and encourage the growth of larger specimens.

But even this does not justify senseless slaughter. There's something too eternally significant, too close to the heart of things about a tiny egg's becoming a perfect functioning animal, for that animal to be allowed to die without doing some good, serving some useful purpose: food, bait, fertilizer, *some*thing. The sunfish on the shore, the dolphin on the dock, the bluefin in the dump; all are wrongs that must be righted before man can truly be master of his environment.

I suppose I'd be a flop as an aquatic biologist. When it came time to wipe out a pond's population of "coarse fish" to make room for "gamefish," I would be arguing about the gameness of carp and suckers and sunfish—especially sunfish. Of all the sunnie's attributes, I appreciate most its readiness to rise to a fly. Were it not for sunfish, I might have abandoned fly-fishing and all its attendant pleasures after failing to catch a single trout on my first three tries. What kept me going was the memory of several practice sessions on close-to-home ponds when cooperative sunnies, ignoring my sloppy slapping casts and unnatural retrieves, gave me preview after preview of how it would be when a trout finally took.

Recently Jack and I had a few hours for fishing together. We could have cast the surf or trolled a pond or waded a stream, but instead, we decided to drop small cork-bodied poppers between the lily pads of a nearby cranberry bog. Now Jack, besides being a student of American literature, is, like his old man, an incorrigible punster, perpetually primed to weave words into nonsensical wonders. On watching workmen dump dirt into the vacant foundation of an old textile factory, he would be likely to observe that they are "making a mountain out of a mill hole." Should I come home after a day of fishing unsuccessfully for any species by any method, he might call me a "catch as catch can't fisherman." So, when, to his surprise, sunfish, which he never before had caught on top, started rocketing up after our poppers, I couldn't resist reminding him of the book that great writer-fisherman Ernest Hemingway had written on that very subject: *The Sunny also Rises.*

## BLACK BULLHEAD

### *Ictalurus melas*

Small member of catfish family. . . . Often called hornpout or horned pout because of sharp bony protrusions at top and sides of head (be careful when handling). . . . Widely distributed throughout U.S. in warm muddy water. . . . A bottom-feeder, it eats mostly bait, but is not finicky about what kind. . . . Easy to find and catch, a reasonable scrapper, and a popular foodfish, the pout is a natural for children.

Sharp spines at the sides and top of their heads can inflict painful wounds when you're trying to unhook a catfish such as this bullhead. The secret: Hold your fish so that all three spines are firmly secured between your fingers.

High on the list of memorable experiences for a fledgling fisherman is the sight of his first hornpout. Responding to a few gentle tugs, he sets his hook, restrains a few hard boring runs, and quickly subdues what he expects to be another perch or sunfish. When, instead of bright colors and scaly bodies, a long, slender, slimy, grayish-black body is preceded out of the water by an almost-human-looking mustached face, he is fascinated and repelled at the same time.

Ultimately he summons up enough courage to handle the sleek flopping form and remove his hook. Grabbing it around the head, he shrieks and jettisons his hornpout as his hand is stabbed by one of the three bony horns atop and alongside its head.

This is his initiation into the catfish family's fan club. Its members are legion. I am one of them.

What converted me for all time was not the very respectable scraps I enjoyed with two-pound pout in the Merrimack River's quiet backwaters. Nor was it the red fillets we grilled over an open fire on February ice. (Frankly I didn't enjoy them.) What made me a fascinated admirer of hornpout in particular and all catfish in general was a sight shown to me by my four-year-old son Jack the first time we went fishing.

It was on a small New Hampshire pond whose shore, though muddy, was made solid enough by the continuous flow of cool water from the brook that fed it to enable Jack and me to wade while we cast for trout. Or more accurately, while I cast for trout. Typical of inexperienced parents, I had conveniently convinced myself that my son could best learn the esoteric art of trout fishing by watching his highly accomplished old man in action.

But Jack, bless him, soon discovered something infinitely more interesting than his father's backside. Unlike his unintentionally selfish father, he couldn't wait to share it with me.

"Daddy, Daddy, look, look," he hollered, bending forward and pointing to something in the shallow water at his feet.

What he had discovered were recently hatched hornpout. They couldn't have been more than a half-inch long, yet every feature seemed fully developed. Like tiny toys, they ventured warily out of pockmarks in the mud, retreating and backing into their burrows as soon as they sensed that danger threatened.

Jack and I watched them for a long time. When we finished he fished instead of me, and with no need for help from his old man, he caught his first rainbow trout. Today rainbows always remind me of minuscule hornpout on a very significant day in my life. This was the day I learned that joy expands a hundredfold when shared with someone you love. Thanks for the lesson, Son.

# WHITE PERCH

### Roccus americans

Member of sea bass family, along with striped bass. . . . Resembles striper, even to stripes in young. . . . Caught in salt as well as fresh water. . . . Prodigiously productive spawning plus extra-long life of fifteen years and more enables white perch to overpopulate ponds. . . . Prolonged fast action guaranteed on spinners, flies, and most natural baits when a school is located. . . . Excellent light-tackle opponents and supremely good eating.

My first exposure to white perch occurred inside a gas station in a tiny rural town in Maine. Three of us on our way upcountry had awakened to a flat tire. After we had replaced it, I had been elected to jog alongside the car from station to station in search of a new tube for our spare.

The man in the first station I came to didn't happen to have the right-size tube, but he allowed as how he had something else that more than likely would interest me. Sliding an aluminum mess tray from a paper bag, he removed the cover, for all the world like a backwoods *maître d'* from Maxim's of Paris, and held under my receptive nose a dozen small fillets whose fragrance seemed to blend the dawn freshness with the newly mown fields along which I had been running.

"White perch," he said. "Caught 'em an hour ago. The Missus likes to cook 'em fresh."

He couldn't have been more proud if he had been serving golden trout *sauté à la meunière* prepared by a *Cordon Bleu* chef.

While mine host's wife undoubtedly had a lot to do with the fish's delectability, the perch themselves were firm, sweet, and meaty enough to make me a fan forevermore, no matter who does the cooking. My

Margaret's white perch was caught through the same hole in the ice as Julie's yellow. White perch are eagerly sought in tidewater bays and rivers as well as inland lakes, and little wonder. Fry up a few and you'll understand why.

friends in the car no doubt wondered why I looked so satisfied when I came out of the gas station despite being unable to find a replacement for our tube. That evening while trolling for salmon, they must have been even more puzzled when I suddenly swung our 14-foot outboard toward a lee shore. I had detected one of the patches of dimples that the man in the gas station had alerted me for.

"Look for 'em about twilight," he had said. "Can happen any time, but evening twilight's best. Usually means a school of perch is eatin' underneath."

At first my companions scoffed when I dropped a small wet fly beyond the dimples and started stripping in line.

"What's this supposed to be, a substitute for salmon?"

Nothing in fresh water, of course, is a substitute for landlocked salmon when they're hitting, but after better than four hours of no-hit trolling, my friends were pushovers for these perch. By the time I was playing my second, they were trying to tie on worm-and-spinner combinations with hands that wouldn't stop shaking. Following our campfire feast that night, they too had taken out life memberships in the Northern Maine Branch of the White Perch Fan Club.

Not only do white perch keep rods bending throughout spring, summer, and fall, but they're equally cooperative through winter ice. What many anglers are unaware of, though, is that seagoing schools head up many tidal rivers in early spring. A youngster who can cope with the often bitter cold will welcome this chance to don his boots and launch his stream-fishing season better than a month early.

Rod, reel, line, hooks, sinkers, bait, waders, lots of warm clothing, about 18 bucks worth of penicillin tablets, and plenty of bed rest—these were the prerequisites of a white perch session I experienced last March in southern Massachusetts' Agawam River. The tackle and clothing were for fishing, the medicine and sack time for recuperating from the strep throat I wound up with after a few hours of wallowing in ice water with Arctic winds searing my tonsils every time I opened my mouth to exclaim about the spectacular performance of this unheralded, unexploited, and pretty much unknown tidewater fish.

So okay, after a winter's inactivity you're even ready to start casting to guppies in pet-shop windows, but this kid cousin to the striped bass can stand tall on its own merits. Strong, fast, and spoiling for a fight during its spring spawning run, the white perch runs hard, bores deep, and makes the most of tidal currents. Many a skeptic has been converted by a 2-pounder on light tackle in a fast tideway.

Take outdoor photographer Terry McDonnell, for example. His reaction to my suggestion that we visit the Agawam was about as I expected from one whose white-perch experience had been limited to fresh water.

"C'mawn," he scoffed, "it's just another panfish. What's all the big build-up?"

I didn't argue, because I knew he'd come. In March, Terry, like the rest of us, has just about run out of last season's replays and is aching to start storing up a fresh supply.

Seaworms, I had been told, were likely to produce best, so we headed for Cape Cod, where bait shops garnish their sales with plenty of accurate up-to-date G-2.

"Right alongside Route 6," said the man behind the counter. "Just pull up, stroll out, and start casting. A flooding tide is best. Use enough weight to keep your worm bouncing along the bottom."

Normally during this spring spree anglers are strung out along the banks of the Agawam like Christmas lights, but when Terry and I crossed a wooden footbridge leading to a sandy elbow of the river, we found only a handful of other fishermen. The absence of crowds, we learned, was because we had missed the best tide. "Top two-thirds of a flood, bottom two-thirds of an ebb," said a man who passed us on the footbridge. His 10-quart plastic bucket, though covered, was translucent enough to reveal the shadows of an impressive catch.

We fished anyway, of course. Just the pleasure of being there was enough: salt smell, current caressing our waders, the pulsing pleasure of winter-mushy muscles making their first casts of the new season. With the tide almost full, we knew fish were in front of us. Maybe a few nudges from an ebbing tide would get them into gear.

The tide hadn't even topped off when I felt my first tender tapping, set my hook, and missed. Couple of casts later, ditto. Then recalling that winter flounder often are caught along with white perch, I tied on an up-and-down rig: narrow long-shanked flounder hook at the bitter end with a #8 Eagle Claw a foot and a half above it on a dropper loop. For weight I slid a half-ounce egg sinker on my line, using a barrel swivel to link this line to the leader containing my two hooks. Not only did this setup enable me to fish flounder right on the bottom and perch just above it, it also permitted fish to run with my bait without feeling the weight of my sinker. Yeah, that's right, like a fishfinder rig.

It worked. Only on small flounder till the tide turned, but as soon as there was a marked flow from upriver to down, the gentle jabs became jarring yanks. On my 5-foot spinning rod and 4-pound line, there was no heaving and hauling. By heading for midchannel and turning broadside to the flow, these fish can put a strain on tackle far heavier than what I was using.

After taking a few white perch on this kind of tackle, your youngster will agree with what I replied last spring to those poor uninitiated landlubbers who visited me in my bed of pain, shaking their heads, clucking their tongues, and accusing me of some minor form of insanity for standing in ice water in the middle of March.

"A strep throat," I told them, "is small price to pay."

## LARGEMOUTH BLACK BASS

*Micropterus salmoides*

Probably most popular U.S. freshwater gamefish. . . . In almost every state. . . . Black-to-green back with dark wavy lateral band (smallmouth is bronze to brown with vertical markings). . . . Dwells in Shallow ponds and close to weeds, brush, and submerged logs for food and protection. . . . Eats mostly minnows, frogs, crawfish, and large insects. . . . Active night feeder. . . . Two-to-10-pound spread in North, much larger in South, where growth period longer.

For many youngsters—myself included—the largemouth black bass provides the first explosive introduction to big-league fishing. The experience has launched enough love affairs with old bucketmouth to have earned her a reputation as America's most popular freshwater gamefish. And little wonder. Built like a bull, tough as a terrier, occasionally topping 10 pounds up North and almost twice that down South, she can be found feeding day and night on everything from dragonflies to field mice in almost any shallow warm-water pond.

The same ponds, by the way, in which you and your son might be passing a pleasant afternoon dunking worms from your drifting skiff for panfish. You know how it happens: his bobber jiggles, he sets his hook, and, oops, a tangle, so he pauses, and while he unsnarls his line, the breeze blows his bobber and the 3-inch shiner on the hook beneath it alongside a sunken log; only under this particular sunken log resides a 4-pound largemouth to whom a struggling shiner means meat on the table. The bass blasts the afternoon apart, puts on an aerobatic performance of Blue Angels caliber, and leaves the lad wide-eyed with his line snarled on an underwater snag.

Size, strength, and stamina have made the largemouth America's most popular freshwater gamefish. Although largemouths are less active in winter, they also can be caught through the ice.

If your son was perceptive enough to notice that log under which his largemouth was lurking, he might have learned an important lesson: largemouths crave cover—brush, stumps, logs, weeds, even overhanging branches—for food as well as protection. Two exceptions are at night, when they prowl in close with their guards down and their danders up, and during spring spawning, when they nest in the shallows.

It was spring, in fact, when I caught my first big bass. Nine years old at the time, I was on an overnight camping trip on an island in New Hampshire's mammoth Lake Winnipesaukee. Slipping out of my sleeping bag at dawn, I strolled along the huckleberried shoreline while a molten sun edged up behind the White Mountains' Presidential Range, gilding the glazed lake and spotlighting a cleared circle in the brown bottom a few feet from shore. Creeping close, I saw Papa Bass patrolling his nest. It was a good, though hardly a great fish, 3½ or maybe 4 pounds, but to my nine-year-old eyes those were battleship proportions, and when, with a sweep of its broad tail, it swung to starboard and engulfed the worm I was wiggling past its premises, I thought, after I had set my hook, that I had pulled the firing pin on a broadside of 16-inch guns.

That night as I lay on my bunk back at camp, even my counselor's congratulations, even the special meal prepared for me by the camp cook, couldn't quell my conviction that I had done something wrong, something ugly and unsporting. The bass had been so vulnerable, so easy to spot and simple to snare, that I never again have kept largemouth bass I've caught on their spawning beds.

But nights, now, that's a different story. Row silently with your son on a still, dark summer night till you're a couple of casts from a tree-lined shore. Then drift and listen. "Thwaaap!" Silence. "Sploosh!" Silence.

"A popping plug," whisper to him. "Cast it toward that last noise. When it lands, let it set; fifteen, even twenty seconds if you can keep still that long. Then twitch it. Once. Hard enough so it 'blurps,' then let it rest again. Pretend it's a frog, a scared, cautious frog, and make it look and swim and sound as much like that frog as you can."

Hope you brought your flashlight. No, it's not a good idea to illuminate a dark pond unless you absolutely have to, but this is one of those occasions! You absolutely have to see the look on your son's face when that bass pulverizes his plug.

## SMALLMOUTH BLACK BASS

### *Micropterus dolomieu*

Acrobat of the black basses. . . . Cagey and selective. . . . Widely distributed coast to coast from original range in north-central U.S. . . . Smaller (2–6-pound average) than largemouth. . . . Bronze to brown back with vertical markings (largemouth is black to green with dark wavy lateral band). . . . Prefers cool rocky lakes and slow graveled streams. . . . Eats crawfish, frogs, small fish, and large insects. . . . Active night feeder.

If ever you should run into fishermen with no noses, relax. They're trout and salmon anglers and they're from northern New England. We have a lot of them up here. Their noses? They cut them off to spite their faces.

Or in less metaphorical language, they concentrate exclusively on trout and salmon when all about them are rivers and lakes rich with bronze battlers that are easy to locate, hard to fool, exquisite to fight, and delectable to dine on.

The smallmouth's spectacular topwater tactics make a comparison with landlocked salmon inevitable. During spring the two can be caught side by side in many Maine and New Hampshire lakes. (Photo: Maine Department of Fish and Game)

"But, of course," as the resident with the 6-inch brook trout will tell you, "they ain't nothin' but bass."

I confess to having been a salmon and trout snob myself until one May morning on New Hampshire's Lake Winnisquam when Bill Stone and I thought we had cornered every landlocked salmon in the world behind a small, rocky, close-to-shore island. After two utterly uneventful hours of trolling, we were primed for anything that even suggested fish, so when we saw the swirls and splashes not 20 yards away Bill immediately goosed his outboard, gliding us silently alongside the action. As usual, his streamer fly was looping across the water before I could so much as cock the bail on my spinning reel. If Bill had lived in frontier days, he surely would have been the fastest gun in the West.

The fish responded to Bill's fly but wouldn't hit. They chased, they swirled, but they always stopped short of actually striking. On his third cast, Bill snagged a small metal container. Inside he found a Mepps spinner, one of my favorite lures.

"Here," he said, tossing it forward, "try this."

Casting it across the cove, I let it settle for a second, reeled three or four turns, and had the tip of my 5-foot rod yanked clear to the water. Before I could raise it and start reeling, 3 pounds of infuriated smallmouth blasted skyward and put on an airborne performance equal to that of any landlocked salmon I had ever hooked. After repeating the performance on three successive casts, I pledged my eternal devotion to this spectacular species and, incidentally, offered to rent my Mepps to Bill for $100 a cast.

Then we made our mistake. With four fish on our stringer, it occurred to us that maybe the bass season hadn't opened yet.

"That used to be the case years ago," said Bill. "Opened June first, I think it was. I'm pretty sure they've changed it, but let's go ashore and check."

So we released our fish, confident that we would be able to return and resume right where we had left off, and headed in. We'd gone less than 100 yards when a boat rounded the bend. Pulling up alongside, we learned from its occupant that smallmouths were indeed fair game, so we about-faced, returned to our island, and, of course, couldn't coax another fish to cooperate.

That morning marked my conversion to smallmouth-bass fishing. An afternoon on a gentle Maine river made me a devotee. I can't even recall the river's name, nor did I think I'd ever be wanting to when two friends and I launched our canoes for what promised to be a pleasant but uneventful downstream drift. I had been assured that smallmouths were present, but I was less optimistic. After all, I thought, smallmouths are big-water fish. Cold clear upcountry lakes like Winnisquam, that's what these free-swinging brawlers need to really flex their muscles.

Then the action started. At every bend and pool and pocket our spoons and plugs and spinners were pulverized by fish whose speed and 2- and 3-pound sizes seemed astounding for such placid pastoral waters. Instead of the long deep-boring rushes and airborne oscillations I expected, I found myself trying to cope with runs whose velocity and direction were as unpredictable as New England weather.

Typical of smallmouths everywhere, these fish had adapted their tactics to their environment. These were not wide-open battlefield brawlers like their lake-living cousins. These were guerrilla fighters, striking suddenly and then rushing for the cover of sunken brush and boulders. With only 4-pound-test monofilament and no knowledge of where these snags might be located, I lost many more fish than I landed.

Even more memorable than the fishing that afternoon was an incident that occurred when we beached our canoes on a gravel bar and paused for a sandwich. The jungle, I was reminded once again, is never very far away for the fisherman.

"Watch," said one of my companions, scooping up a small frog from where the gravel met the grass. "Here's how to find out if fish are in an eating mood. See if a smallmouth doesn't come up when this frog starts kicking across that pool."

At first the frog floated motionless, drifting a few feet downstream. For a moment it appeared that the gentle current was going to carry it ashore where the tail of the pool tapered quickly to a fast shallow stony flow. Through the trees a car passed in a sequence of chrome-and-orange flashes between green-and-yellow leaves. Beyond the far bank a cow grazed contentedly. The soft song of a redwing blackbird somehow seemed to harmonize with the shrill summons of an ice-cream truck in the village beyond the next bend, blending everything from cars to cows, from frogs to Fudgsicles into a quiet compatibility. Violence, surely, could never intrude on this tranquillity.

Then the frog kicked. Just once. Before it could retract its legs for a second push, it disappeared in a burst of spray that shattered my nerves along with my lovely illusion. The rings and ripples disappeared quickly from the pool. Soon it was as if nothing had happened. Another creature had died. No monument to mark its having been here, no eulogy to confirm its contribution. The miracle of birth, the achievement of survival, the devastation of death, and nothing to show for it beyond the temporary satiation of a bigger beast's hunger. There has to be something more, I thought, even for a frog.

There is, of course. What handsomer headstone than the sky's eternal reflection? What lovelier dirge than the water's endless whisper?

# CHAIN PICKEREL

## *Esox niger*

> Strikes anything that moves. . . . Caught year-round throughout Great Lakes–Texas–Maine triangle in ponds, creeks, slow-moving streams. . . . Often caught in same weedy areas as largemouth bass. . . . Sharp teeth can sever light lines.

"Freshwater barracuda" is one of the chain pickerel's nicknames. One autumn afternoon on the bank of a trout stream I learned why. Trout were coming hard for outdoor photographer Terry McDonnell and me, so our hopes soared when we saw fish rising on the far side of a gentle bend. Terry was in the water, so I knelt, camera cocked, on the bank above him, a front-row seat at a performance of jungle savagery that constantly goes on but seldom is seen beneath the surface of tranquil streams and placid ponds.

Laying a #12 White Miller across the patch of weeds to the upper end of a sandy dip, he floated the fly close along the far shore where the current curved casually to his right. In classic, almost predictable

As well as being a favorite through the ice, pickerel will hit anything that moves in open water. In midsummer try sneaking up on a patch of weeds and have your youngster retrieve a shiny lure parallel to it and about 2 feet away. (Photo: Terry McDonnell)

fashion, up streaked a fish, back went Terry's rod, and the struggle started. A splashing dash across the surface revealed that Terry had hooked a golden shiner, but its frantic skittering runs were faster and more frequent than those of a trout twice its size. Desperate, it seemed, terrified; as if it were being chased . . . and it was.

"Pickerel," yelled Terry, as 2 feet of predatory perfection grazed his waders, shot out of the weedbed over which he had cast, and clamped the shiner's neck in its guillotine jaws, scattering scales like tiny glittering snowflakes. From my station on the bank, I could see it all: the stalk, the strike, the run to the bottom; the chomping and shaking, and finally the ingenious turning of the shiner as the pickerel edged its victim's head slowly, deliberately into its long lethal jaws.

"Hey," said Terry, preparing to haul back on his rod after a five-minute wait until I narrated from bankside, "this'll be a first: a 2-foot pickerel on a dry fly."

No, Terry didn't land his pickerel. Had it been hooked, or even snagged in its throat by the shiner's fins, it probably would have snapped Terry's fine leader on its sharp teeth. Nevertheless, before the pickerel finally abandoned this crazy breakfast that kept coming out of its mouth as soon as the shiner's tail entered those long beartrap jaws, we saw the whole brutal scene reenacted not once but twice.

Persistence, then, is one of the pickerel's vulnerable traits. Until it feels the sting of your hook, it's likely to keep attacking a properly presented lure. Other elements of your strategy should be the knowledge that old chainsides pounces readily on anything that moves, especially shiny minnow-imitating spoons and plugs. The pickerel waits for its meals in weedbeds along pond edges, river backwaters, and between-pond thoroughfares. It lurks along weedy fringes, so that a lure retrieved parallel and close to a weedbed is likely to be pounced on, and it responds readily to fast, splashy retrieves.

There's a delusion common among casters of large plugs with heavy treble hooks that the pickerel is a quitter. Don't let your boy believe it. Pickerel konk out quickly on such lures because of their tendency to swamp and swallow what they eat. No fish is likely to perform very well with a bulky plug tethering it by the tonsils. Soon as the lad learns to handle a fly rod, sneak your skiff up alongside a weedbed and have him lay a #6 Mickey Finn streamer about 2 feet from its edge and strip it back right away in fast, splashy, 2-foot spurts. On a single hook and light leader, old chainsides will make a believer out of your boy, especially with its last-act, near-the-net explosion.

From suckers to carp, from cunners to searobins, the species known collectively as coarse fish are children's favorites. Frank Sheehan, illustrious member of the Moose River Roll Cast, Six Pack, and Seven Card Stud Society and one of the world's grownup children, traveled to northern Maine's renowned trout country to catch this chub, and wasn't at all disappointed.

# FALLFISH (CHUB)

*Semotilus corporalis*

A heavily scaled minnow abundant in clear streams and lakes of the Northeast. . . . Commonly called chub and similar in appearance to creek chub. . . . Principal value is as food for gamefish, but larger specimens that sometimes grow to a foot and a half in length can provide creditable light-tackle action. . . . Feeds mainly on insects, but can be caught on worms and lures as well as flies. . . . During spring spawning in nest of pebbles, male actually carries pebbles in mouth.

I know, I know. The chub competes with gamefish for food and space. The chub occasionally feeds on their fry. The chub can drive you straight up a tree trunk when you're casting to trout and it takes your fly. And as for eating qualities, as Thoreau said, the chub's flesh "tastes like brown paper salted." Nevertheless, I am convinced after myriad moments of disappointment and delight, irritation and gratitude, that this much maligned member of the fish family deserves a little drum-beating in its behalf.

First, let's make sure we're talking about the same subject. Unlike a rose, a chub is not necessarily a chub is not necessarily a chub. The fish normally referred to as "chub" actually is the fallfish (*Semotilus corporalis*), a member of the most heavily populated of fish families, Cyprinidae, whose more than 2,000 species include the goldfish, carp, and golden shiner. It has prominent scales on its silver sides, a back of black or brown, and gray or pale-pink fins. Dwelling in clear streams and lakes, the fallfish can attain 18 inches in length, although 8 to 12 inches is common.

Aside from its obvious attribute of providing gamefish with a vast and valuable source of food, the chub (for simplicity, let's dispense with subtle biological distinctions and standardize on this name) is a great day-saver. When high water prevented my two teen-age sons from fishing a Maine river, they cast worms and flies from a lakeside dock and had a delightful time catching chub. Often, in fact, chub have provided me with plenty of respectable action when nothing else would respond. True, they haven't the tenacity of a trout or the style of a salmon, but they're reasonably strong and reasonably fast and they usually are good for one or two rod-bending runs.

Probably the most memorable wallop my friend Charlie Pelletier ever received from any freshwater fish occurred while trolling the narrow channel between middle and lower Pierce Ponds in northwestern Maine. Dusk had fallen on a long day of hard but unproductive fishing. A loud splash followed immediately by a jarring yank convinced Charlie that he was on at last to one of the trophy brook trout for which this pond is famous. Nor did the fight that followed dissuade him of this conviction: a succession of short hard runs into the darkness that taxed the tiny 5-foot rod with which Charlie likes to troll these waters. Oh, to be sure, part of the excitement was a product of frustration after a disappointing day, part of it was in wondering and hoping what would come out of the darkness, but part of it also was attributable to a tough, strong, foot-and-a-quarter fish that was determined not to be caught.

"I've taken bigger salmon and trout," said Charlie, "that couldn't carry that fish's golf bag."

Frank Sheehan, unofficial world champion chub-catcher, has an almost arcane affinity for these fish. Frank could, it has been claimed, catch a chub in a corn chowder, and although I have seen him take them on all kinds of lures in all kinds of waters, I never have heard him complain.

"Usually," observes Frank wisely, "it's not a choice between chub and other fish; it's a choice between chub and nothing. I've had too much more-than-adequate action from chub to have any hesitation about making that choice."

Actually the chub is not an unattractive fish. Given a nose job and a dorsal sail, he could pass for the rare and much coveted grayling. But unlike the aristocratic grayling, the chub does not enjoy any aura of exclusiveness. He's just one of the masses, one of the common crowd, so that despite his admirable combination of availability, size, and cooperativeness, his fans are few.

Well, let it be known that my sons and I are among them, and in appreciation of the many pleasant memories the chub has given us, I offer this poetic paean:

> Rub a dub dub
> Three cheers for the chub,
> A friend of the fisherman, he.
> Though stolid and static
> And not acrobatic,
> He's there when you need him to be.

## BROOK TROUT

### *Salvelinus fontinalis*

Native of northeastern U.S. . . . Now found throughout North America as well as in parts of South America and Europe. . . . Brilliantly hued, with colors and shades varying with locality and season. . . . Need for unusually cold water plus destruction of clean remote habitat have made brookies of over 4 pounds a rarity anywhere except unspoiled wilds of Labrador. . . . Easy to catch on bait, flies, spinners, and small plugs. . . . Strong but not acrobatic fighter. . . . Sea-run variety known as "salter."

My cast was short and sloppy, and as I stripped in line after a minute-or-so delay to let my nymph settle to the bottom, I was sure I had snagged weeds. Too heavy, I thought, for a fish, especially in a suburban club pond that residents of northern Maine, where I had just concluded three

An Opening Day tournament on their fish and game club pond enabled this family to launch their trout season a week early.

days of trout fishing, would scoffingly call a puddle. Lifting my 4-ounce fly rod over my head, I tightened my line with my left hand preparatory to trying to jerk my hook free, when my rod was yanked downward like a dowsing switch over a subterranean sea.

The fish ran hard and stayed deep until my rod's unyielding resiliency wore it down. In less than three minutes I had beaten a 3½-pound brook trout, the biggest fish of its kind I ever had hooked.

I relate this incident for two reasons. First is that club ponds can make handy laboratories for fledgling fishermen. In a few sessions of intelligent angling, a child can learn a lot about trout: at which time of day and season they feed best, for example; where in the pond they tend to congregate, and why; that a nymph works best when retrieved in three short spurts followed by a pause; that a dry fly must be floated without drag if it is to fool a trout; that well-fished flies will consistently outproduce worms.

Without guidance, though, a child on a club pond can only enjoy, not appreciate, what he is doing. Many clubs hold clinics, blending a little basic biology and ecology with observations on the use and abuse of equipment, and this is good. But even better is for a boy to have his own personal grown-up teaching and learning right along with him.

My second point is that the brook trout is a pushover. Almost always ready to eat almost anything, from crickets to kernel corn, its battle is characteristically brief and unspectacular. Oh, there are times when brookies won't budge for a blinding mayfly hatch, and if there are underwater snags handy, brookies will make the best of them, but compared to browns and rainbows, brook trout are easy to entice and to beat.

So what makes the brook trout so special? Catch one in the kind of setting my young sons and I used to enjoy and you'll understand. On summer evenings we floated flies and drifted worms across the sapphire surface of a desolate little beaver pond set like a solitary gem in the hollow between two New Hampshire hills. Our only companions were beaver, who would cruise cautiously among the stumps until they saw us and with a thunderclap of their tails disappear, and red-winged blackbirds that swooped like bright ornaments among the gray trunks of rotting trees. And, of course, the trout: dark, wary, bright-hued, with a wiggly wildness to the lines on their broad black backs.

Gone forever? Ours is, yes. Too close to a new highway, it inevitably was discovered and despoiled by barbarians who fished it empty in a single season. But there are others. The woods are full of them. Drive into the country with your youngster. Not far. Just a few miles beyond the supermarkets and housing developments. You'll find a stream, and when you do, park your car, grab your rods, and follow its flow. Head upstream, away from the city, and you'll soon be in brook-trout country: deep cool pools where deer come to drink and quiet solitary stretches where your only competition might be an occasional otter. Here you will understand why brook trout are so special.

And while you're in the neighborhood, why not strip down, dive in, and join them?

## BROWN TROUT

### *Salmo trutta*

Native to Europe. . . . Introduced to U.S. in 1880s. . . . More tolerant than brook trout of warm water but less than rainbow. . . . Much more tolerant than either species of environmental changes. . . . This quality plus extreme wariness enables browns to grow big. . . . Generally golden-brown in color with brown,

Browns are wary. They spook easily. But it's worth the extra care it takes to fool one when you tie into one of these big spotted cannibals. (Photo: Massachusetts Department of Fish and Game)

black, orange, and red spots. . . . Anadromous variety, called sea trout (two words), and residents of large clear lakes that generally are silver with black spots, often mistaken for land-locked salmon. . . . Take bait and lures of all kinds, but best chance for big brown is with live minnows in shallows after dark.

I've never had much to do with brown trout. Or more accurately, they have never had much to do with me. Oh, I've caught many browns under a foot in length, but somehow the name "brown trout" summons up visions of big hook-jawed cannibals that prowl ponds' nighttime shorelines and preside over streams' bait-rich pools. Giants like these I have met only four times, and on each occasion I was taught a lesson.

Lesson #1 was administered many years ago on a brushy bend of the Squanocook River in south-central Massachusetts. On the inside of this bend, the river's constant currents had piled sand into a narrow curling bar behind which was a waist-high hole. Here, concealed by the bank and shaded by overhanging alders, any trout which appropriated this aquatic Automat could wait in comfort and security to ambush unwary bait.

One day I caught a trout out of this hole, a respectable 2-pound brown that ultimately fell for a nightcrawler drifted repeatedly past its lair. Two days later I returned and drifted another crawler through this same pool. I did it more out of sentiment than expectation, because I hadn't yet learned that a good hole that has been vacated by one trout is quickly taken over by another. The successor to my first brown, a good half-foot longer than its predecessor, taught me never to pass up a promising piece of water no matter how recently it's been fished.

Lesson #2 I learned the hard way. On a broad steep-banked bend in the upper Connecticut River, rainbows were rising to insects that a fresh rain was washing from upstream trees. With flyrod in one hand and worm-baited spinning rod in the other, I slid down the sandy banking. I had only four steps to go when I obeyed a compulsion to start fishing a few microseconds sooner and backhanded my worm into the water. I hadn't even reached the river's edge when a brown that should have been wearing a periscope rocketed up, grabbed my crawler, and headed for a partially submerged branch. A couple of quick in-and-out surges and it was all over: my 4-pound line, frayed by a spot of rust on my reel that I had been "too busy" to attend to, snapped with a heartbreaking pop.

Lesson #3 occurred during a drizzly evening on a long deep stretch of the forest-fringed Nissitissit River, just below the New Hampshire-Massachusetts border. Lingering to make a few more last-casts, I tied on the first lure I grabbed from the pocket of my vest, a brass hellgrammite, and reflected on how absurdly inaccurate an imitation it was: hellgrammites aren't shiny, nor do they move as fast or wiggle as wildly as a curved piece of stamped metal pulled across a fast current. But, I concluded, after three troutless hours, it couldn't make much difference which lure I used.

But it did. In that same water through which I had been pulling every traditional spoon, spinner, and plug I owned without so much as seeing a fish, that crazy counterfeit immediately started affecting browns the way catnip affects cats. Two and three at a time they rolled, some so big I thought their backs would never stop coming. When the spree subsided ten minutes later, I hadn't had a hit, but that, I suspect, was my fault: I almost had found the answer; a little more imagination, a little better improvising should have bridged the gap. Nevertheless, the show was spectacular, and in hopes of someday catching a rerun, I always carry a few crazy counterfeits in one of my vest pockets.

The next downstream bend on the same river was the scene of Lesson #4. Here I watched a man frantically casting spinners from a sandy spit for a half-hour trying to entice a big brown from under the branches of a fallen birch. Twice it had darted out, flashing its fat 2-foot form alongside their lures, but for twenty minutes now it had stayed put.

When the man departed in disgust, I waited the two or three minutes it took him to round the next upstream bend. Then, tying on a half-inch red-and-white spinner, I waded carefully onto the spit and in three casts had this 3½-pounder in my net. The man made no effort to hide his envy later when he saw my trout's tail dangling from the lip of my creel.

"You caught that fish under that fallen birch, didn't you? I cast to it till I thought my arms would fall off. What did you use?"

"Hardware," I answered, "same as you."

But it wasn't quite the same. There was, in fact, one difference, and this enabled me to succeed where he had failed. My lure had been only a third the size of his, and it had wobbled whereas his had whirled. That brown had demonstrated by its two earlier passes that it was primed to strike. After a half-hour during which this man had never changed either his lure or his retrieve, a different size and movement, following a few reassuring minutes during which no casts were made, were all it took.

# STEELHEAD

## *Salmo gairdneri*

Anadromous form of rainbow trout. . . . Return to spawn in specific spot in northwestern rivers where born. . . . Do not die after spawning. . . . Most return in winter, though a few streams have summer runs. . . . Normal span of 5 to 25 pounds. . . . Silver at sea but gradually resume spots and pink lateral stripe in fresh water.

I love New England so much that when I die I want to go to New England. Occasionally, my provincialism has prevented me from enjoying some of the U.S.A.'s feature attractions. Florida in the winter? Too hot. The Rocky

After living in the sea, the royal rainbow trout known as the steelhead returns to its natal stream to spawn and continue a glorious cycle that man, by imprudently polluting, building, lumbering, and mining, threatens to extinguish. (Photo: Washington Game Department)

Mountains? Too high. Atlanta? Houston? San Francisco? Too, too ... too bad, but they're just not Boston.

But in the tidal streams of northern California, I once encountered an attraction more beautiful, more romantic, more exciting than even the unlikely sight of the Boston Red Sox walloping the tar out of the Oakland Athletics. I refer, of course, to that glamorous vagabond, the steelhead.

To say that a steelhead is just a rainbow that runs to sea is like saying that Chateau Lafite-Rothschild 1959 is just a wine. Sure it's the truth and nothing but the truth, but the whole truth it most assuredly isn't. We have sea-run rainbows in our New England tidal streams, but even I am not so presumptuous as to dub them steelhead. Few if any of these fish are true ocean tourists like the Western steelhead. What happens is that when, in the normal course of seasonal events, water levels of tidal streams go down while their temperatures go up, these fish respond to increasing competition for a decreasing food supply by heading downstream. A summer in brackish bait-rich bays can fatten them to trophy size. The biggest I've come across (an outdoor-writing euphemism for "saw but couldn't catch") was on the short side of 2 feet, but in one instance, I have had saltwater rainbows reliably reported topping 10 pounds. This, incidentally, was in the Weir River just south of Boston, where anglers concentrate almost exclusively on cod, flounder, and striped bass. Back East, by the way, we also have a fair saltwater fishery of sea-run brook trout, called salters, and browns, called sea trout (two words), that warrants a lot more attention than it receives.

Ironically, during my Navy days I was literally surrounded by steelhead for two months while recommissioning a cruiser in Bremerton, Washington, yet I never fished for them. At the time, I didn't even know what a steelhead was. Along roads I drove on I saw sign after sign that read "Steelhead Stream," but I thought they were referring to some kind of hardhat bridge construction.

Years later during a business conference at the Boeing plant in Seattle I happened to glance out of the window at the Green River that flows nearby and almost called out the Coast Guard when I saw what looked to my East Coast eyes like an invasion fleet of surfacing submarines.

"Oh, sure," said one of my co-conferees as calmly as if he were commenting on the weather, "those are steelheads."

If I should outlast Methuselah, I shall never understand how anyone can remain calm while contemplating the power and majesty and drama of those marvelous creatures returning from thousands of miles at sea to their natal streams so they can replenish their species.

Eventually a midwinter business trip to California did provide me with an opportunity to try my hand at outwitting a real honest-to-gawd West Coast steelhead.

"A two-day seminar in Los Angeles, then run up to San Francisco for a contract negotiation."

As the boss was saying this, I was mentally reviewing coastal maps, license fees, and seasonal dates to consider what kind of piscine prey I might seek.

"Steelhead," I spouted suddenly.

"What?" asked the boss.

"Uh, uh, steal ahead when the other guy slows down," I replied, thinking fast. "That's the way to win a contract negotiation."

"Good show," said the boss.

Reading the article on the plane removed any doubt about my destination: a detailed discussion of late-season steelhead fishing in the coastal streams north of San Francisco, it was tailored to my requirements. In Los Angeles, a quick between-conference visit to the local fish and game office gave me my license, valuable counsel, informative booklets, plus the good wishes of state employees who must have chuckled at this presumptuous Yankee who expected, in a half-day of hurried fishing, to meet and beat the noble steelie.

Had I known more about this fish, I might have been less rash. As I soon learned, locating, luring, and most of all landing a steelhead are achievements that require mammouth measures of endurance, art, intelligence, and luck.

Endurance is needed for long cold hours in the high fast waters of fall and winter, when most of the steelheads come home. Art is required for laying out long loops of heavy-headed flyline or for bouncing bait along a snag-strewn bottom. Intelligence involves predicting fishes' routes and locating the layovers they rest in year after year. And luck? Well, what fisherman doesn't need an occasional kiss from Dame Fortune?

Luck, as it turned out, was against me. Local outdoor columnists were lamenting the recent rains that had converted the Russian, Gualala, and Garcia rivers to murky torrents. Weathermen sang the same dirge over my rented-car radio as I pirouetted my way through the foggy darkness.

And pirouetted is precisely the right word. That ride from the Russian River to Point Arena requires a Pavlova with four-wheel drive: the churning Pacific 10 feet to your left and what must be a mile and a quarter straight down; sheep pouring like snow squalls from the cloud-shrouded hillside on your right; turns so sharp and sudden you swear you just passed yourself going the other way.

A fast four fingers of nerve balm at a local bar was my first order of business after checking into my motel, and here for the hundredth time I received confirmation of my conviction that real fishermen are great guys. In this case it was two Japanese-Americans, one short, thin, thoughtfully bespectacled, the other fat and continually smiling.

"Sure," said Tom, the short one, "with all you've got going against you, you need all the help you can get. Follow us to Alder Creek in the morning."

Alder Creek's tidal pool has a sort of miniature magnificence, a cameo grandeur that makes you want to tip your hat before you start casting. It's small, maybe a cast and a half across, flanked on the left by a flotsam-fringed beach, on the right by a sheer red-clay cliff. In the sea beyond the dunes the steelies await the right time, the right tide, the final overflow of urgency that propels them in a swift compulsive thrust across the bar and into the waters of their birth.

Most of the dozen or so other anglers along the bank fished roe: a small gauze bag of steelhead eggs drifted and dragged along the creek's graveled bed. My companions, flymen who handled their stout rods and shooting lines with effortless authority, fished the head of the pool, a privileged place reserved for their lofty breed. I cast my favorite New England lure which, I provincially assumed, would revolutionize steelhead fishing but which, of course, did not.

We saw a few small fish, but only one was caught. Tom took it, a spent specimen scuffed and exhausted after its spawning ordeal, and when Tom released it, I watched fisherman rather than fish. There was respect and care and tenderness in what he did. It was a beautiful thing to see.

Back home in Massachusetts the needle was sharp: "Skunked again," scoffed the fireside fishermen. "Three thousand miles and not a fish to show for it." But my smile was impervious to their barbs. I had orbited the moon, swum the Hellespont, slain the dragon, scored the winning touchdown. I was Lancelot, General MacArthur, Louis Pasteur, Frank Merriwell. I, sir, had fished for steelhead.

Today as I look back on that celestial interlude, do you know what stands out most clearly? The absence of children fishing. Even during stopovers at the Gualala and Russian rivers on my way back to San Francisco, I saw only two boys, and they were bootlegging roe from fish they had snagged and slaughtered illegally.

Children ravaging a rare resource for a fast buck; lumber companies silting whole strains of steelhead out of existence; dams denying these fish the final fragile fulfillment of their biological cycles; the big-deal, take-it-for-granted calmness of a man in Seattle: surely a century ago in Massachusetts someone must have seen similar symptoms when dams and dyes and sewage were decimating the droves of Atlantic salmon that had swarmed up the Merrimack and Connecticut rivers since long before factories replaced its forests.

Registering the catch at a shad derby. Nowhere can your youngster enjoy more intimacy with the fish he seeks than when standing in a shallow tidal stream while honeymooning shad shatter the night with their nuptial splashes and even graze occasionally off his waders. (Photo: Massachusetts Department of Fish and Game)

## AMERICAN SHAD

*Alosa sapidissima*

Anadromous member of herring family.... Spawns during spring in coastal but not necessarily natal streams.... Normally does not die after spawning.... Eastern streams from St. Lawrence to St. Johns in Florida, with peak sport in Connecticut.... Larger (2-8 pounds) than Southern cousin, the hickory (1-3 pounds).... Excellent, often aerobatic fighter.... Landing net needed for soft mouth.... Successful 1871 transplant in Sacramento River.... Now caught from southern California to Alaska, with best action in northern California.

"In the spring a young man's fancy ... " Likewise shad. When days start getting longer than nights, and mornings are launched with a thousand golden dandelion winks from lately greened lawns, and fresh cool air cascades into your lungs like mountain streams flowing through shaded ravines, then it is that the American shad comes home.

Home is the headwaters of coastal streams, often the very one in which it was born. Following two to five years in the ocean, the shad returns in the spring of the year with salt on its tail and a gleam in its eye to head upstream and spawn. The stream can be big, like the Connecticut and Susquehanna of the East, the St. Johns of the South, and the American and Russian of the West, or it can be one of the countless small creeks that filigree our coastal shoreline. Each presents its own special assortment of pleasures and problems, and both are guaranteed to give a boy a day—or a night—he'll never forget.

Nights are best on small streams, not just for the action, which apparently increases after dark, but also for the eerie excitement of an environment which sometimes has 5- and 6-pound fish slashing, slapping, swirling all about you and occasionally even walloping you in the waders.

Customarily shad are caught in these shallow headwaters by standing still and dangling a tiny jig in the current an inch or two off the bottom. The jig, shaped like an inverted ice cream cone with a whisk of bucktail or nylon surrounding the hook at its apex, is called a shad dart. Normally emblazoned with red-and-white or red-and-yellow stripes, the dart is best fished absolutely motionless except for the almost imperceptible vibration imparted to it by the current. Irritating rather than appetizing, the dart is pecked at by the nesting shad, telegraphing their tender fleeting taps to fishermen who twitch their rods incessantly like so many cows in fly time. The taps are so soft, so brief, that a fish is hooked, oh, maybe once out of every 30 twitches by an inexperienced angler, maybe once out of 10 after you've developed microsecond-fast reflexes.

When you hook a shad it's worth waiting for. In these tight waters a struck shad goes utterly berserk. I once had one explode less than a rod length in front of me, leap three times while scooting across a 15-foot-wide pool, and break me off on an alder branch dangling 6 inches off the water before I could so much as raise my rod tip above horizontal.

First time your boy finds himself fast to a rampaging shad, let him try to tame it himself, even if this means chasing it downstream in the dark. He'll probably nosedive a few times, but these streams are shallow and there will be plenty of other anglers ready to lend a hand in the rare event of an emergency. I was over thirty when I took off on my first 100-yard, over-my-waders, flat-on-my-face chase of an oceanbound shad. Twenty minutes later as I sat dripping on the bank marveling at the performance of the 5-pound roe fish I'd just released, I wished it had happened twenty, yes, even twenty-five years earlier.

Half-to-three-quarter-inch wet flies also are effective on small streams, especially if they're either white or brightly colored and assembled on gold hooks. A small split shot crimped onto your line immediately ahead of your hook's eye, or copper wire wound around its shank, will hold the fly near the bottom. Patterns seem to matter little. Size, depth, and brightness are what count.

Even bare gold hooks work well, with or without a few red beads and a small spinner above them. I once stood in a pool full of dart-danglers and watched a man take three fish in an infuriatingly rapid row on an unadorned gold hook while the rest of us couldn't buy a bite between us.

Darts and hook-bead-spinner combinations also have been high scorers in big rivers where I've fished for shad, but not by being suspended motionless near the bottom. That's how I began first time I fished the big brawling Connecticut from an anchored boat. Big stream or small, I figured, a shad is a shad. After a half-hour of watching local anglers fighting fish while I fought only an increasingly strong urge to dive in and hook one by hand, I looked closely and discovered the difference in our methods. They were casting upcurrent, letting their lures swing through an arc of about 120°, and then retrieving in short, jerky spurts. As soon as I started following their example, I hooked fish on almost every cast.

Hooked, but not necessarily caught. When a 4- or 5-pound shad streaks to midstream, bores deep, and turns its broad profile to the current, it puts a hazardously heavy strain on anything less than eight-pound-test line. If the line doesn't break, the shad's soft mouth probably will, so keep a landing net handy. Fishing from shore, even though the current is likely to be less strong than in midstream, isn't necessarily easier. The banks usually are so lined with anglers that you have no choice but to stand your ground and play your fish with patience and sensitivity. When a youngster lands a 5-pound shad under these conditions, he's earned his fish.

I wish I could report that shad are as good to eat as they are to catch. Some people enjoy them despite their bones and bland flavor, but the two I've tried have tasted like papier-mâché pincushions. Even their highly touted roe I find unappetizing, but I attribute this more to a squeamish, unadventurous, meat-and-potatoes appetite than to any deficiency on the part of marinated shad eggs broiled in bacon.

If your boy shouldn't care for shad or shad roe, tell him not to be disappointed. Remind him that what he misses out on at mealtime should more than be made up for in the knowledge that when he releases a fish, he might be making a down payment on a date a few years hence with one of its offspring.

## WINTER FLOUNDER

*Pseudopleuronectes americanus*

One of over 200 species in Atlantic and Pacific oceans.... Commonly found in shallow water from Canada to the Chesapeake.... Color ranges from gray to dark-spotted brown.... Best known as bay fish commonly weighing around a pound, although in deeper water sometimes grow to 8-pound "snow-shoes".... Move frequently seeking waters of moderate temperature.... A dextral, or "right-handed," species in that both eyes are on right side of head looking forward.... Tiny mouth limits diet to small worms, fish, and crustaceans, requiring small hook.

If any saltwater fish was made for children, it's the flounder. Easy to find and easy to entice, its respectable light-tackle tussles can be crowned with one of the best meals the oceans have to offer. (Photo: Terry McDonnell)

The secret of successful fishing for winter flounder is water temperature. Because they are sensitive to seasonal changes, these fish move inshore and off according to a schedule whose predictability can almost guarantee action for the intelligent angler. When newspapers announce phenomenal flattie catches in early spring or late fall, most readers just moan about not having been there.

"Lucky stiffs," they lament. "Boy, if I'd known those fish were going to be in, I'd sure have been there too."

But they did know. The blitzing of inshore waters by winter flounder is as vernally dependable an event as returning robins, blooming crocuses, and the traditional turning of a young man's fancy. Not only is this an ideal time for bottom-fishing with your boy from an anchored boat, but it's also an opportunity to launch your surf-casting season better than a month before striped bass arrive. Clam necks or seaworms anchored to a sandy bay bed with pyramid sinkers have snared many an inaugural flounder for son Jack and me, and occasionally we've won a bonus of 10-to-20-pound codfish in the bargain.

Autumn action can be even better. After a summer offshore, winter flounder return to fall-cooled shallows in numbers that literally pave great areas of bay bottom. Recently I received a letter from a New Jersey reader on my *Angler's News* column describing an early-November pilgrimage a friend of his makes to Quincy, Massachusetts, just south of Boston. Driving 330 miles nonstop, he fishes from nine to one o'clock and then turns around and drives home. What makes him endure this masochistic marathon? More than 240 flounder last trip, that's what. I know that a fish a second sounds almost like a mathematical impossibility, but flounder are easily caught, two and even more at a time on multiple-hook rigs such as spreaders. Nevertheless the numbers are awesome, and in the opinion of my correspondent, they also are extravagant. "An endurance contest" is what he calls it.

Once you've located winter flounder, it's easy to catch them, but only if your hook is small enough to fit into their tiny mouths. Try a #8 or smaller, and make sure it's long-shanked so it can be extracted easily. Flounder tend to gulp a bait, swallowing it so fast that even a quickly set hook is likely to imbed its barb deep in the fish's throat.

Ingenious devices have been designed for delivering chum to flounder. One is a weighted box full of ground bait that has a spring-loaded cover. When the box reaches bottom, the cover is jerked loose, releasing the chum. Simpler but equally effective is a wide-mesh cloth bag containing a block of frozen ground bait that is tied to the anchor chain just above the anchor. But even the slight stirring of a muddy bottom when you bounce a heavy sinker can activate flounder's appetite.

Flounder are as enjoyable in the eating as in the catching. Even children, who ordinarily aren't fond of fish, like its firm sweet fillets rolled in flour and fried in butter. Filleting flounder can be a chore if you don't know how, so watch someone with experience before you try it. Otherwise you'll wind up with a few small bits of meat instead of a single solid slab. As with all species, the secret of successfully filleting flounder is to use a super-sharp knife.

# ATLANTIC COD

## *Gadus morhua*

Party-boat favorite. . . . Best known as bit bottom dweller in summer, when rod and reel catches close to 100 pounds are made off New England coast. . . . Less well known are spring and fall migrations when cod can be caught from the surf. . . . Big jigs jerked close to bottom or bait such as clams most popular in deep water, but ravenous appetites make almost anything that's edible appealing. . . . Can be either gray or reddish brown. . . . Close kin and neighbor of haddock and pollock.

The cod is not a clod. This misconception is about on a par with calling Mae West a man, yet for many years I, like most marine anglers in the Northeast, whose cod-catching had been limited to winching a few aboard boats from deep water in midseason, scoffed at the codfish's credentials as a sport fish. Steaked and broiled? Unbeatable. Chunked in chowder? Incomparable. But beyond a little bucking and bulldogging and a few rod-bending runs, well, let's face it—acrobatic, Old Musclemouth ain't. A hernia, I figured, is a hernia no matter how you get it.

Then I joined son Jack for a crack at curtain-raiser cod in a chilly April surf and became an instant fan of this brawny, back-alley brawler. While admittedly no substitute for the classy main-event action of stripers and bluefish off the beach, the cod offers an irresistible combination of size, strength, aggressiveness, and availability that starts long before bass and blues arrive and lingers long after they've left.

"The trouble with most codfishermen," a friend once observed, "is that they're looking for the wrong qualities. They're like the drinker who expects to find the body and flavor and aroma of a vintage wine in a boilermaker. Cod are shot-and-a-beer fish."

April and October generally are the best months for beach, pier, and jetty fishing in the Northeast. Most shore-caught cod are under 20 pounds, although in Rhode Island recent autumn migrations have produced some over 40. I have seen impressive midwinter catches of 5-to-10-pounders by well-insulated pier anglers, but as a rule, bigger cod move offshore winter and summer.

Two of the cod's qualities make it easy to catch: it's a bottom feeder, and it has an appetite like a garbage disposal. When casting from the beach, use bait that's tough and durable enough to stay on a large heavy hook such as a #5/0 O'Shaughnessy. A strip of squid, a blob of skimmer clam, or the neck of a steamer clam work best; crabs, herring (whole or in hunks), and seaworms also are used.

Pyramid sinkers hold well on a mud or sand bottom, but over rocks use a bank type to minimize hangups. Sinker weight, of course, depends on current: the faster the flow, the heavier the sinker. With weights of

Big, strong, plentiful codfish are a good choice for dads who are anxious to get their youngsters into heavyweight fishing. Customarily cod are caught close to bottom in deep water, but their close-to-shore feeding sprees in early spring and late fall enable surfcasters to stretch their seasons by several weeks.

more than 3 ounces, it's especially easy for youngsters to snap lines. For this reason, as well as because of the possibility of tagging a heavyweight, use 20-pound-test-or-heavier line. The same surf-casting tackle you use on stripers is fine for cod.

Some anglers even use surf rods on party boats, but only as a means of avoiding tangles with close-in lines. A stiff 5-to-6-foot rod with revolving-spool reel is ideal, even for a youngster, and these often are available for rent on party boats. Droplines work well, but heavy gloves are a must. Bait just a foot or two off the bottom is the ticket over offshore reefs and wrecks, with shiny bouncing jigs a close runner-up.

## ATLANTIC MACKEREL

### *Scomber scombrus*

School fish whose vast hordes provide anglers north of Cape Hatteras with steady fast action. . . . Absence of swim bladder requires that they keep moving to acquire air. . . . Supremely good light-tackle gamefish. . . . Respond to chumline and strike small shiny fluttering jig most readily.

Mackerel and children were made for each other. A child craves plenty of first-class action on easy-to-manage tackle in easy-to-get-to waters, and the mackerel's special combination of aggressiveness, distribution, and availability fills this bill to the brim. In few other fish are quality and quantity better blended. Best of all, they're active when other species are in their midsummer doldrums.

To locate mackerel, it's necessary to know a little bit about their habits. Migrating northward as waters warm, vast schools of these silver-green 1-to-3-pound fish sometimes extend over acres of ocean. Because they have no swim bladder, they have to keep moving to maintain an adequate supply of oxygen. As a result, mackerel fishermen must continually seek new schools or devise ways to attract and keep them close.

While mackerel can be caught easily from shore, especially from rocky points and jetties against which they often herd schools of baitfish such as sparling and sand eels, this is a hit-or-miss proposition: you must wait for a passing school, and once it moves on, you have no choice but to wait again. When my boys and I have mackerel on our minds, we prefer to anchor our small boat about a half-mile offshore in 20 to 50 feet of water and follow this three-step procedure.

First, we anchor near other boats already fishing for mackerel, some

A school of mackerel can provide all the action per hour that a youngster can handle. My son Jack likes to make the most of their underrated fighting qualities by catching them on a fly rod.

of which are likely to be chumming with ground bait to attract foraging schools.

Second, we chum. We mix a can of cat food in a gallon plastic container of seawater, then ladle out a half cup of the soup about once every twenty seconds until rods start bucking. Then we double our chumming tempo to keep the mackerel's appetites whetted.

Third, we begin our fishing by dropping shiny diamond-shaped jigs to the bottom, jerking and letting them settle four or five times, reeling in a half-dozen turns and repeating the process until we reach the surface. Then we begin again. When one of us hits fish, he announces the number of turns he's reeled in, thereby enabling the rest of us to reach the right depth without delay.

The rig we use depends on whether we're interested in filling our freezer or having fun. Mackerel are eminently qualified for both. Hundreds of them can be caught three and four at a time in very short order by stringing five and six jigs about eight inches apart on 20-pound-test monofilament, but this kind of fishing soon gets tiring. Furthermore, it doesn't do justice to this bantam battler.

The boys and I, we fish for both food and sport. Occasionally, in fact, we even catch mackerel for bait: 8-to-12-inchers kept alive in well-oxygenated water are prime striper fare, and chunks on the bottom have brought many a bluefish to beach. After boating a couple of meals for family and friends, Dan grabs our ultralight spinning rod and starts jigging, Jack casts weighted brightly tinseled flies, and I . . . well, somebody's got to man the chum bucket.

# WEAKFISH

### *Cynoscion regalis*

Plentiful and pugnacious April to November along Atlantic Coast. . . . Water temperature determines time and duration of stay. . . . Best action Chesapeake-New-Jersey-Peconic Bay, Long Island. . . . Recently revitalized after long decline. . . . Generally 1-4 pounds with occasional tide-runner to 10 or better. . . . Eat worms, squid, small fish, and shrimp. . . . Soft

If you can chum in a school of weakfish and hold them around your boat, you can assure your youngster of a day to remember. Note the big fork-tailed bluefish that also adorns these boys' stringer.

mouth makes landing net necessary. . . . Prefer shoals and shallow grass-fringed bays and creeks, but found where food is, including surf. . . . Tip: try small jig off lighted dock at night.

The common weakfish (or squeteague or seatrout, take your pick) is neither common nor weak. Until the late forties they were plentiful south of Cape Cod, but about the time I was becoming smart enough to appreciate their annual invasions and old enough to borrow the old man's car to exploit them, World War II intervened. Nine years later, when I was able at last to mothball my dress blues and dust off my waders, the squets had disappeared, faded into one of their inexplicably cyclical declines.

Then a few years back Arnold Clark, whose rusty red eyebrows rarely are raised for anything less than a 30-pound striped bass, told me about a mother lode of spring squets he had hit down by the Rhode Island border. Heading south like a suitor about to keep a long-delayed date with a childhood sweetheart, I caught over a dozen of these classy colorful creatures on my freshwater fly rod from the muddy fringes of a shallow brackish bay, and we have lived happily ever after.

The catching was not as easy as it sounds. I hooked fish on three of my first five casts with a half-ounce bucktail jig and lost every one. This is what the "weak" in weakfish refers to: their mouths. Just a little excess pressure pulls your hook through a squet's mouth as if it were wet paper.

Ah, but on a 4-ounce fly rod! This is a match made in heaven. By drifting a mudworm with just enough weight to keep it a foot or two off the bottom, I watched my rod bend clear to the water, under the boat, and in one instance clear out the other side.

The squet is as pretty as she is pugnacious. Long, sleek, slender, and gracefully proportioned, the olive of her back and the iridescent greens and purples and blues of her sides appear to be burnished to a gleaming golden glow.

From the Chesapeake area south, the spotted weakfish, with its dark dots displacing the mottled splotches of the squet, is the regional species; in the Gulf, their smaller cousins, the sand and silver, predominate.

A ravenous appetite makes the squet a cooperative quarry at any time when the water is at least moderately warm and salty and on almost any bait—crabs, squid strips, mudworms, mummichogs, and especially sand shrimps—as well as any lure that accurately imitates these baits.

Because the squet is especially sensitive to noise, a blitz can abruptly become a blank when an oar is carelessly dropped or a motor inadvertently gunned. Nights, however, after boat traffic has tapered off, draw squets in close. Then you and your youngster can enjoy fast fishing from brightly lighted piers and jetties, but for real eye-popping excitement, fish in the dark from an anchored boat and let the lad listen to the spooky croaks of a big male squet. (The female of the species is uncharacteristically quiet.)

## BLUEFISH

### *Pomatomus saltatrix*

Rough, tough, rapacious. . . . Swift-moving schools slaughter anything that moves, including small "snapper" blues, thus schools tend to consist of same-size fish. . . . Mainly found on Atlantic Coast in U.S., but also appear in most warm seas. . . . Migrate from Florida in spring to New England in June, heading south with October storms. . . . Long periods of unexplained absence. . . . Deep-water residents, but will invade surf. . . . Gulls usually mark schools feeding on surface. . . . Sharp teeth can sever fingers as well as lines. . . . Best fishing in memory during late 1960s and early 1970s.

When fast-moving bluefish kept scooting out of range of Martha's Vineyard shore casters, this young man solved the problem by chasing them in his kayak.

"Everything that happens prior to your first blue," maintain bluefish devotees, "is just practice." Sleek, swift, and savage, the blue is endowed with a deadly beautiful blend of grace, strength, and stamina. Its jut-jawed, thresher-mouthed construction is one of nature's most efficient fusions of form and function. Children will marvel at their airborne head shaking shenanigans and regard their wild don't-give-a-damn donnybrooks as among angling's most exciting experiences. Young children also will get scared out of their skivvies if they tangle too soon with too big a bluefish. My first blue, a 10½-pounder, hit my trolled eelskin off Cuttyhunk's fabled shore about ten minutes after I had boated a 37-pound striped bass, and so help me, I thought I had tied into the bass's granddaddy.

Fortunately there are plenty of small 7-to-9-inch snapper blues in shoreline shallows from Cape Cod to Florida during the bluefishing season. From about mid-January to March, schools move westward into southern Florida waters, heading north to arrive in force in Cape Cod waters about mid-June. Autumn storms and tumbling temperatures send them south again, usually about mid-October.

After a few bouts with smaller blues, your youngster will be ready to take on the big ones. They shouldn't be hard to find. Although a deepwater fish by nature, blues frequently feed topside. When they do, the carnage and commotion are pinpointed by screaming gulls wheeling and diving for scraps of the bluefish's victims. When fish are visible, you might try coaxing them up with a chumslick of ground fish such as the oily strong-scented menhaden. Otherwise swing a deep-trolled lure along the down-current edges of tidal rips where blues often wait to ambush bait tossed about in the turbulence. Blues also can be caught in the surf, usually early and late in the day before baitfish move out to deeper cooler water. In these cases gulls usually announce their presence.

Because bluefish in a feeding frenzy will ravage almost anything that moves, including an occasional gull that gets careless about picking up scraps, you can catch them during these binges on anything from spoons to plugs, from jigs to bait. They do, however, travel fast and spook easily, so position your boat ahead and off to the side of a feeding school and cast a few feet ahead of the school rather than into its midst. Popping plugs and shiny tin squids work well morning and evening. Deep-trolled bucktail jigs with porkrind tails are excellent daytime producers. A chunk of butterfish or mackerel swinging a foot or so off the bottom is effective in both daytime and nighttime surf. Always, of course, precede your lure with a foot or two of braided steel leader as protection against the blue's super-sharp bite.

On bait, a bluefish's strike is likely to be casual and undistinguished: no marauding eruption, as with a topwater plug, but a sudden stiffening of your line, more of a pull than a jerk, followed by a steady fast run. Don't be disappointed, and above all, don't let your lad drop his guard. Once he sets that hook he'll have his hands full. Pressure, pressure, pressure to keep the fish coming is essential. The slightest slack against the fish's perpetual shaking of its head and chomping of its teeth is likely to mean a lost fish. And this applies even after his blue has been boated; even after it has been rapped two or three times between the eyes with the billy you always should have handy. Blues die hard, and they like nothing better than to make their last meal of their executioner's fingers.

One final suggestion: Catch your bluefish while the catching's good. Blues, alas, come and go in cycles, abounding throughout their range for years at a time, then suddenly becoming scarce as half-ton tuna. In 1971 bluefish schools swarmed north of Gloucester, Massachusetts, for the first time since the mid-1800s; even Down Easters enjoyed the action off the mouths of rivers in southern Maine. While there are those who say that blues peaked in '71 and that their marvelous midsummer rampages will soon be just a memory, subsequent summers have neither confirmed nor denied this prediction for the Fallons. Nevertheless, we're taking no chances. When there's an opportunity for us to fish for blues, we take it.

## STRIPED BASS

*Roccus saxatilis*

Real name changed a few years back to *Marone saxatilis*, but devotees retain traditional name. . . . As one said, "That's like asking me to call my wife George". . . . Called "rockfish" south of New Jersey. . . . Handsome migratory saltwater gamefish with greenish-black back, silver sides, white belly with seven or eight dark lengthwise stripes along scale rows. . . . Often caught in tidal rips and close to rocky shores. . . . Takes bait on bottom, plugs and streamer flies on top, and most anything in between. . . . On East Coast found mostly between South Carolina and Maine, but extends to Nova Scotia and Florida. . . . Some in Gulf between Florida and Louisiana. . . . Successful West Coast transplant in 1886, now ranging from Washington to Los Angeles. . . . Successful freshwater transplants in such places as North Carolina's Kerr Reservoir and South Carolina's Santee Cooper.

Surf casting with little girls can be hazardous to anyone within hooking range, but as Margaret and Julie proved on their first try for stripers, it also can be productive.

"How do I love thee? Let me count the ways . . . " If Elizabeth Barrett Browning hadn't penned these lines about her beloved Robert, I probably would have done so about the striped bass. Once an editor responded to my adulatory remarks about stripers by saying he couldn't understand why so many people get so excited about a single species.

"After all," he said, "they're just another gamefish."

Maybe, after fishing the world over, this man knows something about stripers that I don't know. If he does, I hope I never learn it. We're very happy together, *Roccus* and me.

Once an old-timer alongside whom I was fishing a Cape Cod creek spoke disparagingly of the striper.

"Can't compare with the bluefish," he scoffed. "Not in the same league."

And indeed they're not. But once during a foggy long-ago dawn off Cuttyhunk I had my choice and picked bass.

Sprawled for what must have been a half-acre alongside our 26-foot MacKenzie were frantic butterfish sandwiched helplessly between attackers from below and screaming swooping gulls from above. The fog and the din and the frenzy gave the scene a kind of claustrophobic intensity. First aboard was a blue of about 8 pounds. Gaffed and clubbed, its vicious teeth still chattering menacingly as I extracted the hook, it vomited un-chewed chunks of its victims before another wallop between its angry eyes put it permanently out of commission. When, seconds later, my line snapped taut, I remember saying to myself, "Hope it's a bass."

It was, also an 8-pounder, but the resemblance ended there. Its fight was hard, straightforward, and purposeful, with the same splendidly dis-ciplined kind of style that Joe Louis in his heyday employed to bewilder hapless opponents. When this bass came aboard, it was because our fight was over. It had given its best against reasonable odds and its best hadn't been enough. No sour grapes, no trying to chomp a chunk out of the nearest finger. Vanquished, it lay on the deck with its dorsal high, like a flagbearer with his banner unfurled. I swear, if that bass had had hands, it would have saluted.

Okay, so I romanticize. That's a privilege of poets and middle-aged Irishmen. I suppose when you come right down to the marrow, I'm simply revealing a piece of my own personality, a preference for the combative code of a medieval joust for mortal stakes over the ruthless ravaging of a crazed killer. I love 'em both, make no mistake. In my celestial tidal rips there will be plenty of bluefish waiting to take me on. It's just that there will be more bass, that's all.

And now, having stated my preference, I suppose I am obliged to respond to the inevitable questions about which bass were the most this and the most that and why. Fair enough. Here are some of the stars from my gallery of greats.

## THE FIRST

William Harvey Jagoe, my Annapolis roommate, was renowned for his self-discipline. Plebe year and parades and the captaincy of Navy's tennis team prepared him well for the supreme test of his composure when, as regimental commander, he was passing in review before a plat-form of dignitaries and raised his sword to his head, bellowed "Eyeeees right," thrust his blade forward ... and stuck it into the ground. That he left it there for two thousand midshipmen to march around was regarded by his classmates, if not by the administration, as the greatest example of nautical cool since Dewey cruised casually into Manila Bay.

I expected more of Harvey, therefore, when several years later I hooked my first striped bass from his 12-foot outboard in Maine's York River. Though only a 6-pounder, that fish played the current perfectly, zigging, it seemed, every time we zagged. Harve at the con wiggled and wobbled our craft till it put a strain on my light line and soft drag far beyond what they were designed to endure, and his attempts to net the poor bewildered beast resembled Pancho Gonzales swatting mosquitoes. Terry, Harve's teen-age daughter, sat amidships spellbound by her daddy's salty dialogue.

The catching of one's first striper makes a fisherman feel more accomplished, more secure. Next time tall tales are told, he can talk as well as listen. As an angler, I felt, after landing this fish, that I had earned my first pair of long pants. As an American citizen, however, my confidence had been demolished. Harve was currently flying planes off aircraft carriers.

## THE SMALLEST

A mere 9 inches, but what this cocky little squirt lacked in size it made up in moxie. I caught it on a live eel more than a foot long!

## THE BIGGEST

When it hit I was unprepared. I had just removed a kink from my Monel line and was waiting for my plug to start pulsating as skipper Charlie Haag wiggled it through the foamy turbulence of Cuttyhunk's Sow and Pig's Reef. For a first-timer, the blackness of the night, the bouncing of the boat, and the closeness of the swells booming over submerged—and sometimes not so submerged—boulders was terrifying.

Out here where world records are set, it's easy to convince yourself that immortality is just around the corner. With a novice's exuberance, you dwell on it, ignoring the millions of angling hours that have gone into producing a single 73-pounder, and when the jarring yank slams you against the transom, you wonder if Skipper Haag will be wanting to scoot right into Cuttyhunk to weigh in your new record or if he'll wait a bit and see if you can top it on the next pass.

It was a 45-pounder, this fish, a fine, firm, deep-bellied, barrel-chested brute that I gazed at long and kind of sadly until the great Haag shattered my reverie with a raucous reminder that I was on a fishing trip, not attending a wake.

## THE ONE THAT GOT AWAY

It was in Quick's Hole at the tail end of an all-nighter during which Bill Nolan, after better than a half-century of hard persistent fishing, had caught his first striper over 60 pounds. Wobbling our plugs through the rip, Skipper Frank Sabatowski had just finished reminding us that Bill's cow might have a cousin or two hereabouts looking for breakfast when my line stiffened as if it had snagged a speeding submarine. One, two, three screeching runs and it was all over. No more than a second or two. "Twang" went the wire as my plug slingshotted back through the darkness. Sabby was furious, thinking I had set my drag too soft, until he checked it: tight, maybe even a little too tight. I remember clearly his rugged rumpled features as he handed it back. "Some fish," he said. "Yeah, that was some fish."

## THE MOST MEMORABLE

Picture it: a soft dawn, a fish on, and the only one around to share it is a big deer high on its hind legs frolicking in the surf not 50 yards away.

## THE BEST

But most of all, I suppose you'll want to know which striper I consider best, and I'm going to tell you because it's an easy question to answer. My best striper is always the same: my next one, of course.

# DOLPHIN

### Coryphaena hippurus

Superb fighter, supremely beautiful, gourmet eating. . . . Widely distributed throughout warm offshore waters of both Atlantic and Pacific. . . . Normal size range of 5 to 50 pounds. . . . Also called dorado, *mahi-mahi*. . . . Not a fussy eater but partial to small fish, especially flying fish.

Dolphin are regarded by many as the most beautiful fish in the sea. Certainly they are among the ocean's best fighters. Never let your child catch one without pausing for a moment to contemplate the chromatic drama of death as gold and blue and green and silver fade to a funereal gray. (Photo: Metropolitan Miami Fishing Tournament)

One of the ironies of angling is that the dolphin, possessing probably what is creation's most distinctive blend of color, form, fight, and flavor, doesn't even have a name of its own. Mention dolphin to your youngster and he'll think of that whalelike mammal, the bottlenose porpoise, that befriends children, forecasts storms, and catches all those bad guys on TV.

Let him just once see a school streaking behind your boat after a trolled bait, though, and he'll never confuse the two again. The dolphin's chase is furiously fast, its strikes savage and unrestrained. Once hooked, it fights as hard as any fish in the sea, and it's as acrobatic as it is aggressive.

No one can watch a dolphin's dying unmoved. Within minutes of being boated, its kaleidoscopic riot of shimmering iridescent blues and greens and golds fades into the dull plain pallor of death. Nowhere in nature is there a more eloquent or urgent reminder that no creature's death can be taken casually. Just as flaming summer sunsets and flamboyant autumn foliage signal the expiration of another day, another year, the dolphin's transformation links life and death.

Because dolphins are offshore fish, often found in warm bluewater around seaweed rips, they are caught most frequently by trollers seeking sailfish or marlin. This does not exclude young children from having a crack at them, however. School dolphins are often found concentrated around patches of seaweed, and respond readily to shiny spoons and plugs skipped across a calm surface. In fact, any object floating well offshore in dolphin country is likely to have some hanging around it, so make a few casts close by any flotsam you happen to come across.

Once found, a school of dolphin is easy to keep around your boat. A chum of ground bait works well. Also a hooked fish kept in the water.

Many people consider the dolphin the finest eating as well as fighting fish in the sea. Certainly I'm not about to argue with them. They have too much evidence to back up their claims.

# 5.
# Fishing Locales

~~~~~~~~~~~~~~~~~~~~~~~~~~~~~~~~~~~~~~~~~~

## SHORE OF POND

The best thing about just plain ponds is that they're everywhere. Even the city-builders usually manage to leave at least a symbolic splash here and there, and that's about all you need for shore fishing, that plus a minimum of equipment and an acknowledgment that you're not likely to rewrite any record books.

Early in my married life I worked in a southern New Hampshire city. Industry and sewage had converted its once lovely pair of rivers into conduits of corruption, but sequestered here and there along the city's wooded fringes were a few ponds where panfish still thrived and anglers were still welcome. Often when I had a free half-hour I would reconnoiter down side roads in search of some secret place I'd heard a resident refer to in an unguarded moment or that I'd discovered tucked away among the wiggly contours of the topographical maps I was forever studying.

When a pond looked promising I would grab a rod from the arsenal I always carried in my trunk, tie on a spinner or a plug, and cast close to lily pads and pickerel weed and brook mouths. If it produced, suppertime would be spent discussing my discovery: access, color, and composition of the water, composition and shape of its shoreline, number and kind of cottages. By the end of dessert, my four- and five-year-old sons and I would have completed our battle for a weekend assault.

Our strategy rarely varied: throw out a worm and wait for the bobber to start bouncing. Perch and sunfish always provided plenty of action,

You don't have to travel far to find a pond you can fish from the shore. An imaginative youngster can convert the lowliest puddle into a wilderness lake, and without half trying, so can you. (Photo: Terry McDonnell)

and occasionally a pickerel or small largemouth would remind us of bigger things to come. For a few years, though, the shorelines of simple ordinary ponds were just fine for a father getting back to fishing after a long wartime interruption and his two sons who were just starting.

In time we accumulated quite a collection of ponds. Among our favorites was one close by a highway that we traveled going to and from our summer home in the Monadnock Mountains of southwestern New Hampshire. Even after a weekend on one of the state's largest and loveliest lakes, in which we often caught rainbow and brook trout as well as an occasional landlocked salmon, we always added a half-hour to our two-hour drive home so we could stop by for some bluegill fishing.

Recently, like an old and faithful friend, a pond from out of my past came to our rescue when Peg and I drove to Cape Cod to celebrate a dear couple's fiftieth wedding anniversary. We arrived at daybreak, plugged the Canal for a few hours with no success, and then passed a pleasant half-hour sitting on the steep bouldered bank sipping coffee and watching the ships chug by.

With what we thought was plenty of time left, we drove a few miles out of our way to Cape Cod Bay, trudged across the dunes, and caught flounder in the mouth of our favorite creek until, according to Peg's schedule, it was time to go. Peg's schedule, however, was an hour slow, as we learned by phoning the friends in whose home we were planning to change from fishing to party clothes.

If Peg was puzzled when I turned off the highway and down a wooded dirt road, the lady rocking on her porch across the street from the turnoff must have been even more so when we came out. Like a metamorphosed butterfly, my wife, who had entered the woods wadered and rumpled, emerged fifteen minutes later with hair carefully coiffed and regally arrayed in an ankle-length gown.

During those fifteen minutes, by the way, I managed to catch one pickerel. Considering the heavy brush, mucky shoreline, and weedy water, this was no small achievement, but I don't brag about it any more. Not after a friend reminded me that with my beautiful wife making like Gypsy Rose Lee in the bushes behind me, my catching a pickerel was more indicative of old age than piscatorial prowess.

This pond was representative of most warm-water ponds, where weeds and mud make wading difficult. Without a boat to move you along the shore, you'll have to settle for staying put and waiting for the fish to come to you. One advantage to stay-put fishing is that you can work two rods: while casting with one, you can fish bait on the bottom with a second that you have propped in a forked stick.

Trout and smallmouth ponds, on the other hand, often have solid sandy bottoms or plenty of rocks to stand on. If there aren't too many cottages to prevent it, you and your boy might, on a quiet day, wade and cast, pausing to float a fly to rising fish, or just drop a bait and sit down on the shore together. It's a great way to eat blueberries and count clouds. Try it. Lie down, close your eyes, and see how many different fragrances and birdsongs you can identify.

## BOAT ON POND

It isn't that you'd really sell your soul, or your home, or your wife and kids for an hour of good fishing. Of course not. That's just a way of speaking, a hyperbole, an exaggeration for effect.

Of course, no one has ever made you an offer, so you can't really be sure, and there *are* times when the craving for dunking a worm or flicking a fly puts a monkey on your back the size of King Kong. You snarl, you sulk, you growl, you grumble. Children cower, dogs retreat, wives cringe, and employers look up your name on the salary roster to see if maybe they aren't paying you more than you're worth.

You continue groping through your gray world, oozing gloom wherever you go, until at last a weekend provides that day or two you need for reaching those Penobscot River salmon or those Nantucket Sound bluefish, the only adversaries you consider worthy of your time and talent.

Baloney!

Know what that's like? That's like my six-year-old at the local ice-cream stand refusing to order anything because they don't have her favorite flavor: toasted apricot mocha crunch nut whirl with jimmies. Know how I know? Because I used to be the same way, sulking and full of self-pity, fueling my frustrations with dreams of distant waters instead of drowning them in neighborhood ponds. Then son Jack—may he be eternally blessed—suggested that we take our fly rods down to Mill Pond for an hour or two.

You know Mill Pond. You probably pass a half-dozen of them every day on your way to work. They're those undistinguished accumulations of brownish water liberally laced with vegetation that are the antitheses

Sure, go ahead and dream about big league fish in faraway places, but meanwhile don't ignore the right-under-your-nose action in close-to-home ponds. (Photo: Milt Rosko)

of those clear cold northern lakes where you long to be trolling for salmon and trout. They also happen to be the homes of hordes of accommodating panfish which, when fished on the right kind of tackle and in the right frame of mind, can make you feel as though you've struck oil in your backyard. And prominent among these panfish is *Pomoxis nigromaculatus,* the black crappie, which children always prefer to call calico bass.

She was called a few other names by my son and me that morning on Mill Pond before we learned how to handle her. Crappies, you see, like weedy and brush-filled water, this being where their favorite food, minnows, find easy pickings in their search for the small insects which they in turn feed on. I had rowed listlessly to the back end of the pond, away from the road, the cars, the houses, but away also—far away, I reminded myself—from the cool crystal pools of northern Maine. Vegetation was so thick in the cove I was probing that I was having difficulty in finding a clear patch for Jack to cast into.

"Looks like a bowl of shredded wheat left over from breakfast," I said as he sent a wet fly on its way.

"With molasses," he answered over his shoulder, just as his line tensed, his rod bowed, and his hair stood on end.

This crappie put on an impressive performance, taking advantage of every underwater obstacle to snag Jack's thin leader and break free. With his light fly rod and limited experience in this kind of fishing, Jack was no better than an even match, which is as it should be.

Neither, I soon learned, was I, which is not as it should be for a father in the presence of a son still young enough to retain the illusion that his old man is smarter than a pound-and-a-half crappie.

Many crappies got me snagged, tangled, confused, wet, and highly exasperated before our couple of hours had ended, and they also got me hooked. Now a few free hours is not regarded as one-third of the time required for a bout with some Ipswich Bay stripers but as a prize to be sought after by cutting the grass faster and putting up the screens sooner so I can fish one of the many right-down-the-road waters where *Pomoxis* abounds.

I fish a little smarter these days, too. Although this doesn't help much to reassemble my son's shattered illusions, it does enable me to locate my quarry a little more quickly and beat him a little more frequently. I know now, for example, that crappies assemble in schools and when you locate one you're likely to be in for a field day; that they spawn in the shallows during the spring, where they remain until hot weather, when they move to deeper waters; that they return to the shallows again in the fall; that they have delicate mouths and so should not be horsed in or winched aboard a boat without a net; and that although they can be caught on almost any conventional kind of bait and lure, and by fly-fishing, spinning, or bait casting, my best catches of big crappies are likely to be made on brightly colored jigs of 1/32 to 1/8 ounce retrieved very slowly.

Even armed with such intelligence, I don't always fill my stringer. Nor do I long any less ardently for other fishing in other waters. But I don't sit and sulk and feel sorry for myself either. Not with this kind of fishing just down the road a piece—any road—and a youngster eager to share it with me.

# BROOK

The Amazon, we called it. Not that the birches and beeches that shaded this gentle brook or the deer and chipmunks that drank from it suggested South America's royal river. But there was a wildness about our Amazon that conjured up aboriginal images: chanting dancers around flickering campfires, hunting parties of moccasined redmen; and in it was a population of untamed native trout that demanded tiptoe care and down-on-your-knees cunning to catch. Best of all, our Amazon was close behind our summer cottage on a New Hampshire lake. A ten-minute walk, a slow suspenseful stalk, and we could be floating flies through our brook's jeweled pools.

Rarely did these flies float for long. If we were patient in our approach, our offerings often would be attacked even before they alighted on the water, snared aloft in an explosion of glistening grace that never failed to startle us by its suddenness. But if we stumbled or cast a careless shadow, our flies could float clear down to the lake without so much as a sniff. They knew, those trout.

For Jack and Dan and Mary Beth and Matthew, our Amazon was both classroom and playground. Here they studied the ways of wary fish, learned their wiles and how to outwit them, and this made our children better fishermen. Here they also learned patience and appreciation, teamwork and tolerance, and this made them better persons.

Evening was our favorite hour for these backyard safaris, that soft silent interlude between when I'd climb down from my ladder where I'd been staining clapboards since lunchtime and when Peg would start slicing plump summer-fresh tomatoes for dinner. Down the glade we'd go, laughing, tumbling, past the spring where the toughest-looking frog

There's something intimate and elementary about a brook that gives it a special appeal to children. A brook's small waters are a training ground for bigger streams to follow, but a child can find adventure aplenty in its gentle flow. (Photo: Terry McDonnell)

in New Hampshire stood sentinel over his own private swimmin' hole, then scuttling up the leafy slope to where it leveled off in a broad twisting terrace. In the middle of this terrace flowed our Amazon.

Till we reached this level we romped as noisily as we pleased. We tripped, we tickled, we raced, we tackled without restraint. But when the first person to reach Amazon level—usually Jack with Dan wrapped around his thighs, or vice versa—stopped, crouched, thrust out his arms, and froze, we froze too. Even the forest seemed to fall silent. For a brief moment not even a jay jabbered; the breeze in the branches seemed to be holding its breath.

On a signal from me we all assembled quietly, carefully, below the lip of the ridge. One carelessly cast shadow, one noisy footstep would telegraph our presence. Then by the time we had hands-and-kneed it across the few yards of moss to the Amazon's edge, our trout would be gone. Except for muddy trails marking their paths, there would be no sign of life.

Our strategy rarely varied. First we would try a flat open run where the water sprawled out for 5 or 6 feet before converging between a pair of gray lichened boulders. Whoever had the first turn would drop a fly from behind the trunk of a big beech. Invariably if noise or shadow hadn't spooked the trout, one would strike. Rarely, though, was a second one ever fooled.

Once when Peg had first turn she got cocky. Handing her the fly rod with an imitation mosquito dangling at the end of 6 feet of fine monofilament leader, I whispered instructions, administered a pat of encouragement, and sent her on her way.

"Good luck, Mom," said the boys.

"I hope you catch one," added Mary Beth.

With a cocky raise of her pretty Irish eyebrows and a "Nothing to it" shrug, she edged up over the rise and planted her hand on a patch of mushy moss which, according to her later testimony, "slithered like something, yeeeccch, slimy." Terrified, she leaped upright, emitted a bellow such as New Hampshire hasn't heard since Dan'l Webster used to call his lost cows, and came to rest sitting in a puddle of cold mushy Amazon mud.

No, we didn't catch any trout that day.

# BACKWOODS

You can do it in many ways: back-pack into the barrens, horse it to the high country, fly into the bush, or just pitch a tent alongside some reasonably remote yet reasonably convenient North Country lake. All can assure you of an intimacy with wildness that you're not likely to find anywhere on this side of a rapidly receding frontier.

Every year more beer cans and butt packages intrude higher up the slopes and deeper into the forest. Now in the woods when I come across a patch of particularly pristine ground, I no longer allow myself the ennobling illusion that maybe no other man has walked here. I used to, fully aware that I probably was kidding myself but always harboring the half-hope that maybe I wasn't. Too many times, though, I have stumbled across the gross scars inflicted by callous intruders: the clutter of garbage, the clamor of disk jockeys.

I stopped kidding myself (and started worrying in earnest) some years back when a friend and I hiked to a remote region of northern Maine seeking the mouth of a small stream where it entered a sprawling lake. Here, we were sure, we would find bright, dark, deep-bodied, native brook

Unspoiled wilderness is hard to find these days, but a lot of untamed country is closer than you think. This father and son from New Jersey caught landlocked salmon in Maine's Moose River.

trout in elemental surroundings, and we trudged for hours through pathless timberland and tangled brush to get there. And what did we find? A drunken dude whose radio was tuned to what must have been the world series of rock and roll and whose raucous revved-up outboard must have scared the scales off every trout in the lake.

"Boy," he grumbled, "what lousy fishing!"

It's a terribly fragile thing, this wildness. It takes so little to adulterate the rawest, most desolate of grandeurs. A candy wrapper on a rock, a filter tip by a tree—each is a letter "A" burned into the forehead of the forest. Children must learn this lesson early, and it's up to us to teach them.

Suggestion: you—not them, you—spend a few minutes when you're outdoors to pick up trash. No lectures, no "C'mon, let's all pitch in for old Mother Nature." Just pick up a few bags and cans and wrappers. If there's no receptacle to dump them in, bring them home and put them in your trash barrel. You'll soon have plenty of help in leaving the outdoors a little cleaner than you found it, and when you're dead and buried your tradition of tidiness will be carried on by a generation that cares.

When Jack and Dan were seventeen and sixteen, it seemed time for them to get a taste of loon song and tall timber before they mounted the merry-go-round of college and summer employment, so we set aside four days for tenting alongside Brassua Lake in northern Maine. This was our choice because I knew the area, I knew the route, and we could drive it in six or seven hours. A convenient campground with its cleared sites and fireplaces would enable us to make the most of our brief stay, and the mile-long stretch of Moose River between Brassua and Moosehead lakes offered easy close-at-hand fishing in classically lovely waters for landlocked salmon and brook trout. There also were plenty of big accommodating chub to keep the boys entertained in case gamefish wouldn't cooperate.

Mostly, though, the area was a good one for letting the boys be alone together. The woods and water were still rugged, yet no longer hostile; not totally tamed, yet not domesticated either. I could let them walk the woods and wade the shores, sharing their thoughts, breaking down the barriers of sibling sensitivities, and learning before it was too late, before their juvenile jousts for the bigger piece of cake, their subconscious competitions for the bigger share of attention, could atrophy into irreconcilability, that they're both great guys and that they love and respect and enjoy and admire one another.

Our adventure started long before we left. We studied maps, traced our route, set up our itinerary: buy licenses enroute just over the Maine line; one stop on the way for coffee, at Howard Johnson's on the Maine Turnpike; arrive just before daybreak in time to fish the dawn rise below Brassua Dam. Each of us had his pre-departure assignment: Dan dug worms, Jack tied flies, and I made sure we had all the rods and reels and lines and lures and hooks and sinkers we'd need. Mother, of course, was quartermaster, packing enough clean clothes and baking enough goodies to supply a reenactment of the Normandy Invasion. On D(departure)-Day the boys and I cast off in style at a local restaurant, where we fueled up on a turkey-ham-roast beef smorgasbord.

With the boys old enough to lend a hand with the driving, none of us bore too heavy a burden, yet none of us slept enroute. Once off the turnpike and heading north along the Kennebec, we were too conscious of the closeness of history: lumber drives and Indian raids, Benedict Arnold's epic but unsuccessful expedition against Quebec. The clustered shadows of each tiny town—Solon, Bingham, Moscow, Carratunk, the Forks—exuded a frontier flavor, the prospect of seeing another deer sustained suspense. In all, we must have sighted thirty.

Despite a savage, lightning-laced storm as we ascended the desolate height of land below Jackman, a storm which I swear the boys were convinced I had had staged for their entertainment, we pulled up alongside the gate leading to Brassua Dam right on schedule at daybreak. A five-minute walk and we were swinging streamers and floating worms through big brawling waters that Jack and Dan had seen the likes of only on calendars. As the sun seeped through the birches behind us, warming our backs and spangling the riffles, the boys fished to music that spanned the spectrum from the rumbling tympani of the dam to the tinkling cymbals of songbirds.

Our stay was ... well, it was swell. Enough trout and salmon to make a few meals, enough cooperative chub to keep our rods bent in between. Jack and Dan ambled and explored together, laughed a lot, scrubbed dinner dishes with sand and lake water, and fell (jumped?) into the river a few times. The tent went up and down without a hitch thanks to the boys, the meals were cooked, if not *à la Cordon Bleu*, than at least competently thanks to their old man.

We didn't hear much of the loons, though, and that was too bad, because of all nature's noises, this is the most elemental, the one that lingers longest; except, of course, for the cry of your newborn child. The reason we didn't hear the loons is another reminder of why there isn't much wildness left and of why we'd all better get off our collectively complacent keester and do something about it before it's all gone. What happened was, a pair of ignorant apes pulled into an adjoining campsite, set up loudspeakers on the fenders of their camper, and proceeded to get ossified while barnyard falsettos blared into the night about shattered dreams and unrequited love. Finally at one o'clock in the chilly morning I stormed out of our tent in my skivvies and threatened those two delinquent disk jockeys with a stereophonic enema if I heard so much as one more wail.

Maybe in the long run the experience will be more beneficial for the boys than a few notes of loon song. As Dan said during the drive on the way home, "I wouldn't have believed it if I hadn't heard it with my own ears."

## ICE FISHING

In northern latitudes, outdoorsmen participate in a form of refrigerated recreation known as ice fishing. For many years I was of the opinion that the only civilized form of ice fishing was done in nice warm living rooms for olives in martini glasses. I was so cynical, in fact, so convinced that only masochists and Eskimos would voluntarily endure a day on a frozen lake, that I published these paragraphs in an article entitled "Ice Fishing: Agony or Ecstasy?"

There's a little June in January when you can enjoy hot food with dear friends around a warm fire while waiting for your flags to go up. For real fulfillment, cook and eat your catch on the spot.

Ice fishing begins with chipping 6-inch holes through 20 inches of ice, one hole for each line, one hour for each hole, then having a small boy point out several dozen vacant holes that are no longer being used. Live minnows are lowered through the holes on lines attached to "tip-ups," ingenious wood-and-spring arrangements that allow you to leave your lines unattended while you sip antifreeze. Tip-ups are designed so that a gust of wind or an especially active minnow causes a red flag to whip up and wag like an admonishing finger. If your eyeballs have not yet iced over, you rush to the hole, pull in the line, swear, reset the flag, relower the minnow (a thoroughly confused fish by this time), and return to your Prestone.

Fish occasionally are hooked through the ice, but seldom are landed because the hole usually has frozen solid by the time you get there.

Frostbite can be avoided by staying home. Other less effective precautions include (1) eleven layers of thermal underwear, (2) liberal doses of internal insulation, (3) continuous movement, preferably in pursuit of a cuddly blonde, and (4) going home.

Do not, repeat *not*, light a fire. It melts the ice and gets your feet wet.

Avoid bobhouses at all costs. Beguiling as might be the warmth and comfort of their well-appointed interiors, remember that the true fisherman, like all true artists, must be willing to suffer for his art. To quote the great Walton (Si Walton of East Moosehaunch, Maine), "Any man who won't do his fishing out in the open ain't worth a hog's leftovers."

My cynicism was not merely academic. I had tried ice fishing. Unfortunately I had tried it under the guidance of my congenitally improvident neighbor, Vernon Merrill, who dropped by one winter Sunday and suggested that we head north and catch a few lake trout in New Hampshire's Lake Winnisquam.

"But Winnisquam is a hundred miles away," I protested.

"I'll drive fast."

"But the afternoon is almost over."

"I'll drive faster."

"But I don't know anything about ice fishing."

"I know everything."

"But I haven't any gear."

"I'm the Abercrombie and Fitch of northern New England."

Obviously I was not going to outargue Merrill, and since this was prior to my learning that he is disaster-prone, that he not only does not provide against cataclysms, he causes them, I succumbed, reasoning that ice fishing at Winnisquam could not be any more painful than watching Curt Gowdy and Frank Woolner catch striped bass on TV.

I was wrong. It was infinitely more painful. First there was the cold, a heavy, thick, penetrating, pervasive frigidity that kind of oozed up my too-thin pant legs and down my unmuffled neck till my chest felt as though it were being crushed in an icy vise. Then there was the wrecking bar, a heavy, awkward, unsharpened hunk of iron that was as appropriate for chopping holes through 2 feet of ice as a jackhammer would have been for cutting diamonds. And finally, there was Merrill. While I chopped, he reconnoitered, a procedure consisting of his ambling affably about the ice sharing his favorite chilblain chaser with fellow fishermen.

"Gotta find out where the fish are hitting, Jackson," he explained as he headed into the dwindling daylight. Watching him raising his bottle in Arctic conviviality, I thought warm thoughts ... of rising trout on sunny streams, of stripers swirling off a calm beach, of salmon leaping behind my boat ... and I swore off ice fishing forever.

Years later I capitulated to my family's pleas to punctuate our winter wearies with another attempt. Actually it wasn't my family's pleas so much as Julie's and Margaret's soulful wide-eyed supplications that crumbled my resolve. I never could say no to little girls. Peg's "Well, other families seem to enjoy it, don't they?" argument was utterly unconvincing when regarded in the light of our less than illustrious record of "family" endeavors. Our family garden, for example, had fattened only the local woodchuck population. This is a species which the Lord created so beguilingly cute that only the most callous of men could center one in his rifle sight and squeeze the trigger, even while it nibbled tauntingly on his seventy-five-cents-a-pound wax beans. I confess that I did drop some kind of gas bomb down the hole that one of the creatures had dug at the corner of our house, but this succeeded only in persuading the Fallons, not the chucks, to evacuate the premises.

Family camping was set back a century or more by our first try at togetherness in a tent. Mercifully my memory has erased most of the dismal details, but one that will persist forever, probably throughout the entire state of New Hampshire, is the pungent panic produced at two a.m. in the hot August darkness by three-year-old Julie's throwing up—and down and across and all over m'lady's chamber—spraying curdled milk like a butter churn gone berserk.

It was, therefore, with a feeling of foreboding that we set out on a February Sunday for a nearby pond. Predictably, it turned out to be the coldest day in ninety-odd New England winters. Driving to the pond's snow-smothered shore, we disembarked into a wind that literally froze the ketchup solid in its bottle. Cheeks reddened, eyes glazed, fingers stiffened, ears ached, and three-year-old Margaret, recovering from a runny-nose cold, wailed ceaselessly through the two icicles that dangled from her nostrils. Neither dressed nor disposed for what we had bumbled into, we trudged back to our car, hurried home, and spent the rest of the afternoon in front of a blazing hearth watching home movies of August afternoons on sunny Cape Cod beaches.

You can understand, then, why the invitation from my friend Bill Stone a few years later had to be embroidered with a lot of attractions before I could be persuaded to try ice fishing again.

His "Lake Boon, only a short drive from your home, and no North Country weather to cope with" stimulated my interest.

His "Bring the family along and we'll have a cookout" almost convinced me.

His "And I guarantee we'll catch fish" was what tipped the scales.

So about noon on another gray February Sunday, the four excited Fallon children and their apprehensive parents disembarked in the almost empty parking lot of Monahan's Pub between the big blue vans of Bill and our mutual friend Larry Stearns. Larry and his tribe had come along to join in the fun and also to see how their new skimobile performed on the ice.

It performed fine. As a means of collecting firewood, it was ideal. As a shuttle between bonfire and bathroom, it was invaluable. And as a way of enabling Bill to fulfill his promise of action, it couldn't have been better.

Bill was some 20 yards away setting his fifth trap—the last allowable by law—as Larry pulled up alongside the fire where Barbara Stone, Judy Stearns, and all our assorted offspring were exchanging greetings. Normally Bill is a super-sociable sort. Normally he would have hurried right over to greet us. Normalcy, however, no longer prevails when a flag springs up and someone yells, "Fish." There, waving in the wind, was a square of red cloth that set Bill to running like a racehorse . . . with eight children (including me) slipping and sliding behind him.

All my misconceptions about ice fishing's being 90 percent muscle and 10 percent technique were dispelled by watching Bill handle what turned out to be a foot and a half of pickerel. Poised on one knee, he gently lifted the trap from the hole with his right hand while peeling slack from the spool with his left so the fish would feel no tension. Laying the trap on the ice, he snatched line between thumb and forefinger of his right hand with the deftness of a child playing "pick up sticks," letting it run through his fingers until the fish paused.

"Pickerel," he said. "They usually stop like this to turn the bait around in their mouths."

Sure enough, after ten seconds or so the fish resumed its run, slower than before and steadier now that it could concentrate on consuming instead of capturing and killing its prey.

"Ought to be down around its throat," whispered Bill, lowering his right hand and tensing for the strike, "ri-i-i-ght about *now!*"

Up came his arm, in went the hook, and out sizzled line as Bill maintained a steady, just-strong-enough pressure with his fingers. The line, I noticed, was peeling smoothly from the spool because Bill had positioned the trap to the rear of his right hand with the spool just off the ice.

After the fish's initial surge, Bill halted its run by squeezing line. Following a few head-shaking tugs, the fish was eased in steadily, but all the while Bill was poised to pay out line if it should have enough fire left in its boilers for another run.

But it didn't. Its first frantic attempt at escape against the carefully regulated pressure of Bill's fingers had worn it out . . . except, that is, for one sudden shaking of its head when it was halfway through the hole, and this was enough to dislodge the hook. Back through the hole it plunged, its upper half bouncing off the edge, then following its tail into the water. Stunned and pooped, it stayed there for a second or so getting its bearings, during which time I dove to the ice, thrust my hand through the hole, and so help me went all the way in to my shoulder in a vain effort to grab its slippery tail.

"Lesson number two," said Bill. "Don't waste your time trying to hand-grab a slimy pickerel through a hole in the ice."

"Lesson number one," he added. "Don't let the fish fall back in the first place. When I jerked it through, I should have had my left hand ready to sweep it sideways in case the hook came out."

Other lessons I learned from Bill are:

*Topography:* Set your traps at an angle rather than parallel to the shore. This will enable you to fish at several depths as the bottom drops off.

*Time of Year:* The tailend of the season, toward the end of February, seems to be best for warm-water fish such as pickerel, especially following a few sunny days. Under such conditions pickerel are likely to edge into shallower water in anticipation of spring spawning.

*Time of Day:* Late and early are likely to be most productive, same as with open water, although there are inevitable flurries of action in between, especially on mild afternoons that suddenly cloud over.

*Tackle:* The traditional tip-up trap still is most popular. Essentially it consists of three crossed sticks, two horizontal, one vertical. The horizontal pair lay on the ice and keep the assembly level and steady. The vertical, with the line on a spool at its lower end, extends through the hole. At the upper end of the vertical stick is a two-foot ribbon of spring steel with the flag, a small square of red cloth, tied to its end. The ribbon is bent and set to be triggered by a fish taking out line. Another popular technique, especially for crappies, is jigging a shiny inch-long lure on a 2-foot rod. Crappie schools sometimes can be attracted by an occasional sprinkling of crushed eggshells.

*Bait:* Small shiners ensure plenty of action because they're fair game for small as well as large fish, but it's a good idea to bring along a dozen or so big baits—preferably small suckers or chubs—to entice big bass and pickerel. Grubs, prime table fare for small fish, especially sunnies, can be collected from swellings in goldenrod stalks and occasionally beneath the bark of dead trees.

*Technique:* Hooking your shiner just forward of its dorsal fin with a long-shanked #6, lower it to within 6 inches of the bottom. Determine depth first by lowering a sinker and tying a knot in your line when the sinker hits bottom. A small split shot about 6 inches up a 6-foot leader of 8-pound-test monofilament will ensure that your bait will stay close to the bottom.

*Keeping Fish:* Keep caught fish in a pen chopped partway through the ice. A small hole all the way through will fill the pen with water. Don't put your bait in such a pen unless you first cover the water inlet (bait outlet!) with a fine-mesh screen.

By applying these principles, we ended the afternoon with a pen full of crappies, yellow perch, and pickerel. (The children, as usual, outscored their elders two to one.) Later, on a tour around the ice aboard Larry's snowmobile, we also saw sunfish, white perch, hornpout, plus a pair of impressive largemouth bass. High point of the afternoon was dinner around an open fire, with fare ranging from roasted hotdogs to grilled fillets of Cape Cod stripers and bluefish from the well-stocked Stone freezer.

Inspired by this experience, I next tried ice fishing for trout and found equipment and techniques essentially the same as in warm-water ponds: hole, trap, live shiner (or chub or smelt or sucker) swimming free on 6-pound monofilament leader about a foot above the bottom. The only significant variation I've noted is local preferences in bait. In some places it's grubs, in others it's worms; salmon eggs are as popular through the ice as they are in spring streams, and many Massachusetts trout anglers would rather forget their long johns than their canned corn. A couple of kernels covering a tiny hook plus a few more scattered on the bottom have accounted for a lot of Bay State trout. Many states prohibit the use of kernel corn, though, so check before you raid Momma's cupboard.

The trout I'm referring to here are brooks, browns, and rainbows. Normally these are caught from small suburban ponds which, because they are snuggled in sheltered terrestrial pockets, are more comfortable than the broad wide-open northern lakes where lake trout, whitefish, northern pike, and, where permitted, landlocked salmon are the quarry. To beat the weather, many upcountry ice-anglers do their dangling from the heated interiors of bobhouses, which they leave in their favorite locations all season long. On large lakes you'll often find sprawling communities of these one-room retreats complete with urban ills such as trash removal and vandalism. Among them are some interesting examples of architectural and decorative ingenuity. Most, of course, are purely functional structures designed for shelter and privacy, but here and there, among the slapdash tarpaper-and-scrap-lumber creations, standing out like Balenciaga gowns at a basement sale, are carefully crafted, brightly painted habitats with second-color shutters flanking colorfully curtained windows.

Once Jack, Matt, and I made a tour of several on-the-ice suburbs. No fishing; just walking, observing, talking. We didn't arrive at any profound sociological conclusions, but it did seem to us that of all the comments emanating from inside bobhouses, these probably are the most frequently heard:

"Since when does a flush beat a full house?"

"How's a guy supposed to go to the bathroom when he can't even bend his knees?"

"Waddayamean it's my turna check the traps? I checked'm las' week."

On some lakes it's possible to rent bobhouses. On many of Maine's coastal rivers, for example, enterprising residents hire out heated huts to smelt fishermen. By all means see if you can spend a day in a bobhouse with your boy. Its flimsy walls will encourage closeness as well as comfort. To find one for rent, phone a local baitshop a week or so in advance of your coming, then confirm with a second call a few days later. And when you get there, invest a few dollars in having your holes drilled for you by the ubiquitous entrepreneur with the power auger. On midwinter ice that often exceeds 2 feet in thickness you can easily burn up hours of fishing time as well as a lot of valuable vitality. Even at a buck a hole, it's a bargain.

On 2-foot-thick ice, falling through the ice is not a concern for the individual angler. Nevertheless, keep your guard up for the occasional soft spots at the mouths of rivers and around the shores of wind-buffeted islands. Be especially careful if you should drive onto the ice. A lot of trucks, cars, and snowmobiles are lost every year, some of them with their drivers aboard. I recall one grim photo a few years ago showing snowmobile tracks terminating at the ice's edge. The vehicle's driver had been drowned the previous night by following the tracks of another snowmobile that had gone in just a short time before.

Before venturing onto ice, run down this checkoff list.

1. Be especially cautious early and late in the season and immediately following prolonged spells of warm weather.

2. Stay clear of dark patches. When in doubt about an area—after a snowfall, for example—stay away.

3. Avoid open water, especially at river mouths. Strong winds can weaken ice for many feet around openings.

4. Stay close to your youngster, and keep a rope handy in case one of you should fall through.

5. Learn a lake beforehand. The sun's rays reflect back from a shallow bottom and make for thinner ice.

On big lakes and small ponds, then, from behind a jury-rigged wind-break or in the structured comfort of a bobhouse, fishing through the ice offers its own special brand of enjoyment to families realistic enough not to seek in it a substitute for the long casts and open water and leaping fish of summertime angling. What it lacks in action, it more than makes up for in sociability. Interludes of inactivity after holes are cut and traps are set and ice is skimmed and there's nothing to do but wait for a flag offer plenty of opportunity for strolling around, introducing yourself, chatting awhile. You can learn a lot, make friends, and maybe even be lucky enough to meet someone like Donald Downs who hitchhikes almost 20 miles on winter weekends from his home in Rochester, New Hampshire, to Alton Bay on Lake Winnipesaukee, where he sleeps and eats and cooks and fishes and chats with friends in his bobhouse. His only complaint is about his inability to read the labels on his food cans, for Donald is blind.

"Ate a hash last weekend," he told a friend of mine, chuckling. "Thought it was delicious until somebody told me it was dogfood."

Now I ask you, how, with memories like this, could man or boy, woman or girl, ever become discouraged by petty personal problems?

## BOAT ON BAY

With a boy, a fishing trip always should start before daybreak, even when tide and travel time don't require it. Just you and him tiptoeing through a whisper-close world, sharing the soft sounds and shadowed sights of darkness: your home, how it breathes; a distant dog, why it's barking; a lone motorist, where he's heading.

He's heading, of course, for your fish. The only car on a six-lane superhighway, and it can have but one possible destination: that same

From an anchored boat in gentle inshore waters, anglers of all ages can enjoy flounder action all season long. (Photo: Milt Rosko)

square foot of bay bottom that you and your boy have staked out for spring flounder. Sure, this is absurd. The driver undoubtedly is a milkman or a baker or a janitor who always gets an early start, but it's April. The joyous juices of a new season make every man suspect. Speed and secrecy are your only defenses against these interlopers who would presume to fish that flounder-paved fantasy that you and your boy have conjured up over a cold and fishless winter.

But logic prevails. Logic and the lulling heavy-treaded hum of snow tires on the highway. (Always leave your snow tires on for at least one fishing trip. Their macadam melody marks the end of winter as surely as the robin's song marks the start of spring.) Soon your son and you are leaning back, driving leisurely, reassured by reason that on a sunny Saturday such as this there are plenty of bays and plenty of flounder for all the fathers and sons—alas, so few—who are smart enough to fish them.

For breakfast you pick a diner close to your destination where fishermen with rough wrinkled faces and tired eyes and hard hands feed on bacon and eggs and home fries and toast and blacker-and-stronger-the-better coffee. Talk is low, mumbled, colloquial, like tribal chiefs around a campfire. The subtle scents of sweat and dried fish are incense for your son's imagination. His eyes are wide, his lips apart as his counter stool swings him slowly through the panorama.

"And what'll you have to drink?" you ask after he has ordered his bacon and eggs.

"Uh, Dad."

"Yes?"

"Can I have a cup of coffee?"

By breakfast's end the day has dawned. An outboard's harsh chatter meshes the gears of morning. Across the street between sea-bleached buildings you watch while this boat cleaves the quiet cove for a few minutes, then suddenly swings up-tide and drops anchor.

Hey, you think, that's our place. That's where we're going to fish.

"C'mon," you say, "let's get going."

"These mudworms," you explain to your boy when you get to the baitshop, "they're a little longer than we need. Those long ones—eight-, nine-inchers—they're for striped bass; hooked whole just behind the neck and drifted with tide across a dropoff. We'll try that in June after the bass arrive. Today we use half a worm on each hook of our spreader. Like a coat hanger, see, with your line tied to the middle, and one of these narrow, long-shanked hooks on either end."

"Ouch!" he hollers, dropping the worm whose pincers have nipped his finger.

His initiation rite.

"It's okay," you reassure him. "Just a nip. They can't hurt you." But you find yourself rubbing your finger because it, too, feels the pinch.

To your boy your rented boat is a royal barge. It's ancient, battered, splattered here and there along its mottled gray bottom and worn wooden seats with bloody souvenirs of earlier excursions, but he sits regally at its stern: Ahab at the helm, Huck Finn on his raft.

"Watch how I row," you tell him. "Feet here, lean forward, pull back. See how those blades are always upright to the water. Watch closely now. You'll be rowing on the way back."

While he drops and secures the anchor, you rig the rods, bait the hooks, set the reel drags. His drag you set a little looser than your own, smiling as you anticipate the eye-popping epic he will be narrating that night to his Mother: " . . . and they pulled so hard, Mom, that even when I kept right on reeling as hard as I could, I couldn't make them stop."

And they do pull hard, these wonderful winter flounder. You'd forgotten how hard. And their hits, after months in the mud, are hard, hungry hits, not the soft nip-and-nibble of close-to-shore flounder fishing later on in the summer. Best of all, they're plentiful, eating-big, and hit-a-minute hungry.

By the time the tide tapers off, you have all you need, all you care to clean at one sitting, and yet you stay. Partly it's because you hate to break the spell, but also it's because the action has abated, almost ceased, and your boy must learn to love this part of fishing, too. This morning he has learned that the fire one feels while fighting a fish flames brightest when fueled by eager anticipation. Now he will find that fishing satisfies most when reviewed in the ember-glow of action's quiet aftermath.

Already the lad's imagination starts to magnify the morning.

"Hey, Dad, how about that one I lost? That real big one that bent my rod right under the boat? Boy, that was sure some fish, huh? How big do you think that one was?"

Filleting a couple of dozen flounder can be fun with a sharp knife and an attentive audience, and later, on a flat rock alongside the launching ramp, you make it so.

"Like this: cut, pull it back, slice it off. Two nice fillets per fish. Here, hold the meat flat while I strip off the skin. Easy? Okay, now you try it."

Instead of heading home right away, you lunch on the beach. A long walk, barefoot, with cool gritty sand between the toes, to where a distant dune tumbles toward the shore. Talk is of the vastness of the ocean, and where clouds come from, and how come when a gull finds food the others always seem to know. And, of course, of fishing.

"Dad, uh, how much do you think all that flounder we caught is worth? I mean how much do you think we saved by catching it instead of buying it?"

The young provider.

"Oh, twenty, twenty-five dollars. At today's prices. A good day's work."

It's hot now. Daylight is dwindling, but the sand still smoulders with accumulated heat.

"Boy, wouldn't it be nice to take a swim? Wish we'd brought our suits."

"We did. We're wearing them. Last one in is a lousy fisherman!"

And two fully clad males scamper across the beach and plunge into a cool friendly ocean; a man and a boy, but it's hard to tell which is which.

## PARTY BOAT

During the 1930s and 1940s most boys at the seashore saved their money for that Eden of Amusement, "the Center." A day of penny arcade, Dodgem, fun house, roller coaster, soda pop, chocolate-covered, pepper steak, popcorn, and indigestion was the pinnacle of the summer season. Me, I saved my money for party boats.

As soon as I had accumulated enough nickels from running errands, redeeming empty soda pop bottles, and generally "being good," I'd hustle off to Salisbury or Seabrook where 50¢ would buy me a passage on a half-day excursion to a wonderland of rolling ocean and big fish aboard a broad squat vessel under the guidance of a rumpled salt-encrusted superman. To an awestruck lad, the pronouncements of party-boat skippers seemed utterly oracular. With what appeared to be no more than a sniff of the sea and a snap of the fingers, they would predict the presence of mackerel or haddock or cod at a precise point in an apparently undistinguished ocean, and almost without fail the fish would be there.

Nowhere on earth—or in the hereafter, for that matter—would I rather have spent my every waking second. Between trips I smiled a lot and took out the garbage in hopes of conning another coin into my coffer, but my halo was a crown of thorns. Hell, I didn't want to be good. I

An American institution, the party—or head—boat can be an excellent way to start fishing with your child. For a modest fee, bait and equipment normally are provided and action assured.

wanted to go fishing, and especially I wanted to go aboard a party boat.

Then one day when I disembarked from a productive trip carrying a burlap bag bulging with mackerel, I hit upon a scheme which I was sure would enable me to fish forevermore aboard the party boat of my choice: I would sell my catch for 50¢, go on another trip, catch more fish, sell them for 50¢, etc., etc., *ad infinitum*. The Ponzi of the party-boat fleet, I imagined myself spending every summer for the rest of my life shuttling back and forth between haddock holes and mackerel shoals, with maybe an occasional run up to the Center for a pepper steak and a ride or two on the Dodgem.

For a while it worked brilliantly. Housewives were happy to pay a nickel apiece for fresh 2-pound mackerel. The much bigger haddock and cod, of course, I sold for a dime; nobody was going to put anything over on this budding young entrepreneur. Once I accomplished a coup by selling a whole sackful of mackerel and pollock, maybe fifty fish, to a diner owner for 50¢. True, this brought the per-fish price down to about a penny, but then I had made only one call. And besides, once I earned my 50¢, I always made it a practice to give all of my extra fish to my final customer. Good advertising, I figured.

Besides advertising, my enterprise also introduced me to the rudiments of such economic esoterica as mass merchandising, door-to-door selling, and cash flow. Unfortunately, nobody told me about the need for building a capital reserve against contingencies. Inevitably my scheme disintegrated when even the sea-going sachem who guided our craft wasn't able to conjure up 50¢ worth of fish for me, and I had to fall back on errands, bottles, and being good to finance sporadic party boat trips.

I don't know how such an enterprise would work today with fares up around $3 to $5, but I suspect that an energetic youngster with enough sense to sell more than a bare minimum of his catches could make an enjoyable and maybe even a profitable summer for himself. Who knows, with fish flesh currently priced somewhere between squab and chateaubriand, he might even wind up the season owning his own fleet of party boats.

But fun, not fortune, is what has made the party boat an institution along America's seashore. Like the Mississippi paddlewheeler, it has brought profit to a few and pleasure to many.

The party boat's principal source of pleasure is its convenience. Just bring yourself and your son, purchase your tickets, and grab your seats. Lines, bait, guidance, sea stories, and sometimes even a hand with cleaning your catch are all part of about an $8 fare for both of you on an eight-to-noon or one-to-five excursion.

While just going along and catching a few fish is enjoyable, you can increase your enjoyment as well as your catch if you follow these few suggestions.

1. Take a seasick pill about an hour before you embark. Party boats tend to ro-o-o-ol with the swells even on calm days. While you and your boy may have stomachs of stone, bear in mind that most party-boat patrons are landlubbers who are easily transformed by a few beers, a hot sun, and a little rhythmical rolling into miserable regurgitating wretches. Just one victim is all it takes. Nowhere is the power of suggestion more persuasive than on a hot, rolling, smelly boat.

2. Bring your own equipment. Your boy will feel more at home with it and won't have to waste precious fishing time getting used to the tackle that's provided. If you bring freshwater gear, rinse it thoroughly under a dockside freshwater hose as soon as you disembark. No matter how tired you are, don't wait until you get home. On a hot day, salt and rust can ruin a reel in hours.

3. Arrive early. This will enable you to stake your claims on good fishing positions. Bow and stern are best because you can cast across a

wider sector and lessen the likelihood of tangling lines with other fishermen. If bow and stern are taken or unavailable because rough seas make them too dangerous, select port or starboard according to the directions in which wind and tide are likely to swing your boat. The idea, of course, is to be on the side where your line will not drift beneath the boat. By checking boats already fishing offshore, you can get a preview of how your boat will be heading so long as wind and tide don't change appreciably before you get there.

4. Enjoy your boy. Share his suspense on the way out; his exaltation in fighting and beating a big fish; his fascination as he feeds gulls almost from his finger tips during the run back in. With all the distracting details taken care of for you—no motor to mother, no anchor to tend, no fish to figure out—party boats offer an unsurpassed opportunity for concentrating on the supreme pleasure of just having a good time together.

And by the way, if the $8 tab should seem high, just consider the cost of boat, engine, accessories, maintenance, insurance, license, labor; the shortness of the season; the many days when storms and fog keep boats dockside. Consider also the return on your investment with the eating or selling of, say, a mere half-dozen 20-pound cod. Currently these fish are selling for about 50¢ a pound on the hoof. No cleaning, just bring them to a dealer and collect your . . . hey, six fish times 20 pounds times 50¢—that's $60!

I wonder if maybe I was just thirty years ahead of my time.

# JETTY

*Jetty:* a stable platform surrounded by fish.

No, this is not Webster's definition, but anglers who are enterprising enough to exploit the magnetic attraction of jetties for both fish and fishermen won't argue with its accuracy. In a jetty's weedy crevasses gamefish seek resident crustaceans. Against its *cul de sac* sides they herd hapless bait schools. And for getting out into turbulent close-to-rocks action, Gibraltar-steady jetties have it all over boats: no rolling, no bouncing; no motor to mind, no currents to contend with; just cast and catch.

Except, of course, for those times when weekend traffic makes the channel alongside your jetty seem like a saltwater Long Island Expressway; when underwater boulders snag the heavy sinkers you need for coping with the sluicing currents; and when a poorly timed leap onto a slippery tilted slope sends you sprawling as you hustle shoreward to avoid getting cut off by an incoming tide.

Despite the occasional hazards of slippery sloping boulders, jetties can enable you and your youngster to get right out where the action is.

Like everything else in life, then, the pleasure of jetty fishing carries a pricetag. With jetties the price is patience, precaution, and an occasional skinned shin. Patience, if you're like me, probably is not one of your long suits. Oh, I can cast from dusk to dawn without a hit and be happy; that's not the kind of patience I mean. What I lack is restraint when I see fish swirling; the control and composure and clear thinking necessary for an intelligent tactical assessment of a suddenly discovered set of short-lived conditions. When tide and wind and weather and topography conspire to create a perfect churning chowline for striped bass and bluefish, I head for it like a homing torpedo. Once I spotted bass breaking in the Ipswich surf and ran so fast down a steep sand dune that I made three casts from waist-high water before it occurred to me that my waders still were draped over my shoulder. On another occasion I took off across the Weweantic River's spongy marshes toward busting bluefish and disappeared over my head, cameras and all, into a narrow but oh-so-deep tidal trench.

What's merely foolish on dunes and marshes, though, can be fatal on a jetty, so it's a good idea to have a child along to remind you of your responsibilities as well as to share in the fun. Before setting out across your jetty, size it up. How far can you go before boulders cease to be smooth and easy to walk on? Where are the low points that will be filled in first by an incoming tide? Is there a bend where sand has accumulated into a protective bar behind which fish will be waiting for bait? What's the best place to fish?

Ask your youngster this last question. Let him try to figure it out for himself. Let him learn through your collaboration all the subtle factors that get cranked into so seemingly simple a decision.

"That rock over there, Dad. It's broad and flat. Wouldn't it make a nice casting platform?"

"A beauty, but only for about fifteen minutes. Remember, that tide's on the way in. That rock'll be under water soon."

"Okay, then, there's another big flat one farther out, just to the left of that gull. That one's high enough, isn't it?"

"A little too high. How would you land a fish? Our gaff wouldn't reach and there's too much seaweed on those rocks beneath it for safe walking, even in those cleats you're wearing."

Finally, when you've made the right compromise between safety, casting convenience, and likelihood of finding fish, you'll have made it together. He will have participated instead of having just been dragged along in your wake, like a pram behind a power boat.

Neither Jack nor I did any deliberating last time we fished our favorite jetty, on Plum Island at the Merrimack River's mouth. We knew it reasonably well from previous visits, but even better, this time we had been given pinpoint directions from a friend who recently had clobbered late-April cod a week earlier as they cruised in close seeking smelt, crabs, clams, worms, and in keeping with their omnivorous appetites, anything else that crawled, swam, wiggled, or slithered.

*The time:* "Middle third of an ebbing tide. Oh, you can catch a few fish most any time, but the pattern appears to be incoming across the river on the Salisbury side and outgoing on Plum Island. Apparently the fish swing through a long counterclockwise loop and the trick is to intercept them."

*The place:* "Right at the bend in the jetty, just below where it doglegs seaward. This gets you within casting distance of midchannel, but there's no need to try for distance. You'll be just downstream of a sandbar. A choppy line of turbulence will locate it for you. Cast upcurrent of the bar and let your bait swing slowly across it."

*The technique:* "Seven-foot surf rod, 25-pound-test monofilament on an open-face spinning reel with drag set somewhere between the pull of the current and the run of a cod. Hang a couple of clam necks on a #5/0 O'Shaughnessy hook a foot or so above a 6-ounce bank sinker. If your son should be feeling cocky, let him try two hooks, one above the other about 2 feet apart. A pair of 20-pounders teaming up against him in that current just might make him yell 'Uncle.' "

Twenty-pounders we didn't catch that May morning, but there were enough 10-pound terriers to keep Jack and me jumping till the tide tailed off and the majority of fish moved out about an hour before dead low. Less than a week later the run was over. Warming water had sent the fish offshore, and for the rest of the summer, boats dangling bait and bouncing jigs over offshore shoals had a corner on the codfish market.

The cod's exodus, however, merely ran down the curtain on Act One of a season that included pollock, mackerel, flounder, stripers, a few late-season bluefish, and even an occasional coho salmon on its way up the coast for a fall spawning run in New Hampshire's Great Bay . . . which causes Jack and me to wonder if maybe Mr. Webster shouldn't consider sharing our definition of a jetty as a stable platform surrounded by fish.

# HOUSEBOAT

How would you and your son like to catch flounder from your front porch? Or smallmouths from your roof? How would you like to sleep in comfortable bunk beds not just near but right *on* the water, with only ripples and the soft sounds of silence to lull you to sleep? Food? Anything you want. Cook it, serve it, and eat it without even interrupting your fishing. Weather too warm? Just roll into the water for a refreshing dip. Too cold? Just batten down the hatches and light the stove. And when fishing slows down or traffic picks up, just start your motor and move elsewhere.

This is houseboat fishing. Not just an adman's version of this increasingly popular recreation, but the real thing. Jack, Dan, and I verified it a few years back before the boys' summer jobs made it all but impossible

Houseboats are the ideal application of "If you can't beat 'em, join 'em." For three days, Jack and Dan and I lived in luxury on a tidewater bay surrounded by flounder and mackerel.

for the three of us to schedule the same consecutive days off. How glad we are to have grabbed the opportunity when we had it!

Ours was a homemade craft anchored throughout the summer in a sheltered saltwater sound behind Plum Island, on Massachusetts' northern coast. A friend had invited us to use it.

"Hey, it's sitting here empty most of the time anyway," said Jack Young. "Bring the boys and fish yourselves silly. I'll be down evenings to see how you're doing."

This from a man I'd barely known a year earlier, barely seen in between. Jack lives just a twenty-minute run up the Parker River when the tide is right. Now that his son and daughter have married and moved out, he and his wife Edna occupy a comfortable cottage on the maple-shaded main street of a neat New England village. Come the moon tides of May, though, and Jack tows his plywood Taj Mahal off the marsh grass, where he has left it the fall before, and down the Parker to its two-ton-motor-block mooring between the Parker River Wildlife Refuge and the high clustered homes of Ipswich's Little Neck across the Sound.

I met Jack while fishing with a friend. "C'mon," he said, as we swung around Plum Island's choppy southern tip after an afternoon's trolling, "I want to introduce you to a great guy."

He was not exaggerating. Jack's helpful advice and generous hospitality—daybreak breakfasts, lobster lunches, coffee and conversation, a few fingers of chilblain-chaser on chilly October evenings, chauffered boatrides around the bay when stripers seemed to be boycotting my favorite stretch of beach—have been among the biggest dividends from my hours in the outdoors. After three days aboard Jack's houseboat, they're among my sons' biggest dividends, too.

Jack's boat, as I said, is homemade. In simplest terms it looks like about a 40-foot-square raft with a big box on it. Get close, though, and you'll see where care and cleverness have had to complement hard work in putting frames and paint and plywood together. Outside there are hinged booms, one on each side, for tying up boats. When traveling, they are folded in like wings. A couple of feet of the raft's surface permits walking along the sides where the booms are located, and on either end, where the doors to the house are located, about 4 feet of raft are left vacant to serve as front and back porches. Ladders are installed on both ends for reaching the roof. Jack has built a sturdy enough roof to permit sunbathing, fishing, and diving, although his trips topside are made only to raise and lower the flag, his signal to friends that he's aboard, c'mon over, coffee's on.

A kitchen-dining area combination occupies about two-thirds of the inside. Entering through the front screen door, you find a long tavern-type table along a picture-windowed wall on your right, a sink and counter space below another large window on your left, and gas-fueled stove and refrigerator in front of you. Floor and wall cabinets store staples and utensils, while perishables keep nicely in a locker under the kitchen floor. Beds are aft beyond the table, a double-decker on either side, and a privy as clean and private as your neighborhood filling station's is back there too. Gas lanterns provide illumination, but last I heard, Jack was working on a device that would generate electricity with the flow of the tide.

And that's it. Add a below-decks winch, a few chairs, and an awesome arsenal of fishing gear up in the rafters, and you have an idea of where and how my sons and I were going to be living (correction: LIVING) for three midsummer days.

"Here's what you do," Jack had told us. "Drive to the back of the island. Park outside the gate at the end of the Refuge road. I'll leave my 16-footer at Anchorage Point. The 12-footer will be fine for getting me to work and back, and you'll have the bigger boat for toting your gear across and for going fishing."

There was a note on the windshield three days later when Dan waded out to Jack's anchored boat.

"Plenty of lobsters in the carry under the stern. Clams in the burlap bag tied astern. Help yourself. A few bass around. Try poppers tomorrow morning around top tide at Grape Island point. Hottest action on mackerel out around #2 can. Save a few for my lobster pots and *please* keep the screen doors closed. Greenheads have been fierce."

We decided this time to concentrate on mackerel. Jack's boat enabled us to get out to the renowned mackerel Mecca of #2 buoy, to which Jack had introduced me the previous summer, and I wanted to make sure that my sons would have plenty of action.

To ensure this action I planned to employ a trick Jack had taught me a few weeks earlier. Peg and I had driven down in the darkness to start the day plugging a nearby point for stripers, when Jack, with characteristic hospitality, had come over in his outboard and invited us to breakfast. Afterward we headed for the open ocean. Fifteen minutes later, as we swung into the current and I let go the anchor, Jack opened a can of dog food, mixed it with seawater in a plastic bucket, and proceeded to ladle some of the soup into the water every minute or so.

"What are you trying to do," I asked, "attract dogfish?"

"Mackerel," he answered. "They love it. Climb right up the chum line to your boat and stay there as long as you keep ladling. Cat food's even better. More fish in it."

I don't know if it was the dog food that did it, but we soon had enough action to fill an exciting hour and half a bushel basket.

Next morning to ensure the same kind of cooperation from the mackerel, several of which were being hauled aboard neighboring boats as I swung into the current alongside #2 buoy and Dan dropped anchor, I was brewing up a batch of catfood soup even before the boys got their jigs into the water.

The mackerel, in case you've never caught one, is in my opinion one of the most underrated scrappers in the sea. I've caught trout of equal proportions that couldn't touch them for speed, tenacity, and just plain flex-your-muscles-and-run-like-fury fight. Trouble is, they travel in such vaster numbers that anglers rarely evaluate them individually. More intent on filling their freezers by taking four and five at a time on a string of lures, fishermen normally concentrate on quantity and ignore quality.

They're also easy to catch. Anything small and shiny, resembling the sand eels for which they always seem to be foraging, is sure to induce a strike. The ideal lure is a mackerel jig, two to three inches of three-sided metal that tapers from an eye at one end to a hook on the other. Jerked so that it jumps and falls every few seconds, it is irresistible to mackerel whose hunger has been excited by a catfood appetizer. Often with the school only a few feet beneath the surface you can see five, ten, twenty, fish competing for a crack at your jig. Son Jack, in fact, snared two on a single hook.

Since our intention was to keep only enough mackerel to feed ourselves, we were able to get full benefit from their bellicose performance. Dan, using a single jig on ultralight tackle, seemed able with his tiny 5-foot spinning rod and 4-pound-test line to hook them almost at will, but landing them was a different story. With his drag light enough to ensure that the fish would not break off his jig yet tight enough to enable him to keep his fish away from the anchor rope and our lines, he had to play them long and sensitively. Jack, casting a heavily tinseled streamer fly he had tied himself, took longer than Dan to hook fish and made the most of every contest by stripping rather than reeling in his line. Using conventional spinning tackle, I had all the action I could handle between ladling out chum and clicking cameras.

With this kind of fishing every day, who could want more? We could. Dunking worms, we took a few flounder, and on two brief occasions we went after stripers with drifted worms and live mackerel, both times without success. Always, though, we felt the urge to return to the bell buoy for that unique combination of quality and quantity fishing, and as tenants of a houseboat, we were able to do just that.

Houseboats, by the way, are becoming more and more popular. For years they have been seen on fresh water, a few larger ones anchored permanently but most of them light enough to be pushed from anchorage to anchorage by twin outboards. Houseboat cruises on the St. Lawrence have long been a favorite among vacationers. Now they are appearing in the saltwater bays and harbors that offer adequate protection from heavy seas. Occasionally they even are offered for rent, so if you think you might want to see what it's like to live for a while right among the fish you seek, try renting. First, though, study carefully the charts of any tidal waters you plan to cruise. Narrow channels, tricky currents, and shifting bars can put you aground quickly and unexpectedly.

Of the houseboat's many attributes, none exceeds the ability it gives you to enjoy fresh-from-the-ocean seafood. Tops on my list—and this includes the lobster and clams with which Jack Young was so generous—is mackerel, provided it's prepared and cooked the way Jack does it. With a simple slice of a sharp knife, he cleaves a fillet from each flank. Shaking them in a bag of Bisquick, he fries them ever so slowly in butter till the skin crinkles and the firm white flesh glows to a golden brown. Unlike any other mackerel I have eaten, these are neither bony nor oily.

There is, I am told, on the Mediterranean island of Sardinia a seaside hotel which fairly reeks of regal opulence: plush appointments, air conditioning, exotic foods, and servants vying to cater to your every whim. Me, I'll take a houseboat on Plum Island Sound in the compatible company of two teen-age sons.

## SAILING AND FISHING

"Friday about sunset," said Bob Sampson, owner-skipper of the 28-foot sloop *Resolute*, "we'll leave from Pepperell Cove, run downriver on an ebbing tide, and within an hour be dropping anchor at the Isles of Shoals. How does that sound?"

To me it sounded great. Not so much for the sailing. First and foremost, I'm a fisherman. In sailing, speed is supreme, and this normally is incompatible with an angler's need for matching the movement of his craft to the habits of his quarry. What made Sam's itinerary so appealing was our destination. Since my boyhood when, as a passenger on a party boat, I first had sampled the superb fishing around this bleak and almost barren cluster of granite clumps off New Hampshire's narrow coast, the Isles of Shoals had beckoned me back. I looked forward to a return engagement with the mackerel and pollock we used to coax topside with appetizers of ground sand eels and for a chance to sample the scrappy flounder for which Gosport Harbor was fast becoming famous.

The fishing also appealed to my eighteen-year-old son, Jack, who, aboard a party boat a few years back, also had enjoyed a piece of the Isles' action. The sight of a massive mackerel school gorging itself on herring it had herded against a high sea-bleached cliff was vivid in both our memories. But blessed with a youthful appetite for new experiences, Jack also was anxious to try sailing.

For Sam, sailing was the ultimate occupation, the sublime synthesis of knowledge, timing, intuition, exercise, and enjoyment. As inheritor of several generations of seagoing Yankee tradition, Sam took his sailing

Who says sailing and fishing don't mix? We got our best meals on this trip — flounder, cusk, pollock, mackerel — from the sea.

seriously. Anything that interfered with it—and this, I knew, included fishing—was likely to receive short shrift.

But I had a little tradition behind me too. As descendant of a long line of poker-playing Irishmen, I made sure I was holding an ace as my hole card. Sam, I knew, enjoyed nothing better than dining on fresh-from-the-briny seafood, yet he had never been successful in catching a meal while at sea. With Jack's able assistance, I planned to convert him by feeding him.

Our first step in the conversion occurred even while we were still dockside at Pepperell Cove. Sam had rowed to *Resolute,* unmoored her, and brought her under power alongside the Kittery Point Yacht Club's pier, on which Jack and I had assembled stores, sleeping bags, and fishing gear. Even in the silvered calm of evening I might not have noticed the bait scurrying off *Resolute*'s port bow had Sam not scoffed at the rods I was handing Jack to secure along the cabin roof.

"Hmmff," he snorted. "You sure you want to bring those along?"

"These, my cynical skipper," I replied, "are going to keep your galley well supplied with marine comestibles." Then, spotting a patch of splashes,

I handed a rod already rigged with a small shiny jig to Jack, and added, "And to substantiate my promise, watch this."

Jack had seen the busting bait too. Pausing for a second till another flurry positioned the feeding school, he cast his jig a few feet beyond the fish, let it settle briefly, then jerked it hard. As the jig fluttered downward, a half-pound pollock snatched it, and Sam gawked open-mouthed at this Abbott-and-Costello act that apparently could catch fish on cue.

When Jack unhooked what looked to Sam like the start of a tasty meal and dropped it unceremoniously over the fantail, Sam was startled.

"Hey," he hollered, "what're you guys doing with my breakfast?"

"Just practice," I assured him as I took my turn with the rod and effortlessly duplicated Jack's catch.

Enjoyable as this was, neither Jack nor I delayed when Sam announced that it was time to shove off. With mooring lines cast off, Sam eased *Resolute* away from the dock and swung her bow in an easy arc to port. Across the broad Piscataqua we watched the dusk-dimmed panorama of historic Portsmouth: boats and docks and buildings clotting into shadowed clumps that were topped here and there by tall spires gleaming like luminous lances in the August afterglow.

The downriver run was short. Within minutes we were passing Whale-back Light to port. Behind us the gaudy glare of civilization subsided like expiring embers as a gentle swell and a salty breeze made it official: we were at sea. Sam stood silently in the bow sniffing the air, speculating on tomorrow's weather. Jack, at the wheel, concentrated on keeping the Isles' White Island light a few points off our starboard bow. Me, I was thinking about those mackerel and pollock and flounder, and about the 98-pound 12-ounce world-record cod that Al Bielevich had boated out there in 1969.

To entice these fish, I had brought along a can of fish-flavored catfood which I planned to mix in a bucket of seawater. By dumping a dollop of this soup overboard every few seconds, I was sure that in shallow Gosport Harbor I'd soon have flatties sniffing their way up my chumline. Probably pollock, too. Maybe even mackerel, although I expected them to be more responsive to a trolled string of jigs outside the harbor so long as the wind wasn't too strong. I knew that dogfish, which infest these northern New England waters, also might move up my chumline, but they would be more likely to be in codfish country, where the water was deeper and more open. Nevertheless, even if doggies should move in, where could

I enjoy better rod-bending bouts then with these rapacious 3-to-4-foot roughnecks?

The term "snug harbor" was coined with the likes of Gosport in mind. Tethered securely to a solid mud bottom alongside Cedar Island, I had the impression of our being cradled in the strong shadowed arms of Star Island to port and Smuttynose to starboard. With *Resolute* rocking gently and a soft breeze singing in her rigging, I soon was joining Jack and Sam in the bunkhouse below . . . but not before I laid out the following equipment in the cockpit: one stiff-tipped 7-foot spinning rod carrying 20-pound-test mono and terminating in a 4-ounce pyramid sinker with two hooks above it. The lower hook, narrow and long-shanked, 6 inches above the sinker, was for flounder; the upper, a #3/0 O'Shaughnessy, was for bottom-dwellers such as cod with bigger mouths than flounder. Both hooks were tied to dropper loops by 6 inches of 30-pound mono.

One whippy 6½-foot spinning rod with three shiny jigs in series on 15-pound-test mono.

One quart of steamer clams for bottom bait.

One can of catfood in a plastic bucket.

One bar of breakfast candy and two cans of beer to, uh, toast the new day.

And what a day it was! Tiptoeing topside at the first dim hint of daylight, I was greeted by a molten sun edging up over Government Breakwater astern. Every window in the rambling wooden hotel on Star Island reflected its radiance. Gulls squawked as if waiting for something to happen, and within a few seconds of dangling a pair of clam necks to port, I gave it to them. Like a willow switch, the stiff-tipped 7-footer dunked nearly to the water even before I could mix my chumbroth. Despite a tight drag, the fish ran out line in two short hard lunges, then concentrated on a staccato series of head-shaking yanks. By pumping and reeling, I managed to bring to the surface 2 feet of slimy, slithering cusk, that cross between a cod and an eel that's as delicious as it is ugly.

Normally eighteen-year-old sons are not rousted out of bed at daybreak by anything less than the aroma of frying bacon or the availability of the family car. Equally effective on a midsummer morning in Gosport Harbor, I learned, is the splashing of struggling fish and the rustle of a father's feet as he scurries between port and starboard rods that refuse to stay still for more than a few seconds at a time.

"What'll you have?" I asked Jack as he ascended the ladder rubbing his eyes. "Pollock or flounder?"

I don't recall which he chose, but it didn't matter. There was action aplenty for both of us: pollock seemed to be magnetized by our chum and flounder ate our clam necks like kids gulping gumdrops.

Later, after Sam had rolled out of his sack, there also was plenty of eating. Filleting the flounder after we had gotten underway, I shook the meat in a bag of flour and fried up a feed of sweet flaky flesh that made even Sam a believer.

"And all these years," he marveled, holding out his plate for seconds, "I've been anchored over meals like this!"

Because we left the harbor early so we could get in as much sailing as possible, we saw few other boats fishing. I knew, though, that even as we weighed anchor, party and private craft were heading out of Seabrook, Hampton, Rye, Portsmouth, Kittery, and probably even Newburyport to mine the rich lode of mackerel which seems to be the Isles' main midseason attraction.

Mackerel, in fact, didn't seem beyond the realm of possibility for us with only a mild breeze filling our sails. When Sam elected to veer to starboard and cruise casually north of Appledore till the wind picked up, I quickly switched the string of jigs from my 6½-foot rod to my stiffer 7-footer, cast them astern, and immediately started yanking to make them flash and flutter like a school of bait. The mackerel, bless 'em, were as accommodating as the flounder and pollock had been earlier, although a stiffening breeze terminated our trolling after only a few fish.

From here on, the day belonged to Sam, and I didn't begrudge him a minute of it. Hauling and heeling and whatever else it is that salty sailors do, he sliced through the sea while Jack and he took turns at the helm and I reflected on what I had read of the lore and legend of those lonely granite Isles. . . .

How originally they were named the Smith Islands by John Smith of Pocahontas fame, but the name did not endure. . . . How women and pigs had been banned from its shores until 1647, when a young rebel named Reynolds brought a wife from the mainland and was backed in his act by the General Court. . . . How a couple of governors once had divvied up the islands between New Hampshire and Maine, and how their decision is haunting today's shellfishermen. . . . How Louis Wagner rowed to Smuttynose a hundred years ago, brutally murdered two helpless women while their men waited for trawl bait on the mainland, and then rowed back to Rye.

I thought of storms and shipwrecks, of poetess Celia Thaxter's lyrical legacy, and of Dr. John Kingsbury and his Shoals Marine Laboratory, and I vowed silently that one day I would come to know the Isles of Shoals better.

That evening after we had secured *Resolute* to her mooring back in Pepperell Cove, we lingered briefly before loading Sam's dinghy and rowing the hundred yards to shore. "Y'know," said Sam, seated alongside me in the cockpit, "I have only one regret about this whole trip. I wish we'd brought some of those flounder home so Gail could get a taste of what she's been missing."

A splashing commotion from up forward where Jack had been dunking the last of our clam necks announced that he had come through again, right on cue.

"And how many," I asked, "do you suppose that ravishing redhead of yours would like to have?"

# SURF

The fisherman, wound like a watchspring, strode into the Cape Cod surf and heaved a silver sand-eel simulator 40 feet into a 100-yard-wide harbor mouth, where the lure was snatched by a recently turned high tide and swung slowly to the right. Lifting and lowering the rod to let the lure flutter and settle as it swung, the caster cranked the reel's bail closed and continued to raise and lower the rod in a sort of contrapuntal rhythm to the regular rotation of the reel. As the lure yo-yoed tantalizingly into the shallows, a dark form streaked up from below the dropoff at the channel's edge to snatch the glistening tidbit, only to wind up with a mouthful of hook and a tailful of jet propulsion.

Hauling back on the rod, the angler immediately let the fish know who was boss, and throughout the next three minutes of short surging runs and headshaking pauses, there never for a second was any doubt. Relentlessly the reel gained line until the rod led the tired fish through the shallows onto the sand ... as nice a specimen of genus *Prionotus*, family Triglidae, the common northern searobin, as ever drove a striper fisherman to distraction.

The point is that this was not a striper fisherman. It was my six-year-old daughter Margaret, and she couldn't have been more excited or satisfied if she had caught a 5-pound striper. Kneeling beside her catch, she scrutinized its horny back, marveled at its broad "wings," and listened incredulously to its croaks as I, her delighted daddy, removed the hook and released the fish.

The surf can be gentle wavelets as well as booming breakers. On an April afternoon, Jack and I scored this doubleheader on king-size codfish.

Girls are great fun during that gloriously uninhibited interlude before worms become "ucky" and waders become unfashionable; when baiting their own hooks is a way of proving they can do anything those big smarty old boys can do. There is, after all, a charming incongruity in watching a sweet, shy, delicate little doll wind up like a hairy-chested casting champ and heave a lure halfway to Halifax. (It's best, by the way, to do this from behind the nearest sand dune.)

Surf casting, of course, is a difficult and demanding kind of fishing for little girls, but Margaret and Julie had been so anxious to try it that I relented. It was a balmy bathing-suit afternoon, and Chatham's Stage Harbor was close, accessible, lighthouse-and-sailboats-and-sandy-beach lovely, and best of all, it rarely had let me down. In five times of fishing a full tide there, I had taken stripers on four of them. Traffic, I knew, might give us trouble, with speeding boats spooking fish, but then we weren't after world records. A few searobins would satisfy the girls, and the possibility of catching a striper would keep them casting.

A parking lot at the town beach led onto an easy-to-walk dirt road, and in twenty minutes I was rigging a fat, fresh, frisky, 7-inch seaworm on a #4/0 Eagle Claw hook. With a flood tide having just turned, I placed a single small split shot about 2 feet above the hook; as the current picked up I would add enough shot to keep the worm just off the bottom while my daughters walked the worm from the inboard end of the gut seaward.

This is an interesting technique, uniquely applicable to narrow channels with steeply sloping banks alongside which fish are likely to chase bait. It consists simply of casting your worm from the upcurrent end, then walking, rod in hand and bail open, as the worm drifts with the current. By keeping slack out of your line, you can feel fish as soon as they strike. By lifting your rod slowly about halfway to vertical every once in a while, then lowering it slowly, you can give your bait a provocative run-and-retreat action.

On my first demonstration I had walked less than a dozen steps with the tide when my line started pouring from my reel. The run was fast and forceful enough to be a small striper, but when it stopped after only a few feet, I was sure we were into searobins. Setting my hook confirmed it; the fish was frisky but lacking the rough-and-tumble, roll-up-your-sleeves rambunctiousness of a striped bass.

"Here," I hollered to the girls, a few feet behind me on the sand. "Here's a fish."

Margaret waded waist-high into the water, grabbed the rod, and proceeded to reel in with the kind of energy and earnestness usually reserved for half-ton tuna. To give her maximum action, I had set a light drag, and that searobin made the most of it. More often than not Margaret was reeling against a running fish, and when she finally hauled her catch up on the beach, it was hard to tell which of them was more pooped.

Julie as well as Margaret was fascinated by the fish's horny head, broad wings, and croaking noises. Both knelt alongside me as I removed the hook to examine this strange creature and touch it tentatively. For almost a half-hour every drift produced a repeat performance, and the girls took turns, their interest never wavering, their technique improving with each experience.

Then in midchannel I saw what I had been looking for, hoping for, waiting for: a swirl from a feeding striper. I was ready. Removing the girls' hook, I replaced it with a shiny 3-inch lure that resembled the small herring whose schools I had observed in the shallows. I cast a few feet upcurrent of where I had seen the fish . . . and cast and cast and cast. As is usually the case in a busy channel, speeding boats had spooked my fish and for the moment at least, there were no other takers.

"Daddy, can we try it, pleeeeeeese," called my daughters from the shore.

Naturally they, like most children, wanted to do their own casting. Naturally I, like most fathers, thought it safer, more efficient, less susceptible to snarls and snags if I did the casting, then handed the rod to them. To me it seemed that trying to propel an ounce-and-a-half lure with a 4-foot daughter on an 8-foot surf rod was like trying to launch a Saturn V with a slingshot. I was underestimating my daughters, of course. They soon were casting competently by making up in resolution what they lacked in finesse.

Their initial attempts were a little hazardous, but by a simple procedure I managed to escape unscathed. First we would stand at the water's edge and rehearse the casting procedure: reel in excess line, hold line against rod with right index finger, flip bail with left hand, tilt rod back, then whip rod forward, lifting right index finger and releasing line at the instant the lure's weight is felt. Then, as if an air-raid alarm had sounded, I would dive for the beach, hands over head, face in sand, as a wildly swinging treble hook whistled past my graying mane.

Even on so heavy a lure the lassies managed to catch searobins, no small achievement for little girls with big gear totally unaided by their father. They reveled in their newfound virtuosity. Totally independent, they would wind up and whip that lure across the water, a little less than accurate on occasions, their distance somewhat less than limitless, but rarely was there a tangle and never once did they become bored or impatient.

Julie gave the prize performance when, spurning my assistance, she played and landed with the poise and aplomb of a June Rosko a splendid little school striper that hit her lure some 30 feet away as it wobbled through a stream of passing boats.

Later, as we ambled across the dunes to our car, laden with gear and brimful of marvelous memories, I found myself humming a Lerner and Lowe melody from the movie *Gigi.* Its title? "Thank Heaven for Little Girls."

With sons, the drill is pretty much the same as with daughters: an elementary teacher-pupil relationship, altogether delightful, yet a little restricted by a boy's limitations, a little restrained by a Dad's indulgence . . . until one day you make a particularly long cast and notice something wiggling through the water well beyond where your lure has landed. Your first reaction is "Bass!" But it's not big enough for a bass; more likely a frightened bait. Then the sun picks up the thin filament of line leading from this object—now recognizable as a cleverly manipulated counterfeit—to the tip of your son's rod, and suddenly it dawns on you that the young squirt has outcast you. Furthermore, he's working that plug of his with a poise and finesse you didn't know he possessed. Come to think of it, it's been a long while since he's sought your advice.

From that marvelous moment on, you and he fish as equals. No holds barred, no quarter given. The roughest water, the toughest conditions: you tackle them together. You still share secrets (well, most of them), you still trade tricks (except for a few), but all subsequent sessions together in the surf will pit the Goliath of your experience against the David of his impudence. And no slingshots allowed.

This is how it was when Jack, with an idle day between concluding his summer job and starting college, asked if I might be able to join him plugging a favorite stretch of northern Massachusetts shore. As it happened, I could. It was only the beginning of September; the storm windows could wait another day.

Jack had picked a classic almost-autumn setting for our outing. It dawned so bright and cool and clear that we felt, as we drove across the shaky wooden bridge to our island, that the world surely would shatter if we so much as shouted. Flights of southbound geese etched their Vs against an azure sky as a gentle surf spanked an empty beach. The surf was so gentle, in fact, and the beach so empty that we were approaching the end of our 5-mile drive down the island's dusty road before I realized it was time to pull over and disembark. That special sprawl of rocks I wanted to investigate lay just over the dunes. At this time of year, I felt, hungry stripers might be assembling around these rocks for a pre-migration meal.

I had caught stripers here before, good ones, by casting popping plugs and drifting live mackerel from a boat anchored off the outside end of the rocks, but never had I seen anyone fishing from the rocks themselves. There had to be a reason, of course. There always is when attractive casting country is ignored, but I couldn't for the life of me figure out what it might be. Sure, the rocks were awash at high tide, but while the tide was low, as it was now, there should be no problem in simply walking out and casting. By using a topwater plug, one could avoid hangups; by concentrating casts within a couple of broad spans between boulders, one should have enough room for playing a hooked fish. It was tricky territory, but the kind where experience might give Old Man Goliath a rare edge in his duel with David.

The reason for the rocks' unpopularity with shore fishermen became obvious well before we even got to them: they stopped before they reached shore. Now, with the tide almost at dead low, a 15-foot-wide span of ocean separated them from the sandy slope along which we were approaching; as the tide came in, this gulf would widen quickly. This obstacle was emphasized by a lone bait fisherman standing alongside the sandspike that held his rod.

"Naw," he said. "I tried it. Even before this tide turned, the water in that trench was up to my waist. Twenty minutes from now it'll be over your head and sluicing like a squirt gun."

But twenty minutes could give Jack and me maybe a dozen casts at fish that I knew were out there among those foamy boulders just itching to take us on. I could almost see their swirls, feel their strikes, hear their reel-screeching runs. I could smell them, I could taste them, and I wanted in the worst way to touch them, preferably with the cold steel of a hand gaff after I had earned the right in a fair fight.

If we took a chance and were careful not to overplay our hand, I reasoned, the worst we could get is wet. Jack was a strong swimmer, and Lord knows, the day hadn't yet dawned when I couldn't backstroke his butt off. We wouldn't be wearing waders, so holding rods and camera over our heads while the current carried us back to shore should be no problem.

"Five minutes out, five minutes in, and ten to take us a fish," I said to Jack. "What do you say?"

Jack knew a good bet when he saw it. "Let's go."

Five minutes was about right for wading through the chest-high sluice and galloping across the rocks. Ten minutes would have been ample for casting, too, if that bass hadn't waited till my absolutely scout's-honor last cast before scooting out from that clump of kelp and torpedoing my plug.

"Hey," I hollered from atop my rock. "Jack, Jack, over here, look."

But Jack was looking already. And not from the other side of the rocks to which he had gone ten and a half minutes before, but from directly behind and below me where he was standing up to his hips in water that seemed to edge up 6 inches with each successive wave. And he wasn't looking with awe or envy at the 10-pound striper that was bucketing like a loco bronco out among the boulders.

"Dad," he whispered, "I think it's time to go."

So, fortunately, did the bass. It broke off in the next wave.

The man on the beach must have hustled toward us when he saw that we finally were heading in, because he was there on the shore waiting when our noses emerged, followed by our chins, necks, chests, etc. His eyebrows, two-blocked up around his hairline, capped a couple of full-moon eyes, and his stubbled chin hung from his open mouth like a flap on a set of fuzzy drawers. His head moved from upper left to lower right in what must have been a diagonal compromise between a horizontal "I don't believe it" and a vertical "I told you so."

As it turned out, the rest of the day was delightful. Damp, but delightful. There was hot coffee waiting in the car, and we even managed to turn up a pair of cooperative stripers in a a cluster of submerged rocks on the back side of the island. For a while it seemed like old times: no David, no Goliath; just Daddy fishing with his little boy.

This illusion persisted until a few weeks later when Jack announced that he had recorded our experience for his school newspaper.

"Want to read it?" he asked in his best postpubescent baritone.

Naively, I expected a sort of collegiate show-and-tell. What I got was ... Well, here, see for yourself. Not only did it remind me that, like it or not, we now were fishing as equals, but that it wouldn't be long before we would be writing as equals too.

# CONCERNING THE EVENTS IN WHICH I WAS INVOLVED DURING THE MORNING AND AFTERNOON OF FRIDAY, SEPTEMBER 25, 1970
by John Fallon, Jr.


"This water's gonna be a little cold," said my father as we prepared to walk through a shallow stretch of the sea separating Emerson Rocks from the Plum Island beach.

"But," he continued, "I imagine it'll be a lot colder on the way back." At the conclusion of this prophetic statement he sprinted through the calf-deep water to the 50-yard flat stretch of rocks exposed then at low tide. I followed, suspicious and wet.

After setting the two cameras and spare rod safely on a nearby rock, we took our positions on the edge of the rock bed where Dad was sure there were bass. While on my precarious perch (no relation to yellow, white, or sea perch) I noticed that an event which takes place twice daily was leading me to wonder why we didn't wear our waders. Can you guess what event this was? That's right; the tide was coming in. I first sensed this when my sneakers filled up with water even though the rock I was standing on had very recently been high and dry. I switched positions, and for the next ten minutes neither of us had any luck. The tide seemed to be advancing at a rapid rate, but since Dad was not worried, why should I be?

Suddenly I heard Dad yelling. He seemed to have a fish on and shouted for me to join him on his rock. I jumped off my rock into thigh-deep liquid ice and stumbled over to where Dad was in the process of losing a, quote, 10-pounder, unquote. I couldn't fit on Dad's rock, but I was quite content to stand next to him in water up to my waist while trying to fix the bail on my reel.

"They're out there," screamed the calm, knowledgeable saltwater editor of *Massachusetts Outdoorsman* and frequent contributor to various national outdoor magazines.

"I had four hits, then a 10-pounder took it and I lost him." Except for the chattering of my teeth, I remained silent and glanced behind us to where we had left the spare rod and cameras. Waves were beating on the rock and the rod was nowhere to be seen. I asked Dad if he knew where the rod might be.

"Probably got washed off the rock," he replied as he heaved his plug out once again. After reeling in his third "one last cast," we started back. Dad stepped off the rock and lost his footing, tripping face-first into the surf.

"Blub, blub, blub," he mumbled. Although I couldn't catch the exact words, I'm reasonably sure that he didn't say, "Gee, the water is refreshing this morning."

We picked up the cameras just before a wave would have soaked them, and the rod was found floating a short distance away.

Thirty yards of water now separated the rocks from shore. We bravely waded into it and gradually it rose over our belts, chests, chins. When we sloshed ashore there was a fisherman there who told us he had been afraid we wouldn't be able to get back. Dad had the gall to tell him that we knew what we were doing.

So much for Emerson.

We returned to the car and drove to the end of the road, where we stopped, got out, and ate lunch. I could not see any sense in wearing waders, but Dad, having slipped into a pair of dry pants, decided to wear his. We had no trouble getting out to our favorite point, but, for anyone interested in bug-watching, the mosquitoes were quite bothersome at times.

I think we both used poppers for about half an hour without luck before Dad started casting a shallow swimmer into a rip. On his second cast he connected with a mammoth bass of the 4-to-5-pound class. Before I knew what was going on, Dad had the creature beached. After being clubbed on the head, the bass began to shudder and, crying aloud, gave up the ghost.

An hour or so of inactivity followed before Dad once again latched onto, and beached, another enormous monster in short order.

Later, when I was flycasting off to Dad's right, I became curious (yellow) to see if anything was happening in Dad's vicinity and glanced toward him at the precise moment that he had chosen to fall off his high rock into the water again; this time with his waders on. He later explained that his original intent was to jump from one rock to another one nearby, but the fish stringer had become entangled around his legs and consequently his plans were altered to a great extent.

A short while later we returned to Emerson Rocks. Naturally, Dad took the fish with him instead of leaving them in the car where no one could marvel at them.

There was a family on the beach as well as a few older couples out for a stroll. I'm sure they all admired our great catch, but no one dared to come too close. I guess they must have seen us in action on the rocks earlier.

Only one rod was in working condition by this time and I was elected to take it out to a nearly submerged rock and put on an exhibition of true grit for the fans. The title of my show was "Man Against the Elements," and it was very appropriate. I climbed onto the rock from water that was up to my waist. There, while standing on the rock, I withstood the onslaught of wind and waves (which broke right over the rock) in order to valiantly cast a plug into the "bassy-looking water." Naturally I didn't wear my waders. I connected on my first cast, my second cast, my third cast; in fact, I connected on every cast, but all I connected with was seaweed. As soon as Dad sensed the seriousness and hopelessness of the situation, and stopped laughing, he called me back to shore, from where I did a little casting with no results.

In conclusion I would like to say that this kind of fishing is not restricted to the rich. You don't have to fly to Alaska or South America to enjoy it. Here are a few more helpful hints.

A. Plan ahead so that everything can go wrong.

B. Bring waders so that at the last moment you can decide not to wear them.

C. Carry as much equipment as you can. The more you bring, the more you can lose or break.

D. Remember that although stupidity is a great asset for this kind of fishing, it is not a necessity.

E. And last but most important, don't believe everything you read in outdoor magazines.

# Epilogue: Fishing
# With Grown-Up Children

It finally happened. After ten years of trying, the Moose River Roll Cast, Six Pack, and Seven Card Stud Association arrived at its destination and was not—repeat, *not*—greeted with the invariable, inevitable, and demoralizing "Man, you guys should have been here *last* week!" This week *was* last week, the perfect combination of weather, wind, water, and assorted other ingredients that we never had quite been able to blend in our score of assaults on Maine's Moose River.

Our first harbinger of success was the crestfallen look on the normally jubilant face of Bill Stone when he returned from his annual mid-May excursion two weeks earlier. Normally Bill decimates the Moose's trout and salmon populations, but this year his creel was as empty as a taxpayer's wallet on April 16. "I'd have been just as well off with my ice-fishing traps," he said. "Thirty-nine-degree water, and more of it from this winter's abnormally heavy snowfall than I've ever seen. Another two weeks and it should be just right."

It was. Mrs. Harmon, pleasant proprietress of the Moose River Cabins, where we were staying, confirmed Bill's prediction, and so did several residents of other cabins in the area.

"River's gone down four feet in the last two days," said one gentleman.

"Fella took a 6-pound squaretail last evening in the pool right below where you're staying," said another.

"Wow," said we.

Most encouraging were the authoritative words of Ernie Perkins, proprietor of Brassua Lake Campgrounds, from whom we were renting boats for our run to the lake's legendary upper end where the Moose River enters. Ernie is a gentlemanly guide with two outstanding attributes: he is husband to a woman with a phenomenal capacity for looking pretty and acting pleasant at any time and under any circumstances, even, we learned, in response to an early reveille by five unshaven bearded brutes; and he possesses a knowledge of local fish and fishing that is exceeded only by his reputation for telling it like it is. When Ernie said, "Ayuh, right about the tail end of the smelt run, ought to be good," we shoved off like the first wave for Omaha Beach, Vern and Charlie in one boat, Frank, Vin, and I in the other.

Before starting our motors, allow me to introduce the illustrious membership of the MRRCSPASCSA:

*Charlie Pelletier:* Our bantam Bunyan. . . . Genial and generous, the original "give you the shirt off his back" guy. . . . A wit so versatile it can charm a child or shatter glass. . . . If snoring were fishing, he'd be Lee Wulff.

*Vin Gugger:* King of cooks, campers, and companions. . . . Warm and

All fishermen are nine years old, and every one should be lucky enough to have his own Moose River Roll Cast, Six Pack, and Seven Card Stud Association.

wise, solid and sincere. . . . Nobility of nice guys. . . . Patient and persistent in pursuit of fish, but not of poker hands. . . . Known to have fallen asleep holding a full house.

*Vern Merrill*: "Name's Vernon, not Vermin." . . . Long, loose, and lean. . . . Retired Navy chief with an armload of gold good-conduct hashmarks denoting twenty-two years of never having been caught. . . . Half Indian and half antelope in the woods.

*Frank Sheehan*: Big-city boy, enslaved by the comforts of civilization, yet incongruously at home in the outdoors. . . . Bon vivant with worms in his pocket. Lucius Beebe in waders (extra-large). . . . Nine hours' sleep, four meals, three naps, and a half-dozen snacks a day, and bring on your privations.

*Me*: Trustworthy, loyal, helpful, friendly, courteous, kind, obedient, cheerful, thrifty, brave, clean, and reverent. . . .

The morning was perfect. Unlike the day before, when Brassua had kicked up like a North Atlantic convoy run, with driftwood—fleets of floating logs and roots and stumps—substituting for submarines, today was so calm and cool and bright and breezy that the 6-mile run to the river's mouth was more delight than delay: the whispering flight of ducks overhead; a trout rising in an island's shady lee; distant mountains and quiet water; and finally, as we approached our objective, a forested ridge burgeoning with new yellow-green growth that seemed to spill like foamy fresh rivulets into a pine-green sea.

The river flowed from the forest, spreading down a gentle slope for 100 yards into a pool that poured leftward into the lake. The current, though fast, could be handled easily by our four-horse motors, enabling us to troll slowly up the slope swinging our lines like kite tails in the current. Each pass took twenty to thirty minutes, at the conclusion of which we turned downstream to start a new run at the pool's end.

No, we didn't catch a thousand fish. No, we didn't set any world—or even state or local—records. But we had good fishing, as good as any mortals are entitled to expect: maybe an average of a strike per boat per pass, of which we landed perhaps fifteen or twenty trout and salmon between us. Combined with compatible companionship and cool bugless comfort in a place that surely must be on the edge of Eden, this kind of action induced the following comments from my fellow MRRCSPASCSA members:

*Vin*: Well worth waiting for.

*Charlie*: I didn't even mind running out of beer.

*Vern*: See what can happen when you listen to me.

*Frank*: Like a hot fudge sundae.

It wasn't quite like a hot fudge sundae. The cherry was missing, the crowning confection in the form of something special, something enduringly unusual. I got it the following morning in the maelstrom below Brassua Dam, where the river leaves the lake.

With the river still too swollen for effective fishing, it was more of a sentimental exercise, a final hour or two of farewell fishing in one of our favorite pools before we headed home. So unoptimistic was I that I left my net in the car a quarter-mile up a dirt road from the dam. In Shakespearean drama this would be called my fatal flaw, the single simple act that unleashes the tides of tragedy, after which everything proceeds inexorably toward its dreadful preordained destiny.

Despite the wild water, I was able to fish with at least a modicum of effectiveness by using my 5-foot spinning rod and 4-pound-test line. Casting directly into the current was like flying a kite in a hurricane, but by casting a weighted bucktail into a small pocket behind a rock and raising my rod high I was able to work my fly for a few seconds on each cast before it became sucked into the surge. After quickly taking a small salmon, it was obvious that a net might be a handy thing to have, so when Vern announced that he was returning to the car for a reel replacement, I asked him to bring back my net.

He did. About fifteen minutes later in response to Charlie's frantic summons to hurry. Alas, if only it had been 14½ minutes, the mantle over my fireplace might boast the handsomest brook trout ever to throw a fly. Five times I had it on the surface, a vast expanse of speckled fish flesh that loomed large enough to have Jonah in its belly and Ahab on its back. Just as Vern and Charlie rounded the corner of the damkeeper's cottage, a wave washed my prize against a rock, and when the water subsided, my fly, but not my fish, was fast to the granite.

It's hard to react properly to the dashing of a dream, even when as a mature adult you know that the loss of a prize brook trout is pretty small potatoes in a world of war and hunger and injustice. But you need to be reminded.

"Be grateful for the five minutes you had him on," said Vin. "Not many of us are likely to have that experience, ever."

"You're just going to have to pay more attention to ole Vern, Jackson," said Merrill. "All these years I give you the benefit of my wisdom, and when the pressure's on, you blow it."

"Here, have a beer," said Charlie.

"Tough break," said Frank. "What's for breakfast?"

# Glossary

~~~~~~~~~~~~~~~~~~~~~~~~~~~~~~~~~~~~~~~~~~~

ANADROMOUS: Refers to fish that live in the sea and return to freshwater rivers to spawn. Among these are shad, Atlantic salmon, and most striped bass. Catadromous fish such as the American eel live in fresh water and spawn in the ocean.

ANGLER: A sportfisherman. The name is derived from *angle,* a term still used in many countries to designate a hook.

ANGLEWORM: An earthworm used for bait.

BACKING: Heavy line wound on a spool underneath lighter, less coarse line used in casting. An inexpensive linen line, for example, though poor for casting, is strong enough to restrain a running fish that takes your 150 to 200 yards of monofilament. Because it costs only a fraction of what a good monofilament costs, its use as backing can save you and your son several dollars with no loss in casting or playing capability.

BACKLASH: A tangled line resulting from the overrun of a revolving-spool reel.

BARNACLE: Small, hard marine crustaceans, approximately hemispherical in shape, that cling to rocks, boats, and pilings. Lines break easily on their rough and sometimes sharp surfaces.

BASS BUG: A floating fly-rod lure that imitates frogs, mice, and large insects. A popular lure for largemouth and striped bass.

BEACH BUGGY: A motor vehicle, generally custom-made, for transporting fishermen along sandy beaches.

BILLFISH: Fish such as marlin, sailfish, and swordfish whose upper jaws are elongated into a point.

BOBBER: Any of several plastic or wood devices used to keep bait a desired distance below the surface. The bobber's movement signals a fish's biting your bait. Also called a float.

BREAM: In the South, a term for several varieties of sunfishes.

BUCK: A male fish. The term normally is used to differentiate between the sexes during spawning. Also JACK.

BUCKTAIL: Hair from the tail of a deer. The term often is applied to the combination of such hair and the hook to which it is tied. Bucktails can be used by themselves on single or treble hooks, or as trailers on plugs and spoons.

CADDIS FLY: Freshwater insect whose almost 800 species provide fish fodder in wormlike larval as well as winged-adult stages.

CATADROMOUS: Refers to fish such as the American eel that live in fresh water and enter the sea to spawn. Anadromous fish (shad, Atlantic salmon, most striped bass, etc.) live in salt water and spawn in fresh.

CHARTER BOAT: Large powerful vessel available for hire by individual or group seeking big-water fishing. Cost includes bait and tackle, and on the larger charters a mate backs up the skipper and instructs passengers. Two to four anglers can fish simultaneously, although normally this is limited to two.

CHOP: Light waves caused by wind or tide.

CHUM: Ground fish food used to attract fish. Usually a spoonful of the mush is thrown into a tideway every few seconds, enticing fish to follow the scraps to their source. Also can be placed in a burlap sack and hung over the side for topwater fish, or tethered to your anchor for bottom-dwellers. Oily fish such as menhaden are especially effective, but almost any fish, or clams, crabs, and mussels, can be used.

Cow: A large female fish.

CRAYFISH OR CRAWFISH: Small lobsterlike freshwater crustacean. Excellent bait, especially for trout and black bass.

DRAG: The brake on a reel designed to make it more difficult for a fish to take out line. Also refers to an artificial fly's moving on or under the water faster than the current.

ESTUARY: The mouth of a tidal river.

FALSE CAST: In fly-fishing, swishing the line back and forth prior to casting, in order to extend your line or dry your fly.

FATHOMETER: Electronic instrument for determining depth of water or location of fish. Transmits signal which is reflected from target and returned to transmitter. Time for round trip is used to electronically calculate distance to target, which is recorded on paper tape or designated on numerically tabulated indicator.

FEATHER: In rowing, to twist the wrist at the completion of a stroke so that the oar blade is horizontal.

FENDER: A bumper hung over a vessel's side to prevent scraping against a dock or other vessel.

FERRULE: Metal plug-and-socket combination fitted on matching ends of a rod so they can be fitted together. Always lubricate male ferrules with oil from your hair, forehead, or behind your ear to avoid sticking.

FISHFINDER: A rig used principally in surf fishing, which enables a fish to run with your bait without having to pull your sinker.

FLY BOOK: A multileaved walletlike container for storing and carrying flat flies such as streamers.

FLY BOX: A container, usually compartmented, for storing and carrying flies such as dries, which cannot be pressed flat without injury.

FORAGE FISH: Small fish of various species with no sport or commercial worth but valuable as food for larger gamefish. Examples are darters, sand eels, mummichogs, and many kinds of sculpin.

GAFF: A large unbarbed hook on a handle for landing fish on a beach or lifting them aboard a boat. Hand gaffs for surf fishing are about 2 feet long, boat gaffs usually 6 to 8. Pier gaffs are oversize barbless treble or quadruple hooks on heavy line that can be dropped the long distances from pier to water to snag a hooked fish and haul it up to the pier.

GILLNET: A vertical mesh, weighted at the bottom and floated on its top, for trapping fish. The net's mesh size is selected according to the thickness of the fish being sought. When a fish inserts its head through one of the net's openings and finds that it cannot pass completely through, it tries to back off and catches its gills in the webbing.

GRILSE: Adolescent Atlantic salmon returning from the sea.

GUIDE: One of the metal rings along a rod's length through which line passes. Ring, snake, and roller guides are standard types. Sometimes guides are lined with smooth hard material such as agate or special alloys to avoid grooves. The guide at the end of the rod is called the tip-top. Also, of course, a person who is hired to help a fisherman find and catch fish.

HARDWARE: In rod making, those metal parts such as ferrules, guides, tip-tops, and reel seats. In fishing, metal lures such as spoons and spinners.

HATCH: An emergence of newly hatched insects from fresh water. In fly-fishing, a hatch usually refers to mayflies. On a trout stream a hatch frequently triggers a rise of feeding fish.

HEAD BOAT: Vessel carrying large numbers of anglers on regularly scheduled fishing trips. Per-head cost may or may not include bait and tackle, but if not, these usually can be rented. Sometimes called PARTY BOAT.

HELLGRAMMITE: Larva of the dobsonfly, found under rocks in streams. Hellgrammites 2 to 3 inches long are considered by many to be best all-round bait for black bass. Be careful, they pinch.

HYBRID: Crossbreed of two closely related types of fish for improved characteristics such as faster growth, longer life, and better disease resistance. The tiger trout, for example, blends the brown trout with the brook or speckled trout; the splake combines the speckled trout with the laker.

ICE OUT: That instant during the spring when winter ice disappears from a lake.

ICHTHYOLOGY: The study of fishes.

JACK: A male fish. See BUCK.

JIG: A piece of metal, usually lead or stainless steel, with a hook in one end. The metal can be spherical, flat and round, or otherwise streamlined. A jig's hook often is dressed with feathers or bucktail. Line is tied to an eye in the body of the metal head. In use, line is alternately yanked and relaxed when trolling or retrieving, to impart a fast-slow, rising-retreating action. To jig a lure is to use it in this fashion.

LEADER: A length of wire or line attached to the main line's forward end. In salt water this usually is wire or heavy monofilament for protection against abrasion from rocks and sand and against severing by sharp-toothed species such as barracuda and bluefish. In fresh water, fine wire sometimes is used when fishing for muskie, pike, pickerel, and walleyes. In fly-fishing, long fine leaders bridge the gap between the flyline and the fly. Usually these taper to a fine tippet so flies can be dropped gently onto the water.

LINE DRESSING: A paste or liquid applied to flylines to make them float.

LIVE-LINING: Employing live bait. Traditionally the term refers only to the use of swimming bait such as herring, mackerel, and mullet in salt water and various minnows in fresh water, and to the techniques for employing them. By some fishermen, however, it includes the use of all live bait, such as frogs, worms, and crawfish.

LONGLINE: Commercial techniques of floating multi-hooked lines that sometimes are several miles in length. From a main floating line short dropper lines are hung, each containing several baited hooks. Most frequently this technique is employed by Japanese to catch tuna and billfish.

MAYFLY: By far the most popular food of trout, from bottom-dwelling nymph, through the dun emerging from the water, to the fully mature winged adult. Eggs laid in the water hatch into nymphs. After a fall and winter on the bottom, the nymph rises to the surface in spring or summer, splitting its skin and hatching into a winged adult. In about twenty-four hours it once again sheds its skin, and within a few hours thereafter, it mates, lays its eggs, and dies. North America has over 500 mayfly species which occupy almost every body of fresh water and can be observed day and night throughout spring and early summer in one stage or another of their evanescent life cycle. When your youngster gets cocky about his prowess in catching trout with bait or lures, you can take the wind out of his sails by having him try to perform with his favorite bait or lure while standing in the midst of a mayfly hatch with trout rolling and rising all around him. Without a well-presented mayfly imitation, he might as well be skipping stones. Better yet, let him try dropping, say, a #12 Dark Cahill into the midst of the melee and learn the supreme satisfaction of competing successfully with the real thing.

MILT: A white milky substance containing sperm that is ejected by a male fish to fertilize a female's eggs.

MINNOW: Small forage fish of several species that are netted, trapped, or raised commercially for bait.

MOSSBUNKER: Colloquial name for Atlantic menhaden, a small oily school fish often ground for chum or used whole as bait for striped bass and bluefish.

MULLET: One of various inshore fishes popular as both bait and food. Of the more than 100 species in the world, mullet are most abundant around Florida, although they are found along our entire East Coast and the southern part of our West Coast.

MUMMICHOG: Popular small baitfish found in coastal shallows from eastern Canada to Texas.

NATIVE: A term that originally referred to fish that were indigenous to an area, such as the brook trout in the eastern United States. Now it is used more commonly to indicate a fish born rather than stocked in a body of water.

NYMPH: The larva of an underwater insect after its wings have begun to appear, or a fly fashioned to imitate this larva.

OUTRIGGER: A long metal rod on sportfishing craft which is rigidly secured slightly aft of center, one on each side of the craft. Outriggers are used to troll heavy baits far enough outboard of the bait being trolled from the fighting chair so that there will be no interference.

PANFISH: A group of small freshwater fishes not big enough to be considered gamefish. Panfish are found in almost every pond, lake, river, and stream. Examples are crappie, bullhead, perch, rock bass, and various sunfishes. The term is used with increasing frequency in reference to small saltwater species such as porgies and surfperch. All provide excellent easy-to-find action on light tackle.

PARTY BOAT: Same as HEAD BOAT.

PLANKTON: Drifting microscopic animals that provide a valuable supply of food for small fish.

PLUG: An artificial lure, usually of wood or plastic, designed to resemble a baitfish in size and color. Normally a plug is armed with one treble hook in its tail and two under its body. One of the body hooks sometimes is removed to increase the sport, but this should be done only with careful consideration of the effect it will have on the plug's balance and hence its action. A plug's body can be jointed as well as solid. Popular plug types are the popper, swimmer, diver, and darter.

POACH: To take fish illegally. Also to cook fish by a method similar to boiling, but in a special bouillon.

PORKRIND: A strip of a pig's hide used as a lure. Often these are attached to the hook of another lure, such as a leadhead bucktail jig, although they sometimes are used by themselves on bare hooks.

PRIEST: A small, usually weighted billy club used to knock out freshly caught fish. Always have a priest handy in a boat when you might catch species such as bluefish, sharks, and barracuda whose teeth can cause serious injury.

PURSE SEINE: A large net for catching schooling fish. With its bottom weighted and its top floated, the seine is strung in a vertical position around a fish school. A line through rings spaced along the seine's bottom is drawn tight, closing the net like a purse around the fish inside.

RACE: Churning water where currents collide.

REDD: Gravel spawning bed in which fish such as the Atlantic salmon deposit and fertilize their eggs.

RIP: A condition of turbulence in salt water where tidal currents collide with one another or with wind, rocks, or underwater undulations.

RISE: A fish coming to the surface to feed, as when a trout rises to a dry fly. The rise normally is marked by a swirl on the surface of the water.

ROE: Fish eggs. Sturgeon roe is caviar. Roe from other fish, most noticeably the shad, is considered a delicacy. A favorite steelhead bait is a small nylon bag of steelhead roe bounced along the bottom.

SALTER: A sea-run brook trout.

SAND SPIKE: A tube stuck in sand and used by surf fishermen for holding their rods. Normally these are made of aluminum and their bottoms are cut at an angle for easy insertion into sand.

SCULL: To propel a boat by pushing and pulling an oar from side to side over the stern.

SEA TROUT: Sea-run brown trout found mostly in rivers of Canada and eastern United States.

SEATROUT: Popular saltwater gamefish of the drum family similar to the weakfish.

SHOOTING HEAD: The front level section of a weight-forward flyline.

SINKER: A metal weight, usually lead, that can be made in various shapes and sizes and is designed to pull your bait or lure to a desired depth. The pyramid sinker, for example, is shaped to anchor a bottom-fished bait close above a sand or mud bottom, while a split shot might be used to hold your trolled streamer fly just far enough under the surface to attract landlocked salmon.

SNELL: A short line, usually monofilament, with a hook at one end and a loop at the other. Because the snell usually is heavier than the line to which it is attached, it provides protection against abrasive rocks and fishes' teeth.

SOLUNAR TABLES: Data tabulated by the late John Alden Knight and currently published by his daughter-in-law, Mrs. Richard Alden Knight, for predicting daily feeding times of fish and game. Maintaining that best fishing is likely to occur in fresh as well as salt water when the moon's tidal pull is weakest, Mr. Knight calculated these times for locations throughout North America and devoted many years to confirming his calculations.

SPENT-WING: A dry fly with hackle feathers tied at right angles to the hook's shank to suggest a spent mayfly.

SPIDER: An easy-to-cast artificial fly, usually dry, with extra-long hackles that enable it to drift gently down to the water's surface.

SPINNER: The mating stage of the mayfly, when many of these insects flutter and seem to be spinning over the water. Also a blade-shaped metal lure designed to spin as it is pulled through the water. Although a spinner more often is used to attract attention to a bait or lure with which it is used in combination, hooked spinners, such as the Colorado, also can be effective when used alone.

SPLIT SHOT: Small cylindrical lead sinker that is split and opened so it can be crimped on a line with pliers. Originally designed only for one-time use, split shot now come with small tabs which when squeezed reopen the shot, releasing the line and enabling an angler to reuse the shot.

SPOON: A lure shaped in the general configuration of a spoon. When trolled or retrieved after casting, the spoon wobbles or flutters.

SPREADER: A device which enables you to fish with two baited hooks side by side without their leaders becoming tangled. The leaders are tied to eyes at the ends of a horizontal piece of stiff wire about a foot in length. In the center of the wire is a piece of metal with two eyes, one above the other. Your sinker is attached to the bottom eye, your line to the top. The spreader is a favorite of flounder fishermen.

STINK BAIT: A favorite of catfish and carp fishermen with strong stomachs and clothespins on their noses. Everyone seems to have his own favorite formula, most of which start with juice from rotted fish. Ultra-ripe cheese and oil of anise are popular ingredients. Sometimes doughballs saturated in the goop are molded around a treble hook, but an easier method is to fish a piece of sponge that's been immersed in the mess.

STONEFLY: A favorite food of fish that inhabit clean, cool streams. There are almost 400 species of this six-legged twin-tailed insect in the United States and Canada.

STREAMER FLY: An artificial fly designed to resemble a small baitfish.

STRIPPING: In fly-fishing, the act of pulling line from a reel when preparing to make a cast. Also, retrieving line in fairly fast and regularly spaced intervals. In fish culture, the act of forcing eggs or milt from ripe fish.

STUMPKNOCKER: Refers in the South to several varieties of sunfish.

SURF FISHING: Seeking inshore gamefish with lure or bait from a saltwater shore.

SWIVEL: A device, usually of brass or stainless steel, for connecting line to leader or leader to lure whose purpose is to prevent line twisting. The barrel swivel has a closed eye at either end, while the snap swivel has one eye and one safety-pin-type snap. For bottom-fishing, a three-eyed swivel can be used, one eye for your line, one for your sinker, and the third for the leader to your baited hook.

TACKLE BOX: A container for fishing tackle. Normally these are made of plastic or a corrosion-resistant metal such as aluminum. Today most tackle boxes contain compartmented trays that fold inside when the cover is closed.

TEASER: A secondary lure used in addition to the main lure to increase chances of fish striking. A popular freshwater arrangement is to have a second fly, usually of a different pattern from the first, tied on a dropper loop a foot or so up the leader to double the first fly's enticement value. In salt water, a strip of porkrind or plastic tubing sometimes is tied a few feet ahead of a plug to suggest a large fish such as a mackerel chasing a small fish such as a sand eel. Jealousy can make a gamefish strike plug or teaser, with doubleheaders occurring often when casting into a feeding school.

TERMINAL TACKLE: Any items of equipment such as swivels, leaders, sinkers, hooks, and lures that are attached to the end of a fishing line.

THERMOCLINE: The middle layer of water in a pond or lake where temperatures change very rapidly during summer between the tepid epilimnion layer at its top and the cold and stagnant hypolimnion at its bottom.

TIDES: Movement of the ocean toward and away from land because of the moon's and sun's gravitational pull. Tides flow in and out twice daily, with a given tidal condition occurring about fifty minutes later each day in accordance with the rising of the moon. In certain mid-Pacific locations such as Tahiti, tide always is low at sunrise and sunset and high at midnight and noon.

Tides are important in determining where and when fish will feed. Although no rule applies everywhere under all conditions, one that usually applies is that on an ebbing tide fish wait off the mouths of rivers and creeks for food. Suggestion: Examine shorelines at low tide to locate holes, sloughs, sandbars, rocks, wormbeds, etc., where fish may be found when a flooding tide covers them.

A flooding tide moves in, an ebbing tide moves out. Slack water is that infinitesimal instant between flood and slack when flow seems to cease. Spring tides are unusually high and occur twice each month, at full and new moons. Neap tides, occurring midway between spring tides, are abnormally low. Because many mudflats are not exposed at times of spring tides, a good selection of mudworms is hard to find in baitshops.

TIDE TABLES: Tabulated times of high and low tides for every day of the year for key coastal locations, with corrections for intermediate points. Usually contain data on moon phase and tidal flow as well. An invaluable aid for marine anglers, and often published as an advertising giveaway.

TIP TOP: The line guide on the tip of a fishing rod.

TROLLING: Fishing from a moving boat by towing a lure or bait astern.

TROTLINE: A long heavy line from which hooks are suspended on short dropper lines every few feet. Normally a trotline is extended across a stream, although it can be anchored and buoyed at any desired angle. This is a popular commercial method of catching catfish.

ULTRALIGHT: Designation for spinning tackle where line is less than 3-pound-test and rod less than 3 ounces. Although difficult to master, this method offers many tactical advantages against wary fish in clear shallow water.

WADERS: Waterproof footwear of either hip-high or chest-high style. Chest waders, though sometimes hot and cumbersome, are a better all-round investment for both freshwater and saltwater use. The boy hasn't been born who won't try to take that "just one more step" that always seems to be into water that is slightly deeper than his boot tops. Buy them big enough for a pair of woolen socks, and make sure that their soles provide a rough contoured no-slip surface. Steer clear of flimsy plastic designs. Initially they might save you a few dollars, but they puncture readily on barnacled boulders and thorny bushes, and their seams split easily when you have to stretch your legs to climb a banking or ascend a rock.

Winter Kill: The suffocating of fish in iced-over lakes because green plants do not produce enough oxygen to support life. Normally this occurs because heavy prolonged snow cover prevents enough sunlight from penetrating the ice.

Wire Line: Heavy trolling line, made usually of Monel, stainless steel, or copper. Main advantages are that it gets lures to extreme depths without a heavy drail or planer, and its rigidity enables a troller to impart action by jigging. Unless it is continuously pressured by the thumb when being released, however, and laid evenly across the reel spool while being retrieved, it can drive you to distraction by its kinking. Wire line is not a weapon for the inexperienced youngster.

# Index